ROBERT
BARTON

ROBERT BARTON

A Remarkable Revolutionary

CHRIS LAWLOR

The History Press

In memory of Professor Raymond Gillespie, late of Maynooth University, who did so much to help me on my academic path over the years. Ar dheis Dé go raibh a anam dílis.

Cover picture: Portrait of Robert Barton by Sir John Lavery, oil on canvas, 1921. (Collection and image © Hugh Lane Gallery, Dublin)

First published 2024

The History Press
97 St George's Place, Cheltenham,
Gloucestershire, GL50 3QB
www.thehistorypress.co.uk

British Library Cataloguing in Publication Data.
A catalogue record for this book is available from the British Library.

ISBN 978 1 80399 816 9

Typesetting and origination by The History Press
Printed and bound in Great Britain by TJ Books Limited, Padstow, Cornwall.

MIX
Paper | Supporting
responsible forestry
FSC
www.fsc.org   FSC® C013056

Trees for Life

Contents

List of Illustrations

About the Author

Dr Chris Lawlor is a former head of the history department of Méanscoil Iognáid Rís in Naas, County Kildare. He won the County Kildare Archaeological Society's Lord Walter Fitzgerald Prize for Original Historical Research in 2003 and the Irish Chief's Prize for History in 2013. He was also the winner of the Dunlavin Festival of Arts Short Story Competition in 2001 and the Ireland's Own Short Story Competition in 2022. He has contributed numerous articles and chapters to many journals and compilations, and his twelve previously published books include The Little Book of Wicklow and The Little Book of Kildare. He continues to write in his retirement.

Acknowledgements

I wish to thank my family, academic mentors and historians, the ever-helpful staff of the various libraries, archives and repositories who helped me to bring this work to fruition, and Ele Palmer, Nicola Guy and the team at The History Press.

Thank you to my wife, Margaret Lawlor; Declan Lawlor; Jason Lawlor and his wife Mary; Michael Lawlor and his wife Orla. Thank you for all your support, encouragement and help. Thank you also to my grandchildren, Caitlin, Cian and Bronagh, for often lifting my spirits.

Thanks also to each of the following: Prof. James Kelly, St Patrick's College, D.C.U.; Prof. Mary Ann Lyons, Maynooth University; Dr Daithí Ó Corráin, St Patrick's College, D.C.U.; Dr Ida Milne, St Patrick's College, Carlow; Hugh Beckett, Irish Military Archives; Lisa Dolan, Irish Military Archives; Vincent Buttner, National Archives of Ireland; Vera Moynes, National Archives of Ireland; Selina Collard, University College Dublin Archives; Aisling Lockhart, Manuscripts and Archives, Trinity College, Dublin; Anne Marie Saliba, Hugh Lane Gallery, Dublin; Frances Clarke, National Library of Ireland; Glenn Dunne, National Library of Ireland; Damian Murphy, National Inventory of Architectural Heritage; Colum O'Riordan, Irish Architectural Archive; Brian Crowley, Kilmainham Gaol Museum; Ciarán McGann, The Houses of the Oireachtas Service; Peter Brooks, Royal Agricultural University, Cirencester; Dr Mari Takayanagi, Parliamentary Archives, London; Sophie Bridges, Churchill Archives Centre, Cambridge; Adam Green, Trinity College Library, Cambridge; Kaili Smith, Imperial War Museum, London; Catherine Wright, Wicklow County Archives;

Gerlanda Maniglia, Wicklow Local Studies Department; James Durney, Kildare County Archives and Local Studies; Maura Greene, Dunlavin Library; Joan Kavanagh, Rathdrum Historical Society; Peadar Cullen, West Wicklow Historical Society; John Dorney, The Irish Story website; Tommy Graham, History Ireland; Florence Grace and Maura O'Neill, Dunlavin Writers' Group; Tom Noone, Mary McCabe, Andrew Keating, Kathryna Phibbs and Joseph Kelly, Meánscoil Iognáid Rís; Rita Evans and Joe Walsh, former colleagues.

Special thanks to Dr James Lee, Dunlavin, who restored me to good health at an important time in my research.

List of Abbreviations

A.C.C.	Agricultural Credit Corporation
B.A.	Bachelor of Arts
B.M.H.	Bureau of Military History
D.C.U.	Dublin City University
DE	Dáil Eireann
D.I.	District Inspector, R.I.C.
D.I.B.	Dictionary of Irish Biography
Dip. Econ.	Diploma in Economics
D.M.P.	Dublin Metropolitan Police
E.S.B.	Electricity Supply Board
G.A.A.	Gaelic Athletic Association
G.H.Q.	General Headquarters
G.O.C.	General Officer Commanding
G.P.O.	General Post Office
H.M.	His/Her Majesty's
I.C.A.	Irish Citizen Army
I.M.A.	Irish Military Archives
I.P.P.	Irish Parliamentary Party
I.R.A.	Irish Republican Army
I.R.B.	Irish Republican Brotherhood
I.T.G.W.U.	Irish Transport and General Workers' Union
I.V.F.	Irish Volunteer Force
J.P.	Justice of the Peace
M.A.	Master of Arts
M.R.A.C.	Member of the Royal Agricultural College

MS	Manuscript
M.S.P.C.	Military Service Pensions Collection
N.A.I.	National Archives of Ireland
N.L.I.	National Library of Ireland
O.T.C.	Officers' Training Corps
Ph.D	Doctor of Philosophy
R.I.C.	Royal Irish Constabulary
R.T.E.	Radio Teilifís Éireann
T.C.D.	Trinity College Dublin
T.D.	Teachta Dála (member of Dáil Eireann)
U.C.C.	University College Cork
U.C.D.	University College Dublin
U.C.D.A.	University College Dublin Archive
U.V.F.	Ulster Volunteer Force
W.C.C.	Wicklow County Council
WS	Witness Statement (to Bureau of Military History)
WW.C.A.	Wicklow County Archive

Introduction

RATIONALE AND BACKGROUND

In December 2021, I participated in a History Ireland 'Hedge School' entitled 'Robert Barton: forgotten man of the Irish Revolution?' with other contributors John Dorney (The Irish Story website), Joan Kavanagh (Rathdrum Historical Society) and Catherine Wright (Wicklow County Archives), chaired by Tommy Graham (History Ireland).[1] I have always thought that Barton was an under-studied figure in Irish history, particularly given his central role during the Irish revolutionary years and the socio-economic effects of his later public service at the head of the Agricultural Credit Corporation and, especially, Bord na Móna. The title of the 2021 Hedge School reinforced my view. As a plenipotentiary in the Irish delegation sent to London to secure a political agreement in the wake of the War of Independence, and as a signatory of the Anglo-Irish treaty, Barton's role was integral in the birth of the Irish state ... yet, amazingly, he still awaits a biographer. It is incredible that this is so, and the more I thought about it, the more convinced I became that some kind of brief study of Barton's life, times and contribution to Irish history should be written. In particular, I thought it would be fitting, as we leave the decade of centenaries behind us, that some account of the part played by Barton, and his contribution to the events of that decade a hundred years ago, should be placed on record. That thought was the genesis of this study.

Of all the people involved in the Irish Revolution of c.1913–23, it fell to Robert Barton to choose acceptance or rejection of its negotiated settlement, the Anglo-Irish Treaty, and it is no exaggeration to say that in

December 1921 he singly carried the full weight of a nation's expectations on his shoulders during the final hours before the agreement was fully signed. Given his prominence at this crucial time, this study seeks to establish just who he was, to examine his part in the Irish Revolution with particular reference to his central role as a key player during the treaty negotiations, to give a brief overview of his later life and, finally, to evaluate his legacy as a political figure. Please note that all quotations in the text, appendices and endnotes retain the original spelling and punctuation (including upper case letters).

This work does not purport to be a definitive biography of Robert Childers Barton. He lived a very long – and very full – life, eventually passing away at the age of 94. It would take many years of extensive, in-depth research to cover Barton's eventful existence during those ninety-four years. As the title suggests, this study concentrates on Barton's contribution to Irish history during the revolutionary period, and in particular during the period 1916-23 – from the Easter Rising to the Civil War. It also briefly covers his early life before 1916 in an effort to give an overview of the influences that brought him into the Irish national movement, and very briefly addresses his later life after 1923 in an effort to outline his enormous public service within the new Irish state as it morphed from the Free State to the Republic, and the effect of his work on the new Ireland. However, both his early and later life are only sketched briefly – I did contact Bord na Móna, only to be told that the company (incredibly) does not have an archivist and there is no access to sources. In any event, the principal focus of this study concentrates on the crucial revolutionary period, centred in Barton's case on the years 1921–22, and including the treaty negotiations, the signing of the document, the treaty debates and the eventual outbreak of civil war.

SOURCES

One of the problems of working on this period is the sheer volume of sources available. This is not to say that gaps do not exist; they certainly do – but this was an age of increasing literacy, and this is reflected particularly in the publication of periodicals. National and local newspapers, pamphlets, magazines and other contemporary publications abound. One must beware of bias in the reporting, of course; newspapers could be unionist or nationalist, pro- or anti-treaty in sympathy – just like those who wrote them or those who read them. The most immediate problem working with press sources was often choosing what to include and what to omit. Other printed sources, including election flyers and political pamphlets, also contributed to the overall picture. The most significant manuscript sources for the revolutionary period from 1916 to 1923 were undoubtedly those held in the Irish Military Archives (I.M.A.), Dublin. These include Robert Barton's witness statement, and some information relating to Barton is also found in other witness statements such as those of his sister, Dulcibella, and Mrs Austin Stack. The I.M.A. also contains many other records from the period including, for example, I.R.A. pension application files. The National Archives of Ireland and the National Library also hold some relevant material, and sources from other Irish archives outside of Dublin such as Kildare County Archives and Local Studies Department and Wicklow County Archives, and some British repositories, also helped to put flesh on the bones of Barton's eventful life and valuable contribution to the Irish state. Secondary sources specifically relating to Barton (or his family) are thin on the ground. Apart from my own short piece from 2014,[2] they are confined to articles or chapters such as those by Michael Fewer,[3] Catherine Wright,[4] Turtle Bunbury,[5] and Pauric Dempsey and Shaun Boylan.[6] Unsurprisingly, though, Barton appears *en passant* in many general publications dealing with the revolutionary period, most notably Pakenham's *Peace by ordeal*,[7] and Macardle's *The Irish Republic*.[8] Occasionally (when it was necessary to denote the passage of time in Barton's constituencies), events in the village of Dunlavin have been referenced. The village was chosen because it was centrally located in both of Barton's constituencies (located, as it is, on the north–south border of the baronies of Upper and Lower Talbotstown in the West Wicklow constituency and on the east–west county boundary in the constituency of Kildare-Wicklow), and because a study of the area during the Irish revolutionary period has been published previously.[9] I have tried to weave the various snippets found in relation to Barton in both primary and secondary sources into some form of coherence in this work.

Almost half a century ago, Professor Patrick Corish (whose lectures in Maynooth I was privileged to attend), delivered a stark warning to historians writing about mid-seventeenth-century Ireland by telling them that they 'risk disturbing ghosts'.[10] This is even more the case, I think, when one is writing about events that happened a century ago, or less.

Moreover, many of the events of this formative time in our history were deeply divisive, and have moulded political attitudes, in some cases right up to the present day, so Barton's role may be perceived in different ways by various groups. One thing is certain: more and more primary sources relating to this period will be opened up for research, and will be made available online, as the years progress. The new information will complement what has already been discovered – but it may also contradict some sections of it. It will be for future generations of historians to make sense of any new findings and to re-interpret Barton's words and actions in a new light. It is my sincere wish that some Ph.D. student or historian from the world of academia will take up the challenge of researching and writing a more comprehensive biography, and to any future student of Barton's life, times, legacy and contribution to Irish history, I humbly offer this study, with its many imperfections, as a starting point.

Chris Lawlor
Dunlavin
March 2024

1

Early Influences
(1881–c.1893)

Robert Barton's background was not that of a typical Irish revolutionary. At least, it is not the background that one would expect for such a
figure, as it is somewhat arguable whether there is a 'typical' background
for an Irish revolutionary. For example, republican Theobald Wolfe Tone
(known as 'the Father of Irish Republicanism') came from a wealthy Kildare
Protestant family;[1] Home Rule leader Charles Stewart Parnell came from a
Protestant landlord family;[2] Countess Constance Markievicz came from an
elite, privileged family;[3] and other Irish nationalist and republican leaders
during the eighteenth and nineteenth centuries emerged from unexpected
and surprising backgrounds. Robert Barton was born on 14 March 1881
into an elite, unionist, Protestant, landlord family in County Wicklow,
whose wealth was increased by their interest in the French vineyards of
Barton and Guestier. Bob Barton's parents were Charles William Barton
of Glendalough House, Annamoe, and his wife, Agnes, daughter of Rev.
Canon Charles Childers, H.M. Chaplain at Nice and canon of Gibraltar.[4]
The Barton family of Glendalough House were also pillars of the local
Church of Ireland community, and on 14 September 1894 the 13-year-old
Bob joined the Derrylossary branch of the Church of Ireland Temperance
Society.[5] As an adult, Barton readily proffered the information that his
father, Charles William, 'was a loyal supporter of the British administration
here [in Ireland]'.[6] Moreover, Charles Barton's political views caused him
to fall out with his more famous neighbour, Charles Stewart Parnell, who
became the president of the Land League and the charismatic leader of the
Irish Parliamentary Party in their campaign to gain Home Rule for Ireland.
According to R. F. Foster, Robert Barton's father and Parnell were 'close

friends as young men, but politics sundered their friendship completely. Barton was a strict Unionist.'[7] Despite this falling out, Parnell was invited to Glendalough House to view a big tree that had been blown down in a storm in 1888, and Barton remembered his nanny pointing out the great 'uncrowned king of Ireland' to him as he gazed out through his playroom window.[8]

The young Robert Barton grew up at Glendalough House, in the company of his older, orphaned cousin, Erskine Childers, who had moved to Annamoe to live with his Barton cousins in 1876. The Glendalough House cousins would enjoy a lifelong bond of friendship. This imposing residence was located in a beautiful setting of parkland, woodland, river and mountains. It replaced an earlier house owned by the Hugo family. The grounds included a formal garden with yew trees set between the stables and the house, with an enclosed garden beyond. The long, Gothic stables, dating from 1838 (shortly after Barton's grandfather, T. J., bought the estate from Captain Hugo),[9] originally comprised a separate building, but an extension dating from *c.*1880 later joined the stable block to the main house. The house itself also dates from 1838, and is a highly ornate mansion built in the Tudor Gothic style. This is somewhat unusual, as the building of larger, ornate, landlord houses tended to peter out in the mid-to late-nineteenth-century, as by then, the Anglo-Irish had lost much of the confidence needed to build on a grand scale.[10] Generally, big houses built during this later period were simpler, and often smaller, than their eighteenth-century predecessors, which dated from the heyday of the emergence of the Irish landed elite.[11] Glendalough House, with its fanlight doorway, eaved roof, hall enclosed on three sides by a gracefully joined staircase, imposing rooms, ornate chimney pieces (including one piece of possible Russian origin), large windows and castellated features was a statement building.[12] It emanated an unmistakable aura of wealth, power and social control, and compared favourably with other big houses in County Wicklow and beyond. At a glance, it was evident to all, including, in his childhood, the young Robert Barton, that the owners of such a house, which dominated the cultural landscape of the locality, were part of the landed elite, and that they belonged to the establishment that controlled nineteenth-century Ireland.

An account of a visit to Robert Barton at Glendalough House in the 1940s paints a portrait of a wealthy, comfortable lifestyle in impressive surroundings:

Fig 1. Glendalough House, Annamoe, as Robert Barton would have known it. (Image (2/41X1) courtesy of the Irish Architectural Archive)

A long drive with magnificent Wellingtonias and other trees dotted about the park led to a large L-shaped house, with a covered porch and wide steps leading to the entrance hall ... The house smelt as all old houses do, of old oak. He took us first to the Library for drinks. The walls were lined with books which were almost entirely concerned with Irish history. There was also a complete set of Maria Edgworth's novels ... A staid, pale, disapproving butler announced the fact that luncheon was served. We moved into the dining-room which was hung with Erskine and Barton portraits, going right back to the days of Queen Elizabeth, when the Bartons first settled in Ireland. We had a magnificent meal of sirloin of beef with an enormous dish of fresh garden peas, beans and new potatoes, followed by pineapple, fresh raspberries and extraordinarily good sherry. After lunch he took us first to see his immense walled garden and greenhouses, and a vast tree that almost overshadowed the house. [There was] a new rockery with dwarf junipers and cypress trees that he had planted by the sides of a little lake on the hillside, with waterfalls that fell steeply down to a lower lake. We then walked along through a forest of primaeval oak ... This track wound its way past gnarled, bent and withered trees, through vast undergrowth and came out at a stout stone lodge gate that had been the dairy, and then converted into a village school. In the distance I heard the call of curlews on the sides of the mountain called Scard, which is Barton's grouse moor. We crossed a road, climbed a stony, rough, walled lane, and soon found ourselves looking down on a lake, shut in on three sides by the mountains. This was Lough Dan and on its black, cold-looking surface, I saw a rowing-boat painted scarlet. On the way back to the house, he took us up some outside stone steps to a room in which the wife of one of his servants was spinning wool, while her son sat in front of the radio with his ear close to it, listening to a running commentary on the football match between Meath and Kerry ... After a tea, which included some of the finest honey in comb that I have ever eaten, Barton drove us home.[13]

Glendalough House also incorporated part of an older house. Prior to the Bartons, the previous owners were the Hugo family. Captain Thomas Hugo was particularly well known to, but not particularly well remembered by, the ordinary people of the Annamoe region. Hugo, a former High Sherriff of County Wicklow and an ultra-loyalist, had been particularly active during the 1798 rebellion period in County Wicklow.[14] Speaking in a television interview in 1969, Robert Barton, by then an elder statesman, wryly referred to the fact that he had lived in the same place as the notorious Thomas Hugo.[15] As a child, he had lived 'in the heart of the rebel area of County Wicklow' and had 'absorbed quite a lot of national sympathies'.[16] He had also absorbed much of the history and folklore of Glendalough House and its hinterland surrounding Annamoe during his long life. He left behind a collection of this material, with some personal reminiscences, which is now housed in the National Archives of Ireland.[17] According to Barton:

Mr. Hugo of the 1798 rebellion time, was a captain of the yeomanry, who had slaughtered ... many rebels around [Glendalough] House. The house had got such a bad name that it became known as 'the slaughterhouse'. The people that my father and I were employing were descendants of those who were shot in 1798. My sympathies were with them, that's how I originally came into the national movement.[18]

It is interesting that, even in old age, Barton did not refer to the people on his estate as 'tenants'. This may have been due to a genuine paternalistic pride that Barton felt as an employer. However, it may also have been an attempt to distance himself (and his landlord family) from the language of landlordism, as land reform had been a divisive topic during the first half-century or so of the existence of an independent Ireland, first as a free state and later as a republic. In a conversation with an old university friend in 1948, Barton told him that Irish people particularly wanted to displace English landlords who left their properties in the hands of their agents, stating, 'That's almost our oldest grievance, being under the heel of the agent.'[19] Landlordism and its messy, protracted aftermath had left long shadows, and even in 1969, discussions about and arguments over land could become heated. Under the first Minister for Agriculture appointed after the establishment of the Free State, Patrick Hogan, the partial break-up of landlord estates (and, in some cases, demesnes) and some redistribution of agricultural lands was undertaken by the Land Commission. However, Land Commission farm size remained small. Inevitably, in County Wicklow as elsewhere, there were winners and losers in this process. Expectation did not always match reality and, overall, agricultural labourers and smallholders fared badly.[20] The early years of the fledgling Free State witnessed a flight from the land as many smallholders (or, after their deaths, their sons and daughters) sold up and shipped out. Their land was often bought by neighbouring strong farmers. As recently as the late 1990s, during the height of the Celtic Tiger boom years, the author spoke to two County Wicklow residents who had bitter memories of these events, which they both referred to as 'the time of the land grabbing'.[21] Whatever Barton's motives for referring to his tenants as 'employees' (and perhaps he had more than one), these were the people among whom he grew up, and his sympathy for – and empathy with – them strongly suggest that his journey towards Irish nationalism began in his boyhood years, which he spent in the Annamoe area, at least during holiday periods.

2

A Traditional Education and
a Political Conversion
(1894–1916)

As a boy, Robert Barton conformed to the educational model of many of the sons of the Irish landed elite, whether gentry or aristocracy, and received his education in England. He received a public school education at the famous Rugby School in Warwickshire, before progressing to the Royal Agricultural College in Cirencester, Gloucestershire, and on to Oxford University. Barton received his diploma from Cirencester in 1901.[1] He then studied at Christ Church College, Oxford, and was awarded a B.A. and subsequently, on 13 June 1908, a Dip. Econ. (Diploma in Economics) from that august institution.[2] Barton's educational progression fell within the expectations of his family and other members of the landed elite. In many ways, it was the traditional education received by the sons of Irish landlord families; it precisely mirrored, for example, that of Pierce O'Mahony, another young man from County Wicklow's landed elite, from the village of Grangecon, a quarter of a century or so earlier.[3] O'Mahony had established an Irish Home Rule Club at Magdalen College, Oxford,[4] and during his time in Oxford (and probably Cirencester), Barton was also politically active. He lived on the same college staircase as Stuart Petre Brodie (S. P. B.) Mais, who went on to become a prolific author of travel books, journalist and broadcaster.[5] In one of his books, Mais reminisced about how Barton had a profound effect on his own political opinions regarding Ireland. According to Mais, Barton:

> first set me thinking of the English treatment of the Irish and aroused in me a sense of disgust at our barbaric tyranny and of sympathy with the movement to free Ireland from English rule. I have no Irish blood in my veins, but I felt an overpowering desire to serve the Irish cause in any capacity that Barton suggested.[6]

Some years later, in 1914, Mais thought of Barton again. By that time, he was on the staff at Sherborne, a public school in Dorset, and was an officer in the O.T.C. Mais reveals that:

> Two of my colleagues and fellow-officers, both Englishmen, were so angry at Carson's threat of violence in Northern Ireland that they decided to throw in their lot with Sinn Féin and join the Southern

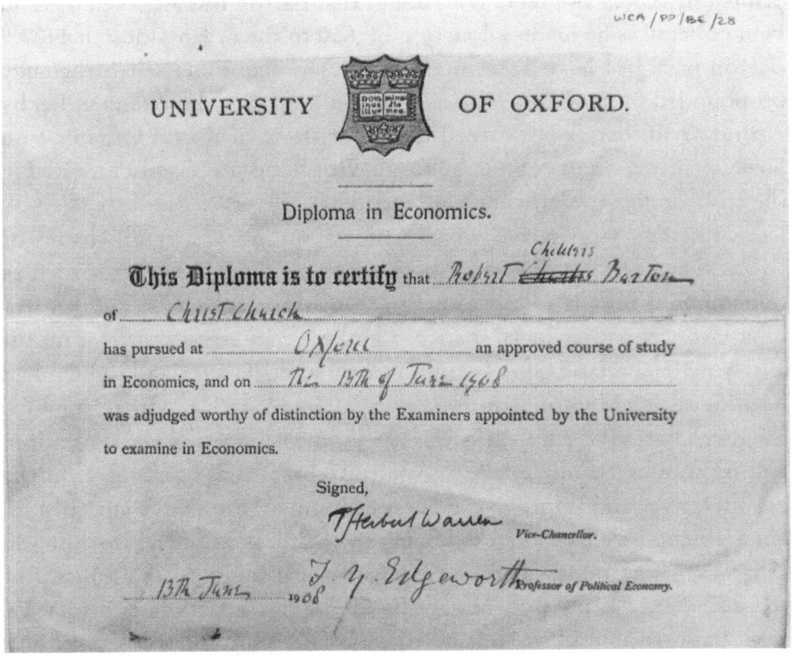

WCA/PP/BE/28

UNIVERSITY OF OXFORD.

Diploma in Economics.

This Diploma is to certify that Robert ~~Charles~~ Childers Barton

of Christ Church

has pursued at Oxford an approved course of study

in Economics, and on the 13th of June 1908

was adjudged worthy of distinction by the Examiners appointed by the University to examine in Economics.

Signed,

T Herbert Warren Vice-Chancellor.

13th June 1908 F. Y. Edgeworth Professor of Political Economy.

Fig 2. Barton's 1908 Diploma in Economics (with distinction) from Oxford University. (Image (Barton Papers, WWCA/PP1/19) courtesy of the Wicklow County Archive)

Irish. I remembered Barton at Christ Church and felt that I too ought to do something about it. We were on the point of doing something about it when our attention was diverted by Germany and we found ourselves embroiled in a war of quite another sort.[7]

There is no doubt that Frank Pakenham was correct in his assessment when he stated that Barton had 'already passed from Unionism to Nationalism by the time he left Oxford'.[8] However, he was not the only nationalist in the otherwise staunchly Unionist Barton family. His sister Dulcibella (known as 'Da') was also drawn to the nationalist cause. Dulcibella was two years older than Robert, and she probably influenced his political opinions. Her later testimony revealed that both siblings 'took in the Sinn Féin newspaper in the early days', which must have irked their parents, who 'were very conservative and would be absolutely opposed to the opinions expressed in that paper'.[9] The newspaper in question was first printed in 1906,[10] and there is no doubt that Barton was attracted by Sinn Féin policies, as he made a donation of £50 to the organisation in 1907.[11] Barton may also have been interested in the economic self-sufficiency propounded by Sinn Féin, the new, fledgling political movement led by Arthur Griffith,[12] as he worked for the Irish Agricultural Organisation Society (sitting on its committee from 1910),[13] and was deeply involved in the co-operative movement championed by Sir Horace Plunkett.

Plunkett's co-operative movement was supported by all shades of political and religious opinion, both north and south. He is principally remembered for his work with the co-operatives, but he had greater objectives regarding social justice. Plunkett wanted to restore a mutually beneficial relationship between urban and rural Ireland, which had been devastated by long-term poverty and emigration. His scheme for the regeneration of rural areas was based on co-operation and education, and he wanted to modernise agriculture, base rural commerce on the co-operatives and improve the rural economy.[14] Plunkett's agricultural aims for rural Ireland mirrored many of the ideas and ideals forming in Barton's young mind. They were also compatible with the policies of self-sufficiency being put forward by Sinn Féin, a party later associated with Irish republicanism, but Barton was far from supporting any form of republicanism at this early point in his life. In 1908, he undertook a tour of co-operatives in the west of Ireland, in the company of his cousin

Erskine Childers (and possibly also accompanied by Horace Plunkett),[15] and having seen the horrendous level of rural poverty in the region,[16] he returned fully convinced of the absolute necessity of implementing Home Rule for Ireland.[17]

Thus, Barton's early support for Sinn Féin was not as radical as it might appear at first glance. The original Sinn Féin Party, founded by Arthur Griffith in 1905,[18] advocated dual monarchism based on the post-*Ausgleich* (1867) Austro-Hungarian model, where the monarch would rule both Ireland and Britain, but the two islands would have totally separate parliaments with full powers within their respective jurisdictions. Dual monarchism was perhaps a refinement on the idea of 'mere' Home Rule, rather than a step beyond it, since both policies envisaged two parliaments under a single monarch (albeit, in the case of dual monarchism, more or less co-equal parliaments). Thus, by 1910 or so, Robert Barton's political ideology had advanced as far as that of his old neighbour, the Home Ruler Charles Stewart Parnell, or perhaps gone a little way (but only a little way) beyond it, as Barton seemed to toy with the idea of a dual monarchy for a while. Nevertheless, either way, it is safe to assume that Barton's political goal was to see the establishment (or re-establishment) of an Irish parliament in Dublin at this stage. The question must now be asked – why did Barton move beyond Home Rule and become more radicalised?

Events during the period 1912–14 conspired to move Barton beyond his comfort zone as a constitutional supporter of Home Rule. These were the years of the 'Home Rule Crisis', which was precipitated when the parliament in Westminster passed a Home Rule Bill in 1912. This had happened twice before (in 1886 and 1893), and these bills had been rejected by the House of Commons and the House of Lords respectively. However, the 1912 bill was different, due to the terms of the Parliament Act, which had been passed the previous year. Basically, the Conservative-dominated House of Lords could now only delay the third Home Rule Bill for two years, after which it would automatically become law. Alarmed Ulster unionists organised themselves to oppose Home Rule, forming the paramilitary Ulster Volunteer Force (U.V.F.) to resist the passage of the new bill. Inspired by Eoin McNeill's article 'The North Began',[19] Irish nationalists countered this threat to the implementation of Home Rule by establishing the Irish Volunteer Force (I.V.F.), to fight for the introduction of Home Rule. This was the situation that prompted S. P. B. Mais' decision 'to throw in his lot with Sinn Féin and join the Southern Irish'. Barton, meanwhile, supported the aspirations of the I.V.F., but the movement split into two sections when the First World War began in 1914.

The Irish Republican Brotherhood (I.R.B.), a small, shadowy, subversive separatist group who espoused republicanism, rejected gradualism and favoured radicalism and armed revolution,[20] had managed to infiltrate the I.V.F. Hence, when the vast majority of the Volunteers answered the Irish Parliamentary Party (I.P.P.) leader John Redmond's call to join the British army when the First World War began, clandestine I.R.B. activity ensured that a rump of militants stayed behind and eventually staged the Easter Rising in 1916. The smaller group of separatist militants who did not support Britain's war effort retained the name 'Irish Volunteers', while those who joined the British army to fight for Home Rule (which they believed must be implemented after the war in return for their military service) were known as the National Volunteers.

Robert Barton, perhaps inspired by his family's military background, or possibly because of a sense of duty and a desire to oppose German militarism, supported the National Volunteers. Perhaps both motives were at play – the one does not preclude the other, and he may have had other motives as well. In his witness statement to the Bureau of Military History (given in 1954), Barton revealed: 'I was a member of the National Volunteers. I worked in the office only and did not drill or parade. I managed the office for [Inspector General] Colonel [Maurice] Moore. I knew Count Plunkett, Bulmer Hobson, The O'Rahilly, Eoin MacNeill and quite a number of other Volunteer leaders.' Barton continued his account thus: 'I was in the office when the split in the Volunteers took place. There was divergence of policy. Redmond wanted to support the war and, of course, Colonel Moore did too, but the Sinn Féin leaders wanted a more nationalistic programme. So great was the divergence of opinion that the two parties split.'[21] Barton actually succeeded his cousin, Erskine Childers, as Colonel Moore's secretary when Childers left the post to join the British navy.[22] However, Barton did not remain long in the position either, as he mentioned in his witness statement:

I carried on until September, after the Sinn Féin Volunteers had broken off from the National Volunteers. I may have stayed on for about two months after the division. At that time, it appeared to me that the National Volunteers were rather a futile body and that I was not doing anything of much use. So, I went home to Annamoe after handing over to [Dermot] Coffey. It was in October, 1915, that I joined the British Army and went to train as an officer.[23]

On 17 December 1915, Captain Erskine Booth, who was stationed at the Curragh Camp, recommended Barton for a commission. Booth's letter of recommendation was fulsome in its praise, stating: 'I have known Robert Childers Barton all his life, and can conscientiously say that I know no man more suitable for a commission … [He] has given up a very large house and farm so that he may do his duty to his country.'[24] This recommendation acknowledged Barton's sacrifice in leaving Glendalough House and the family estate so that he might 'do his duty'. This is the first overtly documented mention of what was to become a recurring motif throughout Barton's long life – his sense of duty. It must surely have been a prime motive in his decision to join the British army during the war. Barton received his commission, and served as a second lieutenant in the Royal Dublin Fusiliers. His brothers, Thomas Eyre and Charles Erskine, were officers in the Royal Irish Rifles. Both were killed in France – Thomas in July 1916 and Charles in August 1918.[25] Fate, however, dictated that Robert would be gazetted and sent not to France, but to Dublin, in the spring of 1916.

3

An Easter Rising
(April 1916 and its
Immediate Aftermath)

When Barton arrived in Kingstown (Dun Laoghaire) on the outskirts of Dublin on the Wednesday of Easter Week 1916, he saw that the city was 'more or less under siege and part of it was in flames'.[1] Barton was unable to travel into the city, so he reported to the Provost-Marshal at Kingstown, who sent him home because he had no uniform! Barton went home to Annamoe, where he remained for 'about a week', before returning to the capital to report to his commanding officer, Colonel Lawrence Esmonde of the 10th Dublins, in the Royal Barracks, as he had been originally ordered to do.[2] Esmonde and Barton knew each other,[3] and in a telling comment, Barton revealed that Esmonde 'knew where my sympathies lay', so he ensured that 'my duties were confined to the barracks'.[4] Barton's sister, Dulcibella, maintains that Esmonde actually asked Barton, 'Do you want to fight?' to which Barton replied 'No.'[5] Esmonde may have been trying to ascertain whether Barton was willing to take an active role in rounding up and arresting suspected rebels and their sympathisers, as by this time the rebellion had been quashed, and many of the rebels had been taken prisoner. Rebels who had been captured at every volunteer position and nearly all of those arrested in the round-up of suspects following the rebellion (some 3,240 men and 79 women) were taken to Richmond Barracks in Inchicore.[6] In fact, the barracks housed more than 3,000 suspected rebels before their sentencing.[7] After a few days at the Royal Barracks, Barton was sent, along with Lieutenant Grant, to Richmond Barracks, to report to Colonel Frazer for 'duty in connection with the prisoners'. Grant was put in charge of prisoners' letters, and Barton was instructed to 'take over the duties of officer in charge of prisoners' effects'. Frazer told Barton that there were a great many charges of looting against the British troops, and the War Office had instructed the authorities in Dublin to stop the looting and to collect what had been looted and return it.[8] Thus began Barton's time spent with the rebel prisoners, some of whom he already knew from his time in the Volunteers – an experience that seems to have had a profound effect on him. Despite disliking his role in relation to prisoners' effects,[9] according to Pakenham, Barton was 'profoundly moved by the faith and stoicism of the prisoners, [and] he came to see them as the representatives of the new spirit in the country, and to reckon it a crime to resist their movement further'.[10]

When he arrived in Richmond Barracks, Barton found things 'in a chaotic state'. He found that 'prisoners' effects were in buckets and bags littered around the office', and he 'first tried to put them into order and to

Fig 3. Devastation greeted Second Lieutenant Barton on his return to Dublin in 1916. (Image (Barton Papers, WWCA/PP1/33) courtesy of the Wicklow County Archive)

find out to whom the properties belonged'. He also noted that 'the bundles had been systematically pillaged'. He set to work painstakingly, trying to restore order from the chaos and to return property to its rightful owners. He 'went around to all the prisoners to ascertain what each had lost' but he was 'unable to return a quantity of property' because he 'could not find claimants amongst the prisoners in the barracks'.[11] He also wrote to prisoners' next of kin, relations and friends. One such letter was written to Mabel Fitzgerald, wife of Volunteer Desmond Fitzgerald, at Loretto Villas, Bray, County Wicklow, in which he informed her that 'a great coat labelled as being the property of Mr Fitzgerald is being forwarded to you at the above address this day'. The letter was dated 21 May 1916 and was signed by Second Lieutenant R. C. Barton as 'officer in charge of prisoners' effects'.[12] He soon found, however, that his rank of second lieutenant didn't carry much weight when he was dealing with superior officers – Barton noted that a major could get information from them far more easily. Consequently, Colonel Frazer appointed Major Charles Harold Heathcote of the Sherwood Foresters to the role, leaving Barton in place to work under him in the prisoners' effects department.[13] This change is reflected in a letter written by Barton to Dr Kathleen Lynn, dated 11 July 1916. He informed Lynn that no action had yet been decided upon regarding property lost in Liberty Hall during the rising, but he assured her that her claim had 'not been lost sight of' and he promised to write again when he had the 'necessary authority'. This letter was signed by Barton 'pro officer in charge of prisoners' effects' [Heathcote].[14] As was the case with the letter to Mabel Fitzgerald, the tone of the letter to Kathleen Lynn was polite and respectful, which one might not expect from an officer in Richmond Barracks in the immediate aftermath of the Easter Rising, considering that both women were directly and actively involved in the rebellion. It seems that the dutiful Barton did his job well and worked efficiently, whether under his own authority or under Heathcote.

Contact with Heathcote may also have contributed to Barton's political awakening, which eventually resulted in his decision to join Sinn Féin. Heathcote served in the Sherwood Foresters, the regiment that took heavy casualties at and around Mount Street Bridge. Ostensibly as a reward for their gallantry (but in a move that smacked more than a little of taking revenge), the Sherwoods were chosen to form the firing squads for the post-rebellion executions. Brigadier J. Young was in charge at Kilmainham Gaol, but Heathcote, as second-in-command of the regiment, was in command of the actual firing squads.[15] Barton referred to this fact in his witness statement, noting that:

> Heathcote was in charge of the firing party at the executions in Kilmainham – at the execution of the first six or seven anyway. He was in charge of the firing party and ... He was present at Connolly's execution. He may have been in charge of all the executions.[16]

Heathcote's role in the executions meant that he was uniquely placed to give Barton many of the gory details of the events in the Stone-breakers' Yard at Kilmainham, where the grisly work of killing the condemned leaders was carried out. For example, Heathcote's description of the execution of James Connolly seems to have left a deep impression on Barton,[17] who deposed in his statement:

> Heathcote told me he [Connolly] was probably drugged and was almost dead. He was not able to sit upright in the chair on which he was placed and, when they shot him, the whole back of the chair was blown out ... They brought out a chair for Connolly because he was unable to stand. They brought him in an ambulance and from that on a stretcher to the chair. I think ... they just laid him in the chair. They shot him through the chest and blew the back out of the chair. I gathered from Heathcote that he was quite unconscious. He was a dying man.[18]

Hence, although Barton did not witness any of the executions in person, the descriptions that he heard from Heathcote evidently stirred a degree of sympathy for the rebels within him. Barton's presence at some of the courts martial held at Richmond Barracks in the immediate aftermath of the rising,[19] including that of Seán MacEntee, increased his empathy with the prisoners.[20] He testified in his witness statement:

> I saw Seán MacEntee court-martialled. It must have been about the middle of May. I was present. Lord Cheylesmore presided at the court-martial. I don't know whether Seán had a lawyer or not, but I know that it was a terrible ordeal for him ... An officer – I think he was a Scots Guard – was called to give evidence and was asked, 'Can you recognise any of your attackers'? He looked round and pointed

to Seán MacEntee and said, 'I recognise him'. I thought it was going
to be very hot for Seán MacEntee, but he did not turn a hair ...[21]

Despite the growth of his nationalist sympathies and the beginnings of a
more radical shift in his political opinions, Barton remained in the British
army until June 1918. The 10th Dublins embarked for France, crossing
to Le Havre, on 19 August 1916,[22] but Barton did not travel with them.
Instead, 'the Assistant Adjutant General in Headquarters, Parkgate Street'
refused to permit him to go with them, and he was transferred to the
11th Battalion so he could complete his work with the prisoners' effects.
Barton's period of service as a British officer in Dublin, from Easter
Week 1916 to June 1918, and his shifting political loyalties during that
time coincided with a wind of change in public opinion throughout
Ireland. Initial opposition to the rising and overt hostility towards the
rebels, which gradually changed to admiration for their bravery and
support for their cause, have been well documented at national level.
Contemporary press reports provide indications of the public response to
the rising. Printing had been interrupted by the hostilities in Dublin, but
the first edition of a leading national newspaper to appear after the rising
(which covered a period of about a week and a half) reported 'flame and
ruins', 'devastation in the streets' and the 'terrible spectacle' of 'scenes
of havoc in Dublin'.[23] Shortly afterwards, another press report spoke of
'the heart of Dublin devoured by furious conflagrations', calling Easter
week 'the darkest week in the history of Dublin' and referring to 'an orgy
of fire and slaughter'. However, the same newspaper also carried news
of the execution of thirteen rebel leaders, and of John Redmond's plea
to halt these ongoing executions. Redmond stated that 'the continuance
of military executions was causing rapidly-increasing bitterness and
exasperation among a large section of the [Irish] population, who had
not the slightest sympathy with the insurrection'.[24] The shift in nationalist
opinion was beginning, and within a few months it would reflect the
sentiments expressed by militant Irish Americans as early as mid-May,
when one of their periodicals led with the headline 'England murdering
Ireland's leaders', averring that: 'England keeps up her brutal work ...
people of Ireland goaded beyond endurance just as in 1798 ... forty-six
Irish Nationalist leaders sentenced to death in a few days ... [causing] great
indignation in Ireland and throughout the civilised world.'[25] However
biased this article may have been, it was correct in respect of the growth of

'great indignation in Ireland', due to both the draconian British reaction to the rising and to the harsh clampdown in the aftermath of the event. This indignation manifested itself from the summer of 1916 onwards by the swing in nationalist sympathies towards the rebels and their cause.

Moreover, the protracted nature of the executions of the rebel leaders and the wave of arrests in the wake of the rising soon made nationalists pause and reflect, and prompted a different tone in the press, both national and regional. The *Leinster Leader* published an editorial entitled 'Fixing the responsibility', stating that the leaders of the rebellion 'have paid the penalty for their acts and over their graves we are silent; it will be for some historian of the future, removed from the passions and prejudices of our day, to enquire into the motives and estimate the culpability of these men'. Meanwhile, the *Nationalist and Leinster Times* editorial pleaded with the authorities to order 'a cessation of further executions. Justice tempered with mercy will be a sufficient deterrent to further trouble, and leniency at this stage will be less liable to leave behind the bitter feelings that result from the rigid administration of martial law.'[26] Local press reports such as these were influential throughout the country in changing people's minds about the rising and its leaders, but they were also dictated by the opinions of their readership. They were both a cause and a consequence of a rising tide of sympathy with the leaders, and increasing nationalist identification with their ideals.

Local and national press reports provide us with an insight into the process by which the sympathies of nationalists began to change, and reading some excerpts from the actual texts of the provincial newspapers available at the time allows one to trace the speed and breadth of this change across the island. The executed leaders, the rebels and those arrested in the aftermath of the Easter Rising changed rapidly from villains to heroes. This change would lead to the inexorable rise of Sinn Féin, which culminated in that party's landslide win in the 1918 general election. Meanwhile, Barton continued to work with prisoners' effects until he was released from the army in May of that year, a month or so before his discharge papers came through.[27] Other Bureau of Military History (B.M.H.) witness statements provide further illumination on Barton's gradual political conversion through his contact with some of the prisoners. For example, we glean from the testimony of William O'Brien that Barton spent a lot of time with Darrell Figgis, and that they engaged in 'long conversation'.[28] O'Brien revealed that Barton told Figgis that if there was any urgent reason for communicating with him, he should ask for 'the officer in charge of prisoners' effects' and not for him by name.[29] This implies that Barton did not want to appear to be over-familiar with prisoners such as Figgis, even though the two spoke at length. This corroborates Barton's own account of events, in which he stated that he 'had known Figgis quite well as a prisoner'.[30] Figgis, who had been involved in the Howth gun running incident, was a nationalist propagandist and became secretary of the 'new', more radicalised, Sinn Féin in 1917.[31] Barton also revealed that, although he was unsure, he thought that Figgis may have put his name forward as a candidate for West Wicklow in the 1918 general election. If this were the case, Barton's time with the prisoners of 1916 led directly to his political involvement as a Sinn Féin candidate two years later.

Other witness statements also show that Barton treated the prisoners and their families very well, and that he spent a lot of time in their company. Robert Kinsella, who was arrested in the wake of the Easter Rising and was 'put on a gun-boat and conveyed to North Wall, Dublin', was also imprisoned in Richmond Barracks for a while. Kinsella stated that he and the other prisoners 'were under Bob Barton, who treated us very well'.[32] Barton also treated the prisoners' relatives and friends well when they visited the barracks. For example, Mrs Batt (Bridget) O'Connor, who received 'a message from a released prisoner that her husband was detained in Richmond Barracks', stated that she 'went to see him the very next day'. She continued her testimony:

> When I went in there was an officer in charge. That was my first meeting with Robert Barton. He was awfully nice. He had an office in the gymnasium building. He brought me along to the prison buildings – N. Block – and there I met Batt … Back in the office Mr Barton, who treated me very kindly, handed me a parcel with the prisoner's effects.[33]

Hugh Hehir provides more information about Barton's relationship with the republican prisoners.[34] The following excerpt from Hehir's witness statement is very telling:

> At that time Robert Barton was an officer in the Dublin Fusiliers and in the course of his duties he visited our block daily and got very friendly with a group of prisoners there owing to the fact that

he had known Darl (sic) Figgis previously. I think his associations at that time with the prisoners were responsible for instilling in him the very national outlook that he later displayed.[35]

If other witness statements, such as those of Robert Kinsella and Bridget O'Connor, point to how well Barton treated republican prisoners and their visitors, Hehir's testimony moves beyond this. William O'Brien revealed that Barton had long conversations with Darrell Figgis, but Hehir's deposition squarely puts Barton daily visiting and on friendly terms with Figgis and his circle of comrades within the prison system. Hehir goes further, suggesting that Barton's relationship with the incarcerated men was the reason behind his political conversion to republicanism. Hehir maintains that Barton's 'very national outlook' was caused directly by contact with the prisoners at this pivotal time during the Irish Revolution. All the indications are that Barton's time in Richmond Barracks had a profound effect on him. He was deeply impressed by the attitude of the captured rebels in the aftermath of the rising,[36] and in the words of Dorothy Macardle, 'the conduct and the logic of his prisoners made ... Barton a convert to the Republican cause'.[37] Frank Pakenham was even clearer on this point when he wrote 'it was as a British officer in charge of prisoners after the 1916 Rising that he [Barton] underwent the experiences which decided him to join Sinn Féin'.[38]

The Appeal of Sinn Féin
(Summer 1916–Summer 1918)

Notwithstanding the political conversion that he experienced at this time, Barton remained in the British army until the summer of 1918. He left in May and his discharge papers came through in June, but his departure was not because of his shifting political views. He left because T. P. Gill, the Secretary of the Department of Agriculture,[1] wanted him to return to Annamoe to farm the land. Barton had an agricultural diploma from Cirencester, and he had always been a progressive farmer, with an interest in land improvement and modern methods of agriculture. Gill's request to Barton was part of a wider drive to return leading farmers to their land in the wake of Germany's decision to renew unrestricted submarine (U-boat) warfare in 1917.[2] With convoys running a renewed and even more ruthless blockade in the Atlantic, resulting in supply shortages, food production on the home front (in both Britain and Ireland) became paramount and was vital for the survival of the British and Allied war effort. Barton makes this clear in his witness statement:

> There came a time when the provision of food was as important as fighting. The English decided to take out of the army the principal leaders of farming in all districts, and T. P. Gill was asked whether there were any persons in the army whom he would like to get back into agriculture. I was one of those he named and I was given my release.[3]

Barton would not have been allowed to resign his commission in wartime,[4] but he was allowed to leave early because of Gill's request that he be returned to Annamoe. However, all the evidence points to Barton having undergone a political epiphany during his time with the republican prisoners in Dublin. One may speculate that he may have wanted to resign his commission earlier because of his support for the prisoners' ideals, or that he would have resigned immediately anyway once the war ended, but that can only be speculation. What is certain is that by late 1918 Barton was a fully-fledged republican. Significantly, Stuart Mais noted that 'though Barton had been an officer in the British army and fought against Germany from 1914 to 1918, he had been put into prison for sixteen months for his Irish sympathies'.[5] Perhaps R. F. Foster best summed up the effect of the 1916 Rising and its aftermath on Barton when he wrote: 'after 1916 he took another path – resigning his commission, joining Sinn Féin, commencing a career as a nationalist which took him into … the treaty negotiating chamber'.[6] Barton's prolonged contact with the rebels of 1916 certainly had momentous long-term consequences for both County Wicklow and Ireland.

Having returned to Annamoe after his military discharge, Barton devoted himself to farming. In his own words, 'I tried to do the best I could for the purpose for which I was released from the army and to show that it was worthwhile.'[7] There may have been another reason behind Gill's request that Barton should be allowed to leave the army and return to his estate. It is possible that Barton's mother, Agnes, who was then 70 years of age,[8] was unable to run the estate properly. Agnes died on 13 August 1918, shortly after the return of her son. Her will named Robert as the beneficiary, and an Inland Revenue form from 1919 (for the purpose of calculating the amount of estate duty due on the death of Agnes) reveals that, in addition to Glendalough House and the estate lands, there were stocks and shares valued at £2,651 0s 1d and a further £2,000 that Agnes had originally placed in a trust for her husband Charles (who died in October 1890), all of which Barton now inherited.[9] He was now back in the place of his boyhood, which he had described as being 'in the heart of the rebel area of County Wicklow', and among his employees, who were 'descendants of those who were shot in 1798'.[10] Moreover, he had returned at a time of huge political change. The Irish question mattered to Barton, and his own nationalistic views evidently matured during this period.

There had been a marked swing in the sympathies of nationalist Ireland, including those of County Wicklow, beginning in the immediate aftermath of the 1916 Rising. Wicklow County Council held its spring quarterly meeting in the council chambers of Wicklow courthouse on 15 May 1916. Nine councillors were in attendance and the correspondence at the meeting included two resolutions, firstly from New Ross Board of Guardians 'condemning in the strongest possible manner the disturbances caused in Ireland by the Sinn Féin organisation and the Citizens' Army, and, as a nationalist board, entirely disassociating themselves with such disgraceful and unworthy scenes'. The second resolution was from Tullamore Urban District Council, recording its 'condemnation of the recent deplorable outbreak in Dublin, and calling upon all Nationalist Irishmen to support Mr John Redmond's constitutional policy'.[11] Correspondence at the next meeting of the County Council on Thursday, 8 June included a letter from the Prime Minister, 10 Downing Street, Whitehall, London S.W., 'acknowledging receipt of the council's resolution on the subject of the maintenance of constitutional rights and law in Ireland following the recent disturbances in Dublin', and one from Mr John Redmond Esq., M.P., House of Commons, London, 'acknowledging the council's resolution re same'.[12] It is telling, however, that, while the County Council condemned the 'insane action' of those responsible for the rising, councillors also demanded an enquiry into the executions of the rebel leaders and the internment without trial of such large numbers of suspects, while appealing to the Prime Minister to restore normal constitutional rule.[13] By November 1916, the County Council attitude had changed and councillors were now dealing with more radical resolutions such as those:

'(1) protesting against the partition of Ireland in any shape or form, and claiming full self-government for an undivided Ireland (2) warning the government of the grave consequences of any attempt to enforce conscription in Ireland which, if at all, should only be imposed by an Irish parliament and (3) suggesting the establishment of a political prisoners' amnesty association for the purpose of securing the release of the Irish prisoners interned in England'.[14]

Wicklow's county councillors had certainly changed their political opinions during the year.

Many rebel prisoners had been transferred to Frongoch internment camp in Wales after the rising. These included some County Wicklow natives, such as Tom Cullen of Blessington.[15] Cullen was now in a place where many rebels strengthened their resolve to continue the struggle for independence after their release. Those releases began during the summer months of 1916, aided, according to the local press, by 'the efforts of Mr John T. Donovan, M.P. [whose] indefatigable exertions in the interests of the imprisoned relatives of his constituents and the people of County Wicklow are deservedly much appreciated'.[16] Tom Cullen had to wait until December 1916 for his release.[17] A local newspaper reported that:

> through the successful exertions of the Irish Party a large number
> of political prisoners were released for Christmas. What makes the
> action of the Irish Party more magnanimous is the fact that the greater
> number of the prisoners so released were bitter opponents of the
> party ... but even if they erred ... they are Irishmen who loved their
> country not wisely but too well, and Irishmen the world over were
> indignant at what they regard as excessive punishment inflicted.[18]

Cullen returned from his incarceration to a changed Ireland, where the fortunes of the Irish Parliamentary Party were declining rapidly and where the rise of Sinn Féin marked it out as the new political force. John T. Donovan's 'indefatigable exertions' and the subsequent 'successful exertions of the Irish Party' were evidently not enough to stem the tide, and County Wicklow was no exception to this new trend of Sinn Féin advancement in late 1916 and early 1917.

As the year 1917 progressed, the rise of Sinn Féin in County Wicklow evidently troubled some traditional nationalist Home Rulers. In April, a published letter from Joseph Cunniam of Ballycullen noted the rising tide of Sinn Féin. Cunniam described himself as 'a firm supporter of Mr Redmond' and as 'a border man of both divisions, East and West Wicklow' but commented on the absence of both M.P.s 'during the last few troubled and critical years'. He stated that, 'Young men from the farming class, whose fathers were rent-slaves forty years ago, now use the freedom won for them to turn on their benefactors, the Irish Party', before going on to suggest that, 'Strolling adventurers from God-knows-where are preaching a new doctrine to us, but this madness will pass away – as it is already doing – and we will all be working together on the right lines.' The writer called for 'closer understanding between representatives and people in Wicklow, so that our young men will not be swayed by silly stories, but have from our elected representatives, an account of work done and work still to do, and a message of hope and cheer which will re-echo from Blessington to Arklow'.[19] Cunniam's concerns for the Irish Party in County Wicklow were well founded, and the resurgent Sinn Féin Party continued to grow in strength throughout the county during 1917.

The 1916 Rising had been attributed to Sinn Féin in press reports about Easter Week. Arthur Griffith was interned after the rebellion and spent time in Reading Gaol. He was released on Christmas Eve 1916, and quickly set to work to rebuild the party during 1917. The name of Sinn Féin was now an integral part of mainstream Irish politics and Griffith put forward the party's platform of abstaining from taking seats in Westminster, establishing a parliament in Dublin and an Irish government to run the country, and appealing to any post-First World War conference to recognise Ireland's right to self-determination as espoused by the American President, Woodrow Wilson.[20] The Sinn Féin Party also continued to advocate economic self-sufficiency and the promotion of native Irish industry. Indeed, a Sinn Féin handbill for the general election of the following year focussed on the demise of many extinct industrial ventures in County Wicklow, and specifically referred to former local industries in Shillelagh, Cronebane, Glenmalure, Ballymurtagh, Arklow, Rathdrum, Greenane, Wicklow, Stratford-on-Slaney, Baltinglass, Dunlavin and Roundwood.[21] Evidently the policies of Griffith and the 'new', republican Sinn Féin (with de Valera elected president in October) had attracted some support in Wicklow and the party was making inroads in the county.

At a large Sinn Féin meeting and aeridheacht (open-air gathering) in Baltinglass on Sunday, 21 October 1917, the more militant stance of the revitalised party was made clear. The principal speaker was Laurence Ginnell, formerly of the Irish Parliamentary Party but now of Sinn Féin. Ginnell (1854–1923) was a native of Delvin, Co. Westmeath. He was elected as a Home Ruler in 1906 and sat as an independent nationalist from 1909 onwards. He strongly criticised the British government for the 1916 executions. On 9 May he accused the British Prime Minister, Herbert Asquith, of murder, and was escorted out of the House of Commons. Following de Valera's electoral victory in East Clare, on 10 July 1917, Ginnell resigned his parliamentary seat and joined Sinn Féin.[22] At Baltinglass, Ginnell told his audience that he was 'proud to see such a fine assembly of the mountaineers of Wicklow; to find so many of the true old blood of the Kavanaghs, the Byrnes and the Kinsellas and the rest, whose forefathers lived amongst the hills and defended them against the invader'. He assured his listeners that the Sinn Féin 'policy now being put before the country was the wisest, the noblest, the surest and the only policy for the regeneration of Ireland'. Advocating economic independence, Ginnell noted that 'today, there is no direct trade between Ireland and any other country ... they must sell to England at a price fixed by England'. 'Ireland', he said, 'wants to build up her trade and commerce, wants to build up a proper system of education, wants to restore the people to the land, wants to drain the land' but he maintained that the Home Rule Bill would not allow them these freedoms. In contrast, he assured them that Sinn Féin was 'a great policy when correctly understood'. According to Ginnell, the Irish people 'will not accept any [Home Rule] settlement now. They say that England has no right to rule in this country any more than Ireland has a right to rule in England. By sending members to Westminster, Ireland acknowledged that Britain had a right to rule in this country.' Ginnell made an impassioned plea, saying that he 'wanted the young men to come in and join the Sinn Féin branches in their district. It was not enough to come there and cheer him. There was a great deal of work to be done and the young women should also join up, because they were very clever in many ways and could give great help.' Ginnell maintained that Sinn Fein 'clubs would be a centre place where Volunteer views would come under consideration'.[23]

Ginnell's linking of Sinn Féin with the Volunteers at Baltinglass was significant. Some two months previously, a large contingent of R.I.C. men, led by D.I. Egan and Head Constable Taylor, raided a public house in Baltinglass in the small hours of the morning. When Mr J. Kitson admitted them to the premises they seized a cache of rifles and bayonets that he had in his possession. The police removed the weapons, which had been in storage for the local Volunteers.[24] The incident demonstrates that the Volunteers were still a force in County Wicklow, and that there were still arms in circulation in the region. Volunteer reorganisation went ahead rapidly, particularly from the first phase of Frongoch releases onwards. Nationally, the link between the two organisations was cemented at the Sinn Féin árd fheis in October 1917, when Arthur Griffith stood down as president in favour of Éamon de Valera, the senior surviving commandant of the Easter Rising.[25] On the day after the Sinn Féin árd fheis, the Volunteers also elected de Valera as their president. One nationalist periodical urged the new leader of the Volunteers to use 'the caution and discretion that should be exercised by a good general at every stage of the combat, for Éamon de Valera is now the General, commanding-in-chief the Irish army', advising him to 'proceed constitutionally and so compel his opponents to break the law of nations first'.[26] Thus, the two republican movements, political and military, presented a common front and were closely intertwined. From October 1917 onwards, the growth of Sinn Féin in Wicklow also involved concurrent growth in the resurgent Volunteer movement. The military wing of the republican movement was also reorganising, and Volunteers in the county were involved in 'parades, field training, dispatch work and intelligence duties' during 1917.[27]

Within a year or so, three major events occurred, all of which had a huge impact on life in County Wicklow and the rest of Ireland. Firstly, the onset of the great flu pandemic adversely affected the county. As Ida Milne has observed: 'The Spanish influenza pandemic silenced whole communities as it passed through, extracting a devastating death toll and even more astounding numbers of sufferers.'[28] A relatively mild strain of the illness first manifested itself in June 1918, but it reappeared in more virulent form in October. County Wicklow was one of the areas most severely affected, with a death rate of between three and four per thousand of the population in both 1918 and 1919.[29] In October 1918, the second wave of influenza was raging throughout Leinster, but particularly in Counties Wicklow, Wexford and Kildare.[30] The second outbreak of the pandemic was still widespread in November 1918, when the Great War ended. The armistice was another major event, and doubtless led to rejoicing among many inhabitants of County Wicklow, particularly within those families who had combat personnel returning from various theatres of war. However, political developments in Ireland had altered the significance of the armistice, and the soldiers, sailors and airmen returning to Wicklow from far-off places would come back to a changed county. Finally, the new political reality was anticipated when a general election was called immediately after the end of the war. This would be the third major event to affect life in County Wicklow before the end of 1918, and Robert Barton found himself centre-stage.

Barton had returned to Annamoe in the summer of 1918, nearing the end of a period of tumultuous political upheaval in County Wicklow. Despite his hardened nationalistic views, Barton had been a supporter of the Irish Convention,[31] established by Lloyd George in July 1917.[32] The convention was chaired by Sir Horace Plunkett,[33] who issued invitations to all Irish parties (both nationalists and unionists) to attend in order to sort out some compromise between the two political groupings. However, the convention was doomed to failure from the outset. The unpopular possibility of conscription being introduced in Ireland hovered constantly over the event, causing Erskine Childers, who had travelled to Dublin at this time, to observe glumly to Dulcibella Barton: 'This conscription will end the convention.'[34] Moreover, the trade unions refused their invitations and, crucially, Sinn Féin did not attend either. The unionists attended, but Sir Edward Carson held out for the partition of six Ulster counties and would not hear of any other possibility. John Redmond, the leader of the Irish Parliamentary Party, was in poor health, and in a final attempt to salvage his political lifetime's work he tried to do a deal with southern unionists. This overture fell on deaf ears – no one wanted such a deal – and Redmond died in March 1918. His successor, John Dillon, then ended the Home Rule Party's association with the convention, which collapsed in April. However, the Home Rulers suffered much reputational damage through their involvement in this failed attempt at compromise, and Sinn Féin's absenteeism from the convention was vindicated by the negative outcome of events. The fortunes of the Irish Parliamentary Party continued to decline, while those of Sinn Féin continued to rise. Barton's departure from the army in May 1918 more or less coincided with the collapse of the convention the previous month. With hopes of compromise in tatters and the convention disbanded when he arrived home to Glendalough House in an altered, more republican and politically aware County Wicklow, Barton turned to Sinn Féin and he finally joined the party in the summer of 1918.[35] He founded a Sinn Féin club in Roundwood, following in the footsteps of his sister Dulcibella, who had already founded clubs in Laragh and on the Barton estate.[36] By this time, Barton had met Michael Collins, who had been impressed by the Wicklow man's treatment of political prisoners after the Easter Rising. Barton had also interested his cousin, Erskine Childers, in the Irish struggle for independence and it was through him that Childers first came into contact with Collins.[37] Barton's political conversion had finally come to fruition with membership of the revitalised republican party, and the brief period of 'peace and quietness' following his return to Glendalough House ended when the 1918 general election campaign began and 'the people of County Wicklow proposed that he should stand as Sinn Féin candidate for West Wicklow'.[38]

5

Selected and Elected
(June 1918–January 1919)

Barton was slightly vague in his witness statement about who put him forward as a candidate in the general election of 1918, but he thought that Darrell Figgis may have been behind the proposal. Although Figgis may have been the prime mover, it is clear that many people from the county approached Barton to stand for election in the constituency of West Wicklow. When Captain Booth penned his recommendation that Barton should be commissioned as an officer in 1915, he stated: 'His character, ability and his thoroughness, thoroughly fit him for the position of a leader of men.'[1] Evidently, many people in County Wicklow and, more importantly, the Sinn Féin leadership in the county and further up the national hierarchy, agreed with Booth's assessment. Barton's own vague but matter-of-fact account of how he became a candidate was as follows:

> … people came to me and asked me whether I would stand as a candidate. Wicklow had no Sinn Féin candidate at the time. Someone had to be found. Of course, I may have been suggested by someone like Darrell Figgis, whom I had known quite well as a prisoner. Someone must have suggested that I would be a suitable candidate if I would stand for West Wicklow. My name was put up to the various Cumainn, or probably to the leaders in Dublin, because it was my business to form the Cumainn. They responded.[2]

The general election of 1918 differed from previous electoral contests in many ways. While unionists would be returned as usual in constituencies where they formed the majority of the electorate, Irish nationalists now had a clear choice between the Irish Parliamentary Party (who favoured Home Rule) and the Sinn Féin Party (who espoused republicanism). The Labour Party had considered running candidates in nationalist areas, but stood aside, leaving the field clear for a showdown between the two main parties. The contrast in fortunes between the two parties at this time was marked. Recent by-election victories had honed Sinn Féin's electioneering skills, and their support was bolstered by the fact that many of their candidates were either already in jail or being pursued and harassed by the British authorities. Among their other advantages were the youthful demographic of their energetic supporters, the attraction of their separatist policies and the fact that they received credit from the public for preventing conscription in Ireland at the time of the 'German Plot'. The Irish Parliamentary Party, on the other hand, was in disarray. The

Fig 4. Small, broadside (10in × 6in) 1918 election advertisement for Robert Barton. (Sourced from www.ccalireland.com/Graphics/database_images/album_files/public_address/political_advertisements/slides/1918-election-poster-robert-barton.html (no copyright))

death of John Redmond meant that it was now led by John Dillon, who was nearly 70 years of age. The party's association with the failed Irish Convention was disastrous for its image and the fact that it had enjoyed a monopoly among nationalist voters for so long also worked against it. Some Home Rule M.P.s had never even fought an election because there was no need to do so. Local party branches and the United Irish League had stagnated and, in some cases even became defunct, because they were unnecessary. The contrast with the energetic Sinn Féin election organisers could hardly have been greater.[3]

In West Wicklow, Barton was opposed by The O'Mahony — who, many years before, had preceded him at Oxford and formed a Home Rule club in Magdalen College.[4] According to Barton, he 'should have been a formidable opponent, but he was not very active ... He was an internationalist. He was very much interested in Bulgaria and he promoted hospitals for Bulgarians.'[5] Having noted his opponent's lack of activity during the election campaign, Barton went on to contrast it with the Sinn Féin effort. From his account, there seems little doubt that West Wicklow followed the general trend of efficient electioneering by Sinn Féin, which was a hallmark of the 1918 general election nationwide:

> I had no difficulty in winning the election and I think I got two-thirds of the votes. We had a very good organisation, devised by Bob Brennan. I remember his being arrested, and I remember James O'Mara taking over at some stage. Bob Brennan was responsible for the efficient working of the election machinery in each constituency. O'Mara took over from him. Bob Brennan laid down the lines for our general instruction and left us to carry them out; we had to report progress to him periodically. Most of the posters we designed and had printed ourselves. I don't think we bothered much about the dead votes.[6] All our business was to bring in the living and we succeeded very well. Polling day was 14 December, 1918.[7]

The election of 14 December that year was also the first one in which women could vote. The Representation of the People Act (1918) had given the vote to women of thirty years and over (subject to a property qualification),[8] and legislation was then introduced to allow women to stand for election themselves.[9] In West Wicklow, a Sinn Féin poster hoped that 'the women of Wicklow would cast their first vote for independence,

Fig 5. Sinn Féin election
poster 1918, addressed to 'The
Women of Wicklow'. (Image
(EPH/E7) courtesy of the
National Library of Ireland)

Robert Barton and a free Ireland'.[10] The military wing of republicanism
aided the cause in the constituency, with local Volunteers still involved in
'drilling and training', and additionally now also involved in 'dispatch carrying and election work under arms' during the latter months of 1918.[11]
The recent threat of conscription and the wave of arrests in the wake of
the 'German Plot' of May 1918 also helped to galvanise support for Sinn
Féin,[12] and the election resulted in a 'landslide', with the 'Irish Party nearly
wiped out', numbering only seven alongside the twenty-six unionists and
seventy-three Sinn Féin members elected across the island.[13] In the event,
the election in West Wicklow also resulted in a landslide win for Barton,
who polled 6,239 votes to the 1,370 received by The O'Mahony of the Irish
Party. There were overt election celebrations in West Wicklow, including
a 'big procession headed by the O'Byrne Pipers', the lighting of a bonfire
in Mill Street and the singing of patriotic songs as 'slap bangs exploded' in
Baltinglass. An 'immense crowd congregated' for public bonfires and the
singing of national songs for 'some hours' in Kiltegan,[14] and many West
Wicklow voters, both female and male, must have celebrated long and hard
when Barton was returned for the constituency. It was evident to all that a
new political era had dawned in West Wicklow – and beyond.

The year 1919 opened with an air of uncertainty and expectation in Irish political circles. On Saturday, 4 January, a local newspaper carried a report of a large meeting in Baltinglass, called for the purpose of supporting the invitation to Ireland of the American President Woodrow Wilson. At that meeting, Thomas Fleming from Shillelagh apologised on behalf of the newly elected Barton, who could not attend. Fleming gave a rousing speech, stating that 'the people of Ireland were not looking for Home Rule. Absolute independence was the object, and when they returned Mr Barton by five to one, they voiced that claim ... seventy-five per cent of the people here in West Wicklow had voted for absolute independence.'[15] Dunlavin man John J. Cunningham also addressed the meeting, offering congratulations on the return of Mr Barton. Cunningham told the gathering that:

> they had proved to the world ... that Ireland stands for complete independence. The Irish Party had brought the country to destruction, and it was not in Westminster that redress was to be sought. The rights of small nations must be recognised at the Peace Conference ... Some people say that abstention from Westminster is wrong. A few months ago, when conscription was sought to be imposed on the manhood of Ireland, the Irish Party opposed it on the floor of the House of Commons, but they failed. The voice of the people on their own soil had done what the Irish Party could not do across the water, and so the fight for independence must be carried on at home. They had shown by their votes that their wish was to see Ireland, their native land, as free as it was in the days of Saint Patrick.

The speeches given by both Fleming and Cunningham were overtly republican in tone, and the meeting ended with 'patriotic songs' and 'a large procession, headed by the local Pipers' Band and members of Cumann na mBan'.[16] On Sunday, 5 January, the recently elected Barton spoke at a meeting in Baltinglass town hall,[17] and the appearance of the Sinn Féin parliamentarian brought the new political reality sharply into focus in West Wicklow, as was the case almost all over Ireland.

Sinn Féin had promised to boycott Westminster and form an Irish parliament in Dublin, and then to appeal to the post-war Paris Peace Conference to recognise Ireland's right to self-determination. The peace conference was due to meet in the French capital later in January, so Sinn Féin had to move fast. They actually tried to intercept President Wilson when he was in London, *en route* to Paris. A delegation was chosen 'by either the Dáil or its Executive' to try to meet Wilson face to face and persuade him to 'secure representation for Ireland at the Peace Conference'. Barton's background and education made him a natural choice for inclusion in the delegation. The other delegates were Michael Collins, Seán T. O'Kelly and George Gavan Duffy. However, Barton remembered that the mission proved to be 'quite futile', as the delegates 'never got any nearer to Wilson than a Second Secretary in the American Embassy, and had no success at all'.[18] While in London, the Irish delegates often met in the Llewellyn Davies' home at 23 Campden Hill Square, Kensington.[19] Davies was married to a daughter of James O'Connor, a former Home Rule M.P. for West Wicklow.[20] She was a close friend of both Gavan Duffy and Michael Collins.[21] This diplomatic effort to meet President Wilson was not the only one to meet with failure. A short time later, another Irish delegation also travelled to Paris and was present during the Peace Conference itself, which began on 18 January 1919.[22] O'Kelly and Gavan Duffy were once again involved, but again they failed to get a hearing, or to arrange a meeting with Wilson, in the City of Light.

Despite these diplomatic failures, it was evident that Sinn Féin had replaced the Irish Parliamentary Party as the voice of nationalist – and now republican – Ireland. The Volunteers were re-forming and Sinn Féin M.P.s were not going to take their seats in Westminster. Many people wondered what the next move in Ireland would be. In the event, Sinn Féin invited all 105 Irish M.P.s to meet in the Mansion House in Dublin. The twenty-six Unionists and six remaining Home Rulers refused the invitation, but twenty-seven of the seventy-three Sinn Féin M.Ps attended. Most of the others were still incarcerated following the 'German plot'. Michael Collins and Harry Boland were absent because they were organising de Valera's daring escape from Lincoln Jail. The Mansion House meeting on 21 January 1919 constituted the First Dáil, and a 'ministry' (Cabinet) was elected.[23] The new T.D.s (as opposed to M.P.s) reasserted the 1916 'Declaration of the Irish Republic', passed the 'Democratic Programme' (principally of social reforms),[24] and issued the 'Message to the Free Nations of the World', which was read to the House by West Wicklow T.D. Robert Barton.[25] The following day, one press report boldly stated that 'The Irish historian of the future will, no doubt, regard the 21st January 1919 as a date that marked a turning point in the political history of this country.'[26] The report was referring to the inaugural meeting of the Dáil, but the day was also pivotal for another reason. On that same day, a small group of Volunteers led by Sean Treacy conducted a raid for gelignite and killed two R.I.C. constables at Soloheadbeg Quarry in County Tipperary.[27] Though there were some sporadic violent episodes elsewhere before this ambush, the Soloheadbeg incident is generally taken as the start of the Irish War of Independence (also known as the Anglo-Irish War) of 1919–21. Following the Dáil's declaration of the republic, the reorganised Volunteers took to calling themselves the Irish Republican Army or I.R.A. With the political route to independence blocked by the failure of the Irish delegations in London and Paris, it did not take long for the military alternative to manifest itself, and violence began to escalate from mid-1919 onwards.

6

Prisoner, Director for Agriculture – and Fugitive
(February 1919–January 1920)

In early 1919, Barton was back in County Wicklow and he soon came to the attention of the authorities. Shortly before the 1918 general election, Barton had held a campaign meeting on 6 December in Aughrim.[1] Tom Fleming, Barton's election agent, had distributed leaflets of a seditious nature, which graphically showed a prisoner being executed.[2] On 17 January, this action resulted in Fleming's arrest and incarceration in Mountjoy Jail.[3] Once he was elected, Barton received correspondence from Fleming, requesting that protest meetings be held in and around his native Shillelagh, in the hope of pressurising the authorities into his release, and the release of Patrick Etchingham, who had also been arrested and imprisoned. Barton organised two meetings for Shillelagh and Carnew, but they were proclaimed. The district inspector of the R.I.C. informed Barton that he would hold the meetings 'at his peril'.[4] Despite this ominous development, Barton went ahead with the Shillelagh meeting, which was presided over by the strongly republican Benedictine monk and educator Fr John Francis Sweetman.[5] In his speech to the crowd, Barton threatened that if anything were to happen to Fleming and/or Etchingham, reprisals would be taken against Field Marshal John French,[6] the Lord Lieutenant and supreme commander of the British army in Ireland, and against Lord Fitzwilliam's land agent in the locality, Frank Brooke.[7] The R.I.C. were present at the meeting, held on 2 February 1919, and they took notes of

the content of Barton's speech.[8] Later that day, Barton went ahead with
the second meeting, again presided over by Dom Sweetman, at Carnew.[9]
At this meeting, Barton repeated a promise that he had previously made
to his Shillelagh audience; namely, that if he were arrested and imprisoned
for sedition he would escape.[10]

Barton and his sister Dulcibella both knew that Barton was now skating
on thin ice and risking arrest. According to Dulcibella:

> Shortly after he was elected, [Bob] spoke at a meeting, I think in
> Shillelagh, and expressed his opinions strongly against the British
> Government even threatening Lord French. When he came home
> that night, he said to me, 'I'll think very little of the British
> Government if I am not arrested after that speech.' I said, 'They
> would never come here to arrest you.' 'No,' he said, 'but I am billed
> to speak in the Mansion House at a meeting.'[11]

Nevertheless, despite the sword of Damocles now hanging over him,
Barton knew that the Mansion House meeting (which was not political, but economic, promoting consumers' co-operative stores) was now
drawing close.[12] Dulcibella tried to persuade Barton not to attend, but
her dutiful brother would not hear of staying at home.[13] He travelled
to Dublin as planned on 21 February and contributed to the meeting.
However, on exiting the Mansion House after it had ended, he was
arrested as he left the building. Barton was charged with sedition in relation to speeches he had recently made in County Wicklow.[14] Moreover, as
sporadic violent incidents began to occur throughout the country, there
were indications that the conflict was beginning to affect everyday life in
the county. Wicklow G.A.A. passed a resolution stating that it 'considered
the action of the Central Council as arbitrary in suspending all civil servants from the G.A.A. without taking the opinion of the Gaels of Ireland,
and calling for an immediate withdrawal of the order'.[15] The G.A.A. ban
on civil servants and public servants such as R.I.C. constables who served
the Crown happened against a backdrop of I.R.A. preparation in County
Wicklow,[16] where 'local commanders were still drilling and training their
members' during much of 1919.[17]

Following his arrest on 21 February, Barton spent the night in the
Bridewell, before being moved to Mountjoy Jail the following day. He
found himself in the company of political prisoners once again, but this

time he was one of the inmates. According to Barton, three other members of the Dáil, Piaras Beasley, David Sears and J. J. Walsh, were also being held there at this time.[18] However, on the night of 16–17 March 1919, Barton was involved in one of the most daring and audacious prison breaks ever carried out in Ireland.[19] The escape was facilitated by aid from Warder Joe Berry and other sympathetic and friendly warders in the prison. They contacted Michael Collins, and an escape plan was hatched. Barton's solicitor, P. H. O'Reilly, visited him in Mountjoy, bringing Richard Mulcahy along,[20] ostensibly acting as his clerk, but smuggling in a file and a hacksaw at the same time. Unseen by the warders, Mulcahy surreptitiously passed the tools to Barton, who promptly hid them in his riding breeches, as he was not in prison clothes. On the night of the escape, Barton cut through a bar of his cell window, and managed to get out into one of the prison yards.[21] Fortune had favoured Barton because his cell had been on the highest storey of the building but an outbreak of influenza among prisoners in adjacent cells meant that he was removed to a ground-floor cell between those of J. J. Walsh and William Sears.[22] Before he left his cell, Barton coolly left an effigy of himself in his bed and a note for the prison governor, stating that he felt that he had to leave due to the discomfort of his present surroundings![23] The rescue party, led by Rory O'Connor,[24] threw a rope ladder over the 20ft-high outer wall, and Barton scaled it before dropping into a blanket held firmly by the rescuers in the street. They retrieved the rope ladder for future use, and brought Barton to a nearby street, where Michael Collins was waiting to congratulate the escapee. Barton got into the car with Rory O'Connor, and they drove via Sackville (O'Connell) Street to the house of Batt and Bridget O'Connor in Brendan Road, Donnybrook. Barton stayed in that safe house for about three weeks, before moving on to 44 Oakley Road, Rathmines.[25] There he stayed with Áine Ceannt,[26] the widow of the executed 1916 leader.[27] Barton's daring prison break was the first ever successful escape from Mountjoy Jail.[28] On 4 April, the Dáil approved Michael Collins' motion to raise a £250,000 loan. Sinn Fein had learned valuable lessons from the fundraising of the Irish National Aid and Volunteer Dependents' Fund in the wake of the Easter Rising,[29] and a promotional film was shot at St Enda's School to promote the new scheme.[30] Barton daringly and brazenly appeared (buying bonds) in the film, and Sinn Féin propagandists were quick to seize on his new-found notoriety, describing him as 'Robert Barton, T.D., first man to escape from Mountjoy jail'.[31] Barton's sister, Dulcibella, was also an active supporter of the Dáil loan scheme, helping to organise its implementation in County Wicklow.[32]

Although Barton was now 'on the run',[33] he was made Director for Agriculture at the second session of the Dáil,[34] which was held early in April.[35] Barton's chief responsibilities in his new role revolved around land. Ireland had very limited urbanisation, and land was life in rural Ireland. Although there had been a series of land acts passed in the late nineteenth and early twentieth century, for many rural dwellers the burning question of the day was still land reform, which sought not only to bring about an end to landlordism, but to redistribute land in the wake of its collapse.[36] Laurence Ginnell's slogan 'the land for the people and the cattle for the road' was popular at this time, and it engendered much correspondence to the new Director of Agriculture from all over the country. Barton discovered that some radical land reformers were making reckless and 'drastic proposals', which he thought would lead to trouble in rural areas, so he immediately 'set to work to promote the Land Bank' to advance funds to aid the landless and cottiers to obtain land by means of land purchase.[37] Barton faced many obstacles and practical difficulties, though. He had to work out of a small room in Áine Ceannt's house and, being on the run, he could not move about freely in broad daylight.[38] He was a wanted man, and three R.I.C. constables who knew him by sight were transferred from Laragh to Dublin, specifically to watch out for him in a 'search and locate' mission. In addition to a lack of mobility, Barton was also hampered by lack of personnel. He employed John Callaghan as his secretary, but he had no typist, so all his correspondence and documentation was handwritten into duplicating notepads containing carbon paper. If any particular documents had to be typed, Áine's sister, Lily O'Brennan, typed them up at night – she was working for Cumann na mBan during the day and was unavailable.[39] Many Dáil departments operated precariously at this time due to the unwanted attentions of the British authorities, but the Land Bank was legal as it was framed and registered under British law. Its objectives were economic rather than political, so the British had no real grounds to move to suppress it. However, its operation was hampered because the Banks' Standing Committee refused to admit it to the bankers' clearing house. At Barton's request, Michael Collins intervened and pressurised the banks into capitulation by sending a messenger to inform the Standing Committee members that Collins would place them in the same category as the Black and Tans if the Land Bank was not given full clearing house facilities.[40] The committee capitulated.

Barton ensured that his department went beyond day-to-day adminis- tration tasks and planned far ahead.[41] In addition to promoting the Land Bank and facilitating land redistribution, Barton also promoted forestry during his time as Director for Agriculture. He formed a Committee on Forestry early in July and obtained money for the purpose of afforesta- tion.[42] Trees were purchased in bulk in Scotland and Barton's department distributed them around Ireland. Every Sinn Féin Cumann was encour- aged to plant at least sixteen in memory of the executed leaders of 1916. Barton oversaw the distribution of the trees to the various cumainn, who paid whatever they could for them.[43] Barton also appointed Alderman Walter Cole as Director of Forestry, with a view to setting up an Arbour Day in late 1919.[44] Cole was not a forestry expert, but was a very efficient administrator, which was exactly what Barton needed. In June 1920, Cole reported to the Dáil on the Arbour Day organised by Barton in November 1919.[45] By identifying forestry as an alternative productive land use within the Department of Agriculture, Barton showed himself to be ahead of his time. In the decades that followed, a separate Department of Forestry was established in the new Irish state, an area where geographically marginal land was especially suited to forestry. Barton realised this fact early, and his pioneering work in regard to forestry laid the foundations for a pro- ductive economic sector to flourish in later decades.

Despite being hamstrung by having to stay in hiding, and encounter- ing many obstacles during his term as Director of Agriculture, Barton managed to get through an impressive amount of work. This was read- ily acknowledged by Art O'Connor, Barton's immediate successor in the Department of Agriculture, when he reported to the Dáil in August 1921.[46] O'Connor stated:

Commandant Barton's administration extended over ten months, and was terminated by his unfortunate arrest by the enemy at a time when he had just got the Department well under way. He devoted most of his energy to devising a Land Settlement Scheme and set- ting up of a Loan Fund in connection with same. The decree (1919) authorising the scheme declared that: 'The provision of land for the agricultural population now deprived thereof is decreed, and a Loan Fund under the authority of the Dáil may be established to aid this purpose.' Later the draft scheme was submitted to the August session, and it was finally presented and adopted in its amended form at the October session of the same year. The scheme and its operations have now extended over the entire country. Within the brief span of its existence, it has made remarkable headway, and has become firmly rooted in the life of the nation. It has proved its worth and need, and will be a lasting monument to the ability, courage, and imagination of Commandant Barton.[47]

Barton also settled disputes relating to agricultural affairs, including a serious one in County Kildare between farmers, who were members of the Irish Farmers' Union, and farm labourers, who were members of the Irish Transport and General Workers' Union. The dispute centred on wages, hours, and conditions of employment. It was important for Barton's department to resolve it, as it was the first of its kind that they tackled, and it appeared to be escalating rapidly as 1919 progressed. A press report on 3 January related to a meeting (in Barton's own constituency) of the Dunlavin branch of the County Kildare Farmers' Union at which R. G. Dixon presided. Since their previous meeting, two members of the branch had been the victims of arson as their hay had been incinerated. A reward of £50 was offered for information about those responsible for the outrage.[48] Incidents of arson during the War of Independence survived in collective folk memory until the later decades of the twentieth century. The targets of the campaign were mostly larger farmers and gentry figures from the landed classes. The oral history of these attacks on property portrayed them as republicans striking a blow against local establishment figures during the Anglo-Irish War.[49] However, contemporary sources such as newspaper reports reveal that the attacks happened against the backdrop of the labourers' dispute, and it seems quite plausible that they were orchestrated in response to this. It is possible (and perhaps probable) that the primarily second-hand accounts given in the late twentieth century merged the two conflicts in local folk memory. It is also very possible that some men were involved in both the agitation connected to the labourers' dispute and the activities of the I.R.A. at this time. Broadly speaking, both campaigns perceived the landed elite of the area as authority figures and hence as adversaries to be targeted. Whatever the real reason behind the arson attacks, they disrupted everyday life in the region. Barton's newly established agricultural committee failed to get the County

Kildare members of the Farmers' Union to come before a Conciliation Board, so Barton appointed Art O'Connor, who was a Kildare T.D., to try to resolve the matter personally. O'Connor was assisted in this endeavour by another Kildare T.D., Domhnall Ó Buachalla.[50] Their intervention was successful and, according to O'Connor: 'a menace which at the time threatened to spread was happily ended'.[51]

In the autumn of 1919, Barton's agricultural committee issued a warning in the press relating to food scarcity. Unfortunately, this led to some food hoarding by farmers. Also at this time, the Minister for Trade and Commerce, Ernest Blythe (who was under arrest), asked Arthur Griffith to appoint Barton to take over the work of the Department of Trade and Commerce in connection with the dressed meat and packing industry. Realising that exporting animals on the hoof was inadvisable, and that value could be added to the meat sector in Ireland, Barton devoted a lot of time to this project before his re-arrest.[52] Notwithstanding the fact that he was not a full minister, Barton also attended most of the Cabinet meetings (at the instigation of Michael Collins) in the latter months of 1919.[53] Many T.D.s, including Barton, were wanted men on the run,[54] so these meetings were held in various locations, including 'Miss Hoey's residence',[55] on Mespil Road, and 'Mrs McGarry's house',[56] on Fitzwilliam Street.[57] At this time, Barton was also working hard to establish the new Land Bank, and he managed to 'put together a scheme for the acquisition and distribution of land and the provision of a loan fund for that purpose'.[58] However, as luck would have it, Barton had only got the Land Bank legislation through the Dáil, and appointed staff to implement the new programme, when he was re-arrested.[59] Following Barton's arrest and imprisonment, Art O'Connor was appointed as 'substitute' Director of Agriculture. However, there was an 'interregnum for three months' in agricultural affairs. Although O'Connor undertook a mission to Kerry in February 1920, he did not officially fill Barton's place at the head of the Department of Agriculture until 15 April 1920.[60] He had a good knowledge of the job and he worked very efficiently in the department. As Barton later reflected: 'The machinery was there and Art carried it on very actively. He set up a Republican Land Commission with land commissioners.'[61] O'Connor himself simply observed that: 'when Mr Barton was in charge, he put together a scheme for the acquisition and distribution of land and the provision of a Loan Fund for that purpose. I endeavoured after his arrest to carry on that work.'[62]

Another Prison Term – and a Truce
(January 1920–July 1921)

While O'Connor was endeavouring to carry on his predecessor's work, Barton was in the hands of the British authorities. His re-arrest had come about extremely fortuitously for them. Barton attended a Cabinet meeting in Mrs McGarry's house on the night of 30 January 1920. During it, Michael Collins received information (which originated from Ned Broy)[1] that there was a to be 'a big round-up in Dublin Castle', and that a number of arrests were to be made that night. Richard Mulcahy's house was on the list, so he was told to absent himself from home. Áine Ceannt's house, where Barton was staying, was not listed, so Collins told him to return there and hide the Cabinet minute book back in the house. However, Mulcahy and his wife were living at No. 4 Oakley Road, and Barton was in number 44 – and one of the fours of the '44' had been rubbed off (or had fallen off) the fanlight over the front door. The military, seeing the number four over the door, raided Ceannt's house under the impression that it was Mulcahy's, taking Barton by surprise and re-arresting him at 4 a.m. on the morning of 31 January.[2] Having been on the run for almost a year,[3] Barton was court-martialled at Ship Street Barracks on 12 February, and was sent to England 'about four days later' to be interned at Portland Convict Prison in Dorsetshire.[4] While incarcerated there, Barton learned the tricky technique of French-polishing furniture.[5] On the whole, Barton was treated well in prison. Indeed, he admitted as much to Stuart Mais, before 'launching into a panegyric on the English prison system'. Mais commented wryly that this must have been 'the first time that a prisoner ever thought well of the system that kept him in captivity'.[6] Barton's admiration for the system did not prevent his working against it, however. He led a prison strike as a protest, seeking the status of political prisoners for imprisoned Irish republicans during his time in Portland. This was not a hunger strike, but a general strike during which Barton and his comrades refused to carry out any work in the prison.[7] Barton's captivity meant that he was out of circulation as the War of Independence intensified back in Ireland, but he still found ways to resist the authorities.

While Barton was striking in jail, his sister Dulcibella also ensured that the family home at Glendalough House played an active part in the conflict by providing a safe house for I.R.A. volunteers on the run. She later reminisced:

I had many volunteers 'on the run' staying in Annamoe. Many of them came from Cork, via Rockwell College. Kevin Barry's brother, who lives at Hacketstown, used to drive them over in a pony trap. They stayed as long as they liked. In many cases they were on their way to Dublin and I was able to get them there by old roads which were only known to Wicklow people … four men stayed in our house for a month. Then the truce came and they dashed back to their units. They were 'on the run', poor boys. [Their names were] John Butler, Sean Hyde, Maurice McGrath and Bob says the fourth was Carew … I had Dan Breen for three or four nights. He was brought from the hospital in Dun Laoghaire, where he was sent after the fight in Drumcondra. I suppose he came by car, but he was carried up the avenue to our house by Eamon Fleming and another volunteer whose name I can't remember. He was very nice and quiet, not at all the rough type that some people think him. When he wanted to leave … Sweetman's car was commandeered; Dan taken to his destination and the car was returned next day … Liam Lynch was another man who stayed at our house. He was a very good-looking man and so quiet and gentle. I had never known him. Like others who came up from Cork he stopped a few days for a rest. Some short time after I read in the paper about the Black and Tans shooting somebody called Lynch in a Dublin hotel and I got a great shock. It turned out to be someone else.[8]

By mid-1920, the War of Independence was affecting daily life in County Wicklow and the rest of Ireland. The local elections of June 1920 were the first to use the proportional representation system of voting on a countrywide scale,[9] and in County Wicklow they returned an overwhelmingly republican chamber of Sinn Féin and Labour councillors.[10] The first meeting of the county council was held on 18 June and the newly elected Councillor Christopher M. Byrne, who was on the run from the authorities, was briefly present.[11] Robert Barton T.D. was unanimously elected chairman of the council. Barton was, of course, elected in absentia, as he was still incarcerated in Portland prison, so Joseph Campbell was elected as vice-chairman and became the acting chairman in the unavoidable absence of the chairman. Barton's election was in protest at his sentence 'by a court-martial of the English army of occupation in Ireland' and 'as proof that the Irish patriot in an English prison is ever dear to his people'.[12] Rapidly changing political developments were certainly afoot in Wicklow during Barton's incarceration.

Political developments were also evident in Barton's home constituency of West Wicklow, where the monthly meeting of the newly elected Baltinglass Number One District Council was held in Dunlavin on Tuesday, 13 July 1920.[13] This was the first time a council meeting was held in Dunlavin, and 'a Sinn Féin flag [tricolour] was unfurled in the courthouse during the proceedings'.[14] Chairman John J. Cunningham presided, and among the items of local governance discussed were cottage rents, a building scheme for labourers' cottages, and maintenance of pumps, sewers and roads. However, other items discussed had a decidedly more political flavour. The following resolution, proposed by John J. Cunningham and seconded by James Byrne, was passed unanimously: 'That this council of the elected representatives of Baltinglass No. 1 Rural District Council hereby pledge our allegiance to Dáil Éireann, the legitimately elected and constituted parliament of the Irish Republic.'[15] The British government had proclaimed the Dáil in September 1919, effectively outlawing it and 'suppressing [it] throughout the whole of Ireland'.[16] Copies of the full resolution from the Rural District Council were to be sent to the republican Minister for Foreign Affairs for 'transmission to the governments of Europe and to the President and Chairman of both the Senate and House of Representatives in the U.S.A.'. Three financial claims were submitted but ignored since they related to the R.I.C. in the district. The forces of law and order were contested between Westminster and the Dáil and the two legal systems were vying for control, so to support the Sinn Féin courts, the clerk J. R. Dagg, who was a Justice of the Peace, was called upon by the council 'to resign his J. P. ship'.

Another political resolution passed at the meeting related to James Larkin, the workers' leader during the 1913 Dublin lockout, who had since gone to America and was imprisoned for labour activities in the U.S.A.[17] This resolution, proposed by Denis Fay and seconded by John J. Carroll, read:

> That we, the members of the Baltinglass No. 1 District Council, demand the release of James Larkin, who is at present undergoing a sentence of between five to ten years in Sing Sing prison in America, and that he be allowed to return to Ireland to take up his duties as General Secretary of the I.T.G.W.U. That copies of this resolution be sent to the American Consul, Dublin, the Republican Minister for Foreign Affairs and the Larkin Release Committee.

Finally, perhaps the resolution most indicative of the troubled times in which this meeting was held, with the War of Independence as its backdrop, concerned Robert Barton. Proposer John J. Cunningham and seconder Denis Fay had no trouble in getting support for the resolution, which read: 'That this council demand the release of our worthy representative, Mr R. C. Barton T. D., and request the [I.R.A.] Volunteers to hold Brigadier General Lucas as a hostage until Mr Barton is set free.'[18] It was evident that the new council ardently supported the republican agenda and the political landscape in Wicklow – and across Ireland – was changing rapidly as hostilities progressed. It was also evident that support for Barton had not waned at home, despite his absence from the political scene due to imprisonment.

Support for republicanism in County Wicklow was strengthened by the activities of the Black and Tans. The first to arrive in the county were stationed in Baltinglass, but they were deployed shortly afterwards in other towns and villages throughout the county.[19] Barton's home, Glendalough House (then operating as a safe house), attracted a lot of attention from the force. Dulcibella Barton remembered that one raid in particular revealed the mixed heritage and allegiances of the Barton family:

> Our house in Annamoe suffered many raids first by the British Army. I was in bed one morning … shortly afterwards the front

Fig 6. Dunlavin Courthouse, where councillors demanded Barton's release on 13 July 1920. (Image taken from author's collection)

door bell rang. I got up and went down to the hall and opened the door. First, I saw no one, but soon a soldier dashed from behind the pillar of the porch and said he was going to search me. He felt me all over looking for a gun. I had nothing on but my pyjamas and my dressing-gown. Then I noticed the place was full of khaki soldiers … A very polite colonel … went into the smoke-room and sat down … while the soldiers raced through the house searching. A soldier then came in and said 'I found two lances and I rubbed them up to see if they had a number'. 'What do you want them for? asked the colonel. I said they belonged to an uncle of mine who was killed in the Zulu war. The colonel was rather taken aback at that. Then another soldier came in and he had a British uniform in his hand. The colonel asked me what I was doing with that. I said 'That belonged to a brother of mine who is buried in France'. Then another soldier came in with a periscope in his hand. He asked me about that and I explained that it belonged to another brother who had served in France. Then a soldier found in the grandfather clock in the hall a .22 rifle that we used for shooting rooks. They took that away … For that raid about 600 soldiers had been brought with ambulances and all sorts of equipment. They were evidently prepared for a big battle. I was quite sorry for the poor colonel, who was really a very polite man and who must have got a great disappointment at finding only me ... We had the Black and Tans several times, going through the house roaring. Any door that they found locked they burst in by putting their shoulders to it ...[20]

The rough treatment meted out by the Black and Tans during searches, arrests and suspect interrogations, and the murder of Robert Dixon J. P. by two off-duty members of the force in Barton's constituency of West Wicklow,[21] hardened attitudes and strengthened support for Sinn Féin and for Barton across Wicklow, even though he remained in prison in England.

Barton's imprisonment had another effect, however – one that would only become apparent at a later stage. There were other political developments happening nationally, not all of which were positive for republicans. Barton spent sixteen to seventeen months in prison,[22] during which an internal rift was developing within republicanism. This rift would lead to internecine strife within the movement, and would have very serious consequences within a couple of years. Tension between Minister for Defence Cathal Brugha and the leaders in I.R.A. headquarters (particularly Michael Collins and Richard Mulcahy) was at the core of the fracture. Minister Brugha felt that he should be in control of the army, and he interfered at G.H.Q. level, giving orders to Chief-of-Staff Mulcahy. However, Brugha was not directly involved in the fighting, and those who were knew that many of his ideas (such as favouring larger battles with Crown forces over hit-and-run ambushes) were impractical and unrealistic for a small, poorly armed force. Piaras Beaslaí opined that Brugha was 'hopelessly out of touch'.[23] The minister also objected to Collins' power base, the I.R.B., questioning their loyalty to the Volunteers (I.R.A.). However, much of the problem centred on a personality clash between Brugha and Collins. As minister, Brugha saw himself as the leader of the republican armed struggle, but the press and media portrayed Collins as a heroic, glamorous figure, whose derring-do and daring exploits were carrying the fight to the British within the capital and beyond. Collins, for his part, had little time for Brugha and his grandiose combat ideas, and often treated him with overt contempt, which only fanned the flames of division and widened the rift. The problem worsened after Acting President Arthur Griffith's arrest in November 1920, when Brugha declined the post. Collins assumed the acting presidency, and Brugha's resentment of Collins grew. The ill-concealed antagonism between the two men continued during the remainder of the War of Independence and beyond, but Robert Barton, being out of circulation and out of the loop, was unaware of this development, having no idea about the depth of animosity between the two republican leaders.[24]

Barton spent about fifteen months in Portland Prison, where he was generally well treated but deprived of sleep.[25] Having led the prisoners' strike there, he was transferred to Portsmouth Gaol in the late spring of 1921, where he served out the rest of this time.[26] In Portsmouth, however, Barton was able to smuggle letters out via the Catholic curate, who was very sympathetic to the Irish cause. An escape plan was arranged, and Rory O'Connor was sent to England to implement it. The plan was a simple one. A warder, who was in possession of a master key, started his shift every morning at 7 a.m. and began every day by going to the kitchen to heat porridge for the prisoners' breakfast. O'Connor and his accomplices, who had already been to the grounds outside Portsmouth Gaol and 'cased the joint', would scale the perimeter wall and hide inside the jail until the warder entered the kitchen. They would follow him in, put a bag over his head and use the key to release Barton, who would be given civilian clothes. The escapees would leave the prison by scaling the wall again and a safe house had been arranged in Southampton for the night, before Barton and his rescuers made the trip back to Ireland. Despite the risky nature of this plan, Barton seems to have had every confidence in its success.[27]

Fate intervened, however, and the plan was never carried out. Events outside the prison walls were moving apace, and they had a dramatic and unforeseen effect on Barton's incarceration. In December 1920, de Valera had returned from the U.S.A., and he had qualms about the 'tit-for-tat' nature of the ongoing War of Independence. In early 1921, he supported Cathal Brugha's idea of staging larger-scale operations with more open battles, prevailing on the I.R.A. and persuading G.H.Q. to launch an attack on the Customs House in Dublin. The attack was carried out on 25 May 1921.[28] The building was burned successfully and five I.R.A. men (and four civilians) were killed, but the total I.R.A. losses came to over a hundred experienced and trained personnel (and their weapons), due to the large number arrested and imprisoned. The propaganda value of this operation was tainted by the loss of some 40 per cent of the attacking force. This was a devastating blow for the Dublin I.R.A., which had to completely reorganise after the event.[29] The propaganda victory had become a Pyrrhic one; such losses were unsustainable, especially in an organisation where manpower, arms and ammunition were at a premium. The War of Independence was now in its third year and there was no end in sight. While the attack on the Customs House was publicly hailed as a morale-boosting victory by the Dáil and the I.R.A., it also brought home the fragility of the republicans' military position, and privately at least, some thoughts were turning towards the possibility of peace negotiations.

By mid-1921, British Prime Minister David Lloyd George was also well aware of the longevity of the conflict in Ireland. He was under pressure from some lobby groups, both in Britain and America, to talk to Sinn Féin. De Valera's return from the U.S.A. afforded him an opportunity to communicate with a leader who had not been directly involved in events such as the assassinations on Bloody Sunday, making him more acceptable to the British public. In December 1920, Lloyd George had protected Ulster Unionists by introducing a Government of Ireland Act, which had established the northern state. In his view, it was time for elections in both parts of Ireland. These happened, but the ongoing War of Independence meant that only Sinn Féin candidates stood in the 'south', as other parties cleared the field for them by standing down.[30] Despite the fact that he would be unopposed, Dulcibella Barton actively supported her imprisoned brother's bid for re-election.[31] In mid-May 1921, Augustus Cullen was appointed as election agent for the County Wicklow contingent of the Sinn Féin candidates standing for election in the constituency of Kildare-Wicklow: Barton, Christopher Byrne and Erskine Childers.[32] By the end of the month, two elections had been held – one in the north, and the second Dáil had also been elected on the 24th of that month (with Barton being returned unopposed for the constituency of Kildare-Wicklow). Lloyd George's need to open talks with Sinn Féin was urgent, as the Government of Ireland Act had decreed that the British government would have to take control over the twenty-six counties if the government of 'Southern Ireland' did not function. This would be costly and the British public would be incensed, so the 'Welsh Wizard' ensured that King George V made a plea for peace when he formally opened the Belfast Parliament on 22 June 1921. The following day, the king's private secretary, Lord Stamfordham, visited Lloyd George, having previously told Lord Riddell that, 'Now is the time to endeavour to bring about a reconciliation. Unless something is done, the effect of the king's speech will die away. There is not a moment to be lost.'[33]

Lloyd George was convinced and used the king's plea as the pretext for inviting de Valera 'as the chosen leader of the great majority in Southern Ireland ... [to] attend a conference here in London in company with Sir James Craig, to explore to the utmost the possibility of a settlement'.[34]

These were the events that negated the necessity for Rory O'Connor's escape plan for Barton. No escape was needed as Barton was released from prison. Although Barton later told Mais that he was generally well-treated in prison,[35] his time behind bars had affected him as 'he was subjected to considerable brutality' (with much sleep deprivation) at Portland.[36] De Valera was worried about his friend's health and thought that Barton was 'on the verge of a breakdown'.[37] The republican side responded positively to Lloyd George's invitation and Barton was chosen as one of the men that they needed for their delegation to London. Hence, Barton was released from prison in early July (as were Arthur Griffith and Eoin MacNeill) to help negotiate a truce with the British.[38] The choice of Barton may have been partly influenced by de Valera's personal friendship with him, but it also demonstrates the high regard in which he was held within the republican movement, where his education, intelligence, pragmatism and ability to concentrate on one topic or problem at a time, to keep it in focus and to drive a hard bargain, were perceived as valuable assets in any negotiations that were to come. On 5 July, Jan Smuts, the South African statesman, arrived in Dublin, travelling incognito, to take up his (unofficial) role as intermediary in the truce negotiations.[39] Smuts had a boat at Kingstown Harbour (Dun Laoghaire), on board which he met with Barton, de Valera, Griffith and Eamon Duggan,[40] who all proposed formal recognition of an Irish Republic. Smuts countered with dominion status, outlining the advantages, but he found the Irish delegation inflexible and difficult to deal with. In particular, Smuts referred to de Valera as 'living in a world of dreams, visions and shadows'.[41] Notwithstanding this difficulty, in Westminster the Cabinet agreed in principle to a truce, and on 8 July General Sir Nevil Macready (who had been appointed General Officer Commanding in Ireland in the spring of 1920) and Lord Middleton (a leading Southern Unionist), met with Barton, de Valera, Duggan and Brugha at the Mansion House in Dublin. Expectations of peace were high among the war-weary Irish public and, according to Macready:

> The crowd [outside the Mansion House] began to shout and cheer, one excited and unwashed old dame seized my hand and kissed it,

others commended me to their favourite saints ... [but] a few hours before, and indeed afterwards, they would have rejoiced to hear [I] had met death at the hands of the gunmen.[42]

It only took about an hour for a broad agreement to be reached – armed attacks, destruction of property and arrests would cease with effect from noon on 11 July. Basically, General Sir Nevil Macready, Commander in Chief, Colonel J. Brind and Alfred William Cope, Assistant Under-Secretary, acting for the British Army agreed as follows:

No incoming troops, Royal Irish Constabulary (R.I.C.), auxiliary police and munitions.
No movements for military purposes of troops and munitions, except maintenance drafts.
No provocative display of forces, armed or unarmed.
It is understood that all provisions of this Truce apply to the martial law area equally with the rest of Ireland.
No pursuit of Irish officers or men or war material or military stores.
No secret agents, noting description or movements, and no interference with the movements of Irish persons, military or civil, and no attempts to discover the haunts or habits of Irish officers and men.
No pursuit or observance of lines of communication or connection.

Fig 7. General Macready entering the Mansion House, 8 July 1921.
(Image (WWCA/PP1/33) courtesy of the Wicklow County Archive)

In return, Commandant R. C. Barton T.D. and Commandant E. J. Duggan
T.D., acting for the Army of the Republic, agreed as follows:

Attacks on Crown forces and civilians to cease.
No provocative displays of forces, armed or unarmed.
No interference with Government or private property.
To discountenance and prevent any action likely to cause disturbance
of the peace which might necessitate military interference.[43]

Barton was a signatory of the terms of the truce,[44] and he and Duggan
were deputed to meet with Macready at G.H.Q., Parkgate, the following
day. According to Duggan, he and Barton met General Tudor (Head of
the Auxiliaries and Black and Tans) and 'dictated' to him how his forces
should behave during the truce. Duggan stated that Tudor agreed to
these terms, 'which were carried out to the letter'.[45] However, this upbeat
assessment may be somewhat simplistic. From the outset, there seemed to
be confusion about the exact terms agreed upon, and different versions
appeared in the press – one set provided by Macready and another by
Sinn Féin. Specifically, there was a lack of clarity about just how far the
Irish could go in the procurement of arms – a question never addressed
satisfactorily.[46] Macready stated that that Barton and Duggan asked for
some changes to the terms published in the press, but 'seemed contented
with what was merely a verbose version of the original terms'.[47] It was
only natural that a certain amount of republican triumphalism surrounded
the implementation of the truce, but the British were decidedly unimpressed by such rodomontade. It fell to Barton and Art O'Connor, who
were acting as de Valera's intermediaries with the British Cabinet, to pour
oil on troubled waters by emphasising that de Valera's published letters
were merely propaganda 'intended to educate the British public as to what
Sinn Féin stood for'.[48] Whatever the truth of the truce meetings and their
outcomes, a tentative ceasefire began on 11 July 1921, and the terms were
crystal clear in stating that the Irish could keep their existing arms and
preserve their military network intact.[49] Meanwhile, Ireland held its collective breath and awaited further developments.

Plenipotentiary Status and High Hopes
(Summer–Autumn 1921)

Rather surprisingly, despite occasional violent incidents, by and large the truce held. The arrangement and implementation of the truce was testament to the persuasive skills of the negotiators, including Barton, to de Valera's trust in him as a confidante, and to Barton's status and reputation within the wider republican movement. However, Barton noticed that all was not well within the movement at this time. He had misgivings about the divisions that were becoming evident at both Dáil and Cabinet level. In his 1954 witness statement, Barton mused:

> As regards disagreement between members of the Cabinet, up to the time of my arrest there was no personal disagreement; on the contrary, we were all on the most friendly terms. When I returned to Ireland after being released from Portsmouth, I found there was internal dissension which had not existed when I was arrested. I returned in June, 1921. We had several Cabinet meetings to decide whether de Valera should go to London, who should accompany him and what would be the programme. Dissension in the Cabinet developed while I was in gaol. Previously we had been a very happy family. When I returned, I found personal animosity between members of the Cabinet; this very much disturbed me. There were differences of opinion between Cathal Brugha, Austin Stack and de Valera on one

side, and Michael Collins and Dick Mulcahy on the other. Ministers were not co-operating in the way they had before.[1]

Notwithstanding this internal cleavage, Barton, now Minister for Economic Affairs, found himself chosen as a member of the first Irish delegation to meet Lloyd George in London. On 12 July he accompanied de Valera, also travelling with Dáil Vice-President Arthur Griffith, Minister for Home Affairs Austin Stack,[2] Count Plunkett,[3] and acting Minister for Publicity Erskine Childers.[4] They were greeted by a huge crowd of London-Irish well-wishers at Euston station – there seemed to be an enormous appetite for a lasting peace and a final settlement of the thorny Irish question.[5] The first meeting between Lloyd George and de Valera was on 14 July. It lasted some three hours. The setting was the room where the heads of state of the dominions met. The room was dominated by a large map of the British Empire, to which de Valera seemed totally oblivious, even when the Prime Minister indicated an empty chair, evidently meant for Ireland, at the Commonwealth table. The Welsh Wizard noted that there was no Welsh word for 'republic' and asked about the meaning of 'saorstát' in Irish. When told that it literally meant 'free state', he observed that he thought that the name would not need to be changed.[6] The atmosphere was both amiable and courteous – relations were cordial, but the expansive Lloyd George was unimpressed by the pedantic de Valera – and vice versa. A personality clash had developed beneath the calm surface and progress was practically non-existent.

Nonetheless, three more meetings took place between the leaders on 15, 18 and 21 July. The atmosphere turned tetchy as it became evident that Lloyd George would not go beyond offering dominion status, while de Valera would not concede on the republic. Strangely, the Irish delegates never attended any meetings – they were summoned by de Valera after each meeting and told what had passed between the two leaders. Robert Barton later reminisced in his witness statement: 'I was not present at any of the discussions. They were confined to de Valera and Lloyd George. As the terms offered by Lloyd George were unacceptable, President de Valera came back to Dublin and we all came back with him.'[7] The British offer was delivered in writing to Barton and Childers late on the night of 20 July. They were partially undressed in their room as they were preparing to retire to bed.[8] According to Barton, 'de Valera's attitude would be that there was no point continuing discussions with Lloyd George'.[9]

Fig 8. Irish delegates leaving for the peace conference in London, 12 July 1921. (L–R: Arthur Griffith, Robert Barton, Éamon de Valera, Count Plunkett and Laurence O'Neill). (Image (WWCA/PP1/33) courtesy of the Wicklow County Archive)

De Valera probably needed no encouragement to adopt this position, but Barton may actually have prompted the Long Fellow's decision. As the proposals were being perused by the Irish delegates, Barton 'said very deliberately, "Mr. President, would it not be treason to the republic to bear these terms back to Ireland?" The president took the same line ...'[10] Barton may not have been present at any of the meetings with Lloyd George, but his friendship with de Valera ensured that he was brought along as a sounding board for the president. In that capacity, Barton's question to de Valera left no doubt that the British offer should be rejected out of hand. The offer was indeed rejected, but Lloyd George asked for a considered reply in writing, a request to which de Valera agreed as long as he had time to consult with his colleagues. The preliminary talks came to nought, but they confirmed and increased the British perception that Barton was very closely aligned with de Valera within the internal machinations of Sinn Féin.[11] The delegates returned to Dublin empty-handed and awaited developments.

The War of Independence had paused but not ended, however – a permanent treaty had yet to be negotiated and many twists and turns lay ahead on the rocky road to political consensus. Although de Valera's initial visit to London did not produce a breakthrough, crucially (as neither side wanted to resume fighting), the exploratory talks of the first delegation resulted in an agreement in principle to keep communication channels open between Dublin and London. The Dáil met in both public and private sessions on 16, 17, 18, 22, 23, 25 and 26 August, and predictably voted against the British proposals, rejecting them unanimously. However, de Valera also stated that 'we are not doctrinaire republicans', a phrase that suggested there was still room for manoeuvre within the tangled politics and conflicting ideologies of the apparent impasse.[12] Barton carried on with the work of his department and waited, perhaps more in hope than expectation, for an initiative from the British government that might have the effect of kick-starting renewed negotiations. Notwithstanding public accusations of bad faith through the late summer and early autumn of 1921, private correspondence continued between the two sides. As de Valera's trusted confidante, Barton acted as courier on two occasions. He remembered:

Many letters passed between President de Valera and Mr Lloyd George before the final invitation arrived for a visit to London by Irish Delegates to explore avenues to a peaceful settlement. Some, if not all of these letters were transmitted on the Irish side through the hands of responsible persons. ... Two were entrusted to me. The first I delivered to Austen Chamberlain. I think it was in his room at the House of Commons. He received me coldly but politely, and promised to deliver the letter to the Prime Minister and to reply through his Government's official channels.

On the second occasion Lloyd George was on holiday in Gairloch, Inverness-shire. The Cabinet considered that, because of the ill feeling in Great Britain towards Sinn Féin, it was inadvisable that I should travel alone, and Joseph McGrath was detailed to accompany me ... I presented our missive to Lloyd George, who was holding some sort of conference in, I think, the Town Hall, Inverness. Lloyd George informed me that it might be a couple of days before his reply was ready and that I could please myself as to whether I waited for it or not; he was returning to Gairloch. I went to Gairloch ... After two or three days, the reply was handed to me by Lloyd George and I returned with it to Dublin.[13]

Finally, it was accepted by both sides that 'conference not correspondence' (without any preconditions) was the best way forward.[14] After some difficulty, Lloyd George eventually came up with a form of words that was satisfactory to de Valera. Irish delegates would attend another conference in London 'with a view to ascertaining how the association of Ireland with the community of nations known as the British Empire may be reconciled with Irish national aspirations'.[15] Barton's hoped-for but unexpected initiative had materialised and more negotiations loomed ahead. As October began, a newspaper report informed the Irish public that, 'The British prime minister's fresh invitation to a conference in London on October 11 has been accepted by Dáil Éireann.' The conference was to 'explore every possibility of settlement by personal discussion'.[16]

Given his track record in negotiating the truce and supporting de Valera at the previous meeting in London, it was always likely that Barton, who held the important full ministerial post of Economic Affairs in the second Dáil, would be included in the team to travel to London for the second round of talks. The likelihood was increased by the reluctance and, in some cases, flat refusal of others to even consider going – Brugha and Stack, for example, would have no hand, act or part in the new delegation, so de Valera probably hoped that Barton's militant republican views would act as a check and balance on Griffith's more moderate outlook. Tellingly, when the Cabinet were meeting to discuss Lloyd George's original proposals, 'Brugha would have none of it and Stack understood Barton "to be with us" (militant rather than moderate about the proposals)',[17] so de Valera was probably correct in his assessment. In short, it is likely that de Valera saw Barton as a supportive delegate, who would ensure that the Long Fellow's views would permeate the negotiations in London. This perception of Barton being chosen as an ally as well as an expert on economic and trade matters gains credibility when one considers that, although Barton could potentially speak on financial affairs, he was apparently given no specific brief by de Valera when he was chosen for inclusion in the delegation.[18]

De Valera's need for a close ally at the negotiating table stemmed from the fact that he decided not to go to London for the new set of talks. This decision was contentious among his contemporaries and, with the benefit of hindsight, it became even more contentious as the years and decades passed and the whole period was scrutinised by successive generations of historians. Instead, de Valera would send representatives, bestowing 'plenipotentiary' status upon them.[19] Crucially, in September 1921 during the Dáil debate on the ratification of plenipotentiaries, de Valera ignored Gavan Duffy's warning that if the Dáil 'sent Lloyd George plenipotentiaries, they would be making him a present of plenipotentiaries with full powers', and he urged de Valera not to endow the delegates with that name. However, the president swept this argument aside, stating that, 'They wanted plenipotentiaries to give to the world the impression that they are sent over with full powers – to do the best they could to reconcile the Irish position with the British position. They should have full powers because if they go over, they needed to have the moral feeling of support of the position to do the best they could for Ireland.'[20] Equally crucially, however, before they travelled to London, de Valera would inform the plenipotentiaries not to accept any agreement without first referring it back to Dublin, thus providing them with conflicting instructions and leaving them confused.[21] These conflicting perspectives regarding the status of the plenipotentiaries in de Valera's absence would have monumental consequences later on. At the time of their selection and de Valera's announcement of his decision not to attend the talks, a somewhat mystified W. T. Cosgrave stated, in the ratification of plenipotentiaries debate,[22] that 'this was a team they were sending over and they were leaving their ablest player in reserve. Now it was not usual to leave the ablest players in reserve. The reserve would have to be used some time or other and it struck him now was the time they were required'. He formally moved that 'the President be chairman of the delegation'. In the same debate, however, de Valera provided reasons for staying behind, explaining that he 'thought it wisest he should not be a member of the delegation, the reason being exactly the same reason that they inserted that second paragraph in the letter, that they wanted to emphasise in these negotiations they were not entering as a political party but as a nation'.[23]

De Valera went on to develop his argument, stating that he:

knew fairly well from his experience over in London how far it was possible to get the British government to go and when they came to that point they would have to deal with the matter in a very practical manner. To be in the very best position for the possibilities of a break down and to be in the best position to deal with those questions as they would arise and not to be involved in anything that might take place in those negotiations – to be perfectly free – he asked the Cabinet not to insist on his going as one of the deputation.

Cosgrave maintained that, as President, de Valera 'should be one of the delegation. He had an extraordinary experience in negotiations. He also had the advantage of being in touch already. The Head of the State in England was Mr Lloyd George and he [Cosgrave] expected he would be one of the plenipotentiaries on the side of England.' De Valera then elaborated on his position, pointing out that,

> he really believed it was vital at this stage that the symbol of the Republic should be kept untouched and that it should not be compromised in any sense by any arrangements which it might be necessary for our plenipotentiaries to make ... It was not a shirking of duty, but he realised the position and how necessary it was to keep the Head of the State and the symbol untouched and that was why he asked to be left out.

Later in the debate, de Valera again said that 'if he were not the symbol he would go'.[24]

> Barton loyally supported his leader's decision at the time. When recounting the events of that time, Barton explained that de Valera : 'would stay here as being the last defence. If negotiations should break down when he was with us, that would be the end, but, if they broke down without him, there was always a last recourse to him. It was good tactics. I remember him particularly referring to the fact that he represented a reserve in the battle which could be thrown in when all else was lost.'[25]

Barton only accepted his own inclusion in the delegation 'with diffidence' because of refusals by Brugha and Stack.[26] De Valera's decision not to travel to London meant that, in effect, he also refused to participate directly. Despite his diffidence, Barton reluctantly accepted his place among the delegates, partly out of loyalty to de Valera, but also, one suspects, partly out of a sense of duty. The Barton family had been reared with a sense of duty – an attitude of *noblesse oblige* – which had manifested itself in military tradition over the years. Barton's uncle was killed in the

Zulu Wars and two of his brothers had died in France during the First World War.[27] Barton was not a man to shirk his duty, however distasteful he found it. Brugha, Stack and de Valera – the three Cabinet members who later opposed the treaty – all had the opportunity to go to London, but all three spurned it. On the other hand, Barton did not want to be part of the delegation either, but when Ireland had need of him, he loyally and dutifully accepted de Valera's nomination (seconded by Kevin O'Higgins), because he perceived it morally as being the right thing to do. Barton's experience as a plenipotentiary was not pleasant and, tellingly, Barton later stated that he thought that de Valera's decision not to go to London 'should have been reversed by the time we [the Irish delegates] reached the final stage [of negotiations]'.[28] All that, however, lay ahead, and on 8 October 1921 the second delegation (without Michael Collins, who did not travel until the following night) departed for London with high hopes.[29] Mirroring his high hopes, Barton was also in high spirits – he was described as 'sprightly, youthful, happy as a schoolboy, eagerly inspecting the ship, climbing up and down ladders, talking to the captain and his officers, and remaining for a long time, hatless and wind-blown, on the upper deck'.[30] Evidently, an air of optimism prevailed as Barton and his colleagues sailed for Holyhead.

9

Background to the Delegations
(October 1921)

Barton's optimism and ebullience continued when he reached Britain. On the train from Holyhead to London, all the delegates were 'relaxed and in excellent humour', with Barton and his cousin Childers 'like students as they exchanged lively remarks and joyfully contributed to the general conversation'.[1] Arriving in London on 9 October,[2] the delegates again 'received a tremendous welcome from a great crowd of Irish people assembled at Euston station'.[3] The negotiations opened on 11 October 1921.[4] The absence of de Valera meant that the Irish delegation was led by its chairman, Arthur Griffith.[5] One of the chief polemicists of the Irish Revolution, Griffith was in essence a man of words, for whom the pen was mightier than the sword. Whether Griffith and de Valera were in full agreement regarding what they wanted to achieve was questionable from the start. Both men wanted an independent Ireland and both could be pedantic and stubborn negotiators but, unlike de Valera, Griffith had not been directly involved in the 1916 Rising and was not viewed as a 'physical force' man by hard-line republicans. Many of these were dismayed by the choice of Griffith as chairman of the delegation. Peadar O'Donnell put it succinctly, if somewhat simplistically, when he observed:

> Griffith, the Home Ruler, was concerned with the powers an Irish parliament could win for itself from the British government. De Valera, a Republican, not doctrinaire but a Republican, concerned himself with what concessions the Irish Republic could make

to Britain, consistent with sovereignty, on certain aspects of defence and foreign relations.[6]

The passive Griffith's chairmanship of the delegation was counterbalanced by the presence of Michael Collins as his assistant.[7] Collins certainly was a physical force man, whose roles in the I.R.A. and I.R.B. during the War of Independence – and whose use of 'the squad' for assassinations – had catapulted him to national prominence. However, de Valera was worried about the levels of compromise to which Collins might agree, so Barton's inclusion was seen as a safeguard against any such action by either Griffith or Collins (or both).[8] Barton was also a Cabinet minister, but his portfolio was economic affairs, so he saw his remit as negotiating the best economic terms possible in any agreement which might result from the talks. Hence, Barton travelled to London with the ambitious goal of gaining full fiscal autonomy for Ireland first and foremost in his mind. Pakenham later observed that Barton 'had never wavered from demanding that full fiscal autonomy should be established from the beginning [of negotiations]'.[9] The other two delegates were chosen for their legal expertise. De Valera actually referred to the duo, Gavan Duffy and Duggan, as 'mere padding', but he expected Barton and Childers (who travelled as secretary to the delegation) to counterbalance the opinions of Griffith and Collins, suspecting that they 'would accept the Crown'.[10] De Valera's choice of Childers as secretary had an ulterior motive. The president knew that Childers would have a strong influence over Barton, who was like a younger brother to him, and that with Childers' support, Barton 'would be strong and stubborn enough as a retarding force to any precipitate giving away by the delegation'.[11] R. F. Foster has suggested that de Valera's 'intention was to balance the delegation to a point where it was almost paralysed'.[12] If this was so, the breakdown of delegates' duties would matter little, as failure would ensue!

This breakdown of duties within the delegation meant that, in practice, the general perception regarding the substantive issue of the actual acceptance or rejection of the terms of any new agreement would fall first and foremost on Griffith and Collins, with Barton attending to the economic negotiations and the lawyers scrutinising any and all relevant documentation, with particular regard to the language used in any agreement. This was also Barton's perception; he certainly saw himself as the economic representative on the delegation at the time, later recalling that he 'took over with [him] to London, as advisers, Smith Gordon and Professor Smiddy',[13] and noting that:

> The economic papers used for the negotiations in London were mainly written by Smith Gordon and Smiddy. When we were discussing trade, Smith Gordon and Smiddy would compile memoranda on what the suggestions made by the British really meant in practice. Smiddy was a Professor of Economics and he made a life study of trade relationships. He gave advice on how far we could go in compromising on complete free trade and agreement to Dominion preference and kindred subjects.[14]

Thus, notwithstanding the fact that he was now a full Cabinet minister and theoretically on an equal footing with Griffith and Collins as an envoy plenipotentiary, Barton may well have seen his own role as being confined to economic and financial matters and he may have perceived himself as lower in the 'pecking order' of delegates when it came to accepting the terms of an agreement or ratifying a proposed treaty. He may have felt somewhat hamstrung by his place in the hierarchy of the delegation. Internal hierarchical uncertainty was one problem facing the delegation as negotiations opened, but it was far from the only one. Inequality was another.

Much has been made of the fact that the Irish and British delegations were unequal in many ways. In terms of leadership, Lloyd George was a very experienced politician. He had been a government minister since 1906 and became Prime Minister of wartime Britain in 1916. In that capacity, he had recently been involved in monumental negotiations in Paris in the wake of the First World War, where he had proved to be a ruthless negotiator. The British team also included Winston Churchill, Austen Chamberlain, Lord Birkenhead, Sir Laming Worthington-Evans, Sir Hamar Greenwood and the Attorney-General, Sir Gordon Hewart.[15] Lloyd George and his men were on home ground in London and could call on a vast array of resources, including skilled advisors in every field of the negotiations. Griffith, on the other hand, was a former journalist who had led an underground government for about a year and a half. After the opening exchanges of the talks, a pleased Griffith wrote to de Valera, informing him that 'on the whole, we have scored today', causing Barton to comment wryly 'poor Griffith! He always scored when he fell for the baited trap'.[16] Griffith's assistant, Collins, was an ex-post office employee who had been a minister in that underground government and one of the military masterminds of the republican movement. Neither had experience in political negotiations. They were away from home, in the 'enemy camp', and had scant resources beyond the advisors and secretaries who had travelled with them. The Irish were on an unequal footing with their counterparts.[17] Barton recalled this inequality later, musing in his reminiscences that:

> It was clear from the start that the English interest was centred on Michael Collins. We Irishmen were nervous and ill at ease, it was our first introduction to diplomacy. The English were at home and confident in surroundings where they had met and out-manoeuvred or intimidated their opponents in a hundred similar struggles. On the walls hung portraits of past prime ministers, the builders of Britain's empire. Opposite to me was the portrait of Sir Robert Walpole and beneath it sat Winston Churchill.[18]

In addition to these disadvantages, there were internal divisions within the Irish delegation. The Collins-Brugha split in Cabinet was replicated within the delegation. Griffith particularly disliked Childers and suspected that he was de Valera's spy,[19] and was sending information of a hostile nature back to the Long Fellow in Dublin. Barton recalled that, 'Griffith had made Childers' position very difficult ... On more than one occasion, Griffith had been very insulting to him.'[20] Pakenham maintained that the antagonism between Griffith and Childers was obvious from the very moment that Childers was selected as a secretary to the delegation, 'furnishing ... a wretched parallel to that between Brugha and Collins'.[21] However, though Barton confirmed, 'Any information I possess I gave to the writer of the book, *Peace By Ordeal*, Lord Pakenham,'[22] this is one point on which he disagrees with the account given by Pakenham. As Barton recalled it:

> The disagreement between Griffith and Childers, which is referred to in *Peace By Ordeal,* did not develop until there was a divergence of opinion in the delegation itself. I had not noticed it before. I think all relations were quite formal, if not cordial, up to that.[23]

Barton's divergence from Pakenham's account is interesting. It may reflect the fact that he had been out of circulation while imprisoned during much of the War of Independence, so he was absent from the Cabinet and the Dáil as the split originated, developed and festered. However, he had returned to his ministerial duties over the summer of 1921, so he should have been aware of what was happening in the Cabinet, and how it might affect the delegates. Barton could come across as a remote figure with a detached, aloof personality, but it is unlikely that he was oblivious to the internecine strife that formed an ongoing undercurrent within the delegation. It is likelier that he concentrated on the policies rather than the personalities within the delegation, and dismissed any early divisions within the team as irrelevancies. This is remarkable though, since Barton was of the same extreme republican hue as Childers. His professed ignorance of the fracture may also stem from the fact that he had hero-worshipped his older, orphaned cousin as a young boy and had a particularly close relationship with Erskine, so perhaps he had a blind spot concerning any faults that Childers may have had. The antagonism between Griffith and Childers was a two-way street, and Barton may not have wanted to besmirch the memory of his executed cousin when he was providing his witness statement in 1954. Whatever the truth of the matter, for some reason, Barton was unaware, or claimed that he was unaware, of any discord between Griffith and Childers until the other delegates became divided regarding what actions they should take as the negotiations neared their final stage. If this were indeed the case, it demonstrated at best that Barton was single-minded to the point of having tunnel vision regarding the goal of the negotiations (which, in Barton's role as Minister for Economic Affairs, was full fiscal autonomy for the new Irish State) and overlooked or ignored personality clashes within the delegation - or, at worst, that Barton's detachment, single-mindedness, aloofness and lack of awareness of his political and personal surroundings put him out of step with his colleagues from the start of the negotiations.

However, perhaps the greatest disadvantage that the Irish delegates faced as negotiations began was their confusion regarding the concept of external association. This nebulous idea was de Valera's brainchild, which involved giving a concession to Britain in return for allowing Ireland to exit from the Empire and establish a republic. The basic premise was that the Irish republic would then enter into a perpetual alliance with Britain, recognising the monarch as the head of the alliance. Thus, Ireland would not actually be a member of the Commonwealth (or Empire), but would be externally associated with Britain and the various dominions.[24] De Valera hoped that this would reassure Britain regarding issues of security, while offering political carrots to British imperialists, Unionists and the hard-line republican wing of Sinn Féin. As de Valera saw it, imperialists would be content to see the monarch as the head of the proposed alliance; Unionists would retain the link with Britain and hard-line republicans would get a republic. Such were the broad brush-strokes, but the fine detail of this novel idea was never worked out, and the Irish delegates only had a vague idea of how it might work. Lacking clarity themselves, they found it hugely difficult to explain the concept to their British counterparts and impossible to win them over to the idea, in which they had 'zero interest' anyway.[25] The British would offer dominion status, and the idea of a republic (with or without the complicated idea of external association attached) was unacceptable to them. Lloyd George had made this clear in a letter dated 29 September, before the negotiations even began.[26] The Irish delegation knew this before they left for London. Barton later noted that:

> In these preliminaries the English refused to recognise us as acting on behalf of the Irish Republic and the fact that we agreed to negotiate at all on any other basis was possibly the primary cause of our downfall. Certainly, it was the first milestone on the road to disaster.[27]

Even Griffith, the chairman of the delegation, only learned of the concept of external association at the eleventh hour.[28] When de Valera was persuading him to go to London, he called Griffith into his office, along with Brugha and Stack. According to Griffith, he told de Valera, 'I'll go ... but I know, and you know, that I can't bring back a republic.' Only then did the Long Fellow reveal his idea of external association, accompanying his vague explanation with an even vaguer diagram (see endnote). Griffith and the others had not heard of the concept before this, and Brugha gave 'reluctant consent' after a half-hour or so of persuasion, when a silent and 'sullen' Stack left with him.[29] Griffith's words proved prescient. They were echoed in R. F. Foster's assessment that 'whoever went to London would have to compromise the Republic'. Foster added that it was 'significant that de Valera did not entertain the idea of going [to London] himself'.[30]

It is indicative of de Valera's esteem for Barton however, both as a personal friend and as an educated man of intellect, that the Wicklow man knew about the new concept of external association before Griffith ... and probably before anybody else. De Valera often used Barton as a sounding board, and he seems to have been the first person entrusted with knowledge of the novel idea. De Valera unveiled the main points of the idea to Barton shortly after the latter's release from prison in July 1921.[31] Of necessity, though, de Valera confined his explanation to the main outlines of the scheme. The nitty-gritty of the finer points could not be explained as they had not been worked out in any degree of detail. Nevertheless, Barton supported de Valera's plan, agreeing that external association was a desirable objective. This may have been partly out of loyalty to his chief, but it is likely that Barton found the idea of being outside the Commonwealth (and the Empire) very attractive. Barton valued both honour and duty very highly and he had sworn an oath to the Republic. For such a man of honour, Barton saw it as his duty to be loyal to that sacred and binding oath, and to the Republic, whose best interests would be served, he felt, by remaining outside the direct sphere of British political influence. Despite the lack of detail and clarity surrounding the concept, Barton appreciated de Valera's thinking and adopted a similar attitude himself (as did Childers – but he was neither a member of Cabinet nor a delegate). Thus, Barton would push the external association idea in the negotiations, but, by his own retrospective admission, he and the other plenipotentiaries were 'hazy' about what external association actually meant.[32] In a memorandum written after the close of the conference, Barton noted:

> The Dail members understood that their delegate's object was external association. The definition of that term was vague and even the delegates had but a hazy conception of what would be its final form. This, however, was clear to us: External Association meant that no vestige of British authority would remain in Ireland. The compromise would be as regards our foreign relations.[33]

Griffith, who had told de Valera that he couldn't bring back a republic, knew, however, that he would have to compromise in some way on the republican principle at the negotiations. Moreover, Collins (and Cosgrave) – who, according to Pakenham, were 'as good republicans as any' – did not place the same emphasis on external association, seeing little difference between it and dominion status ... or, at least, not seeing the difference as fundamental in accepting an agreement with the British. Unfortunately, they failed to realise how fundamental it was to de Valera.[34] Under these circumstances, although his primary role in the delegation was economic and his principal goal was full fiscal autonomy, Barton would also become the chief proponent of external association among the plenipotentiaries,[35] with his approach to the thorny question of Irish defence based on perpetual neutrality, guaranteed by the Commonwealth of Nations.[36] However, Griffith would eventually become annoyed by Barton's constant and, in his view, unhelpful references to external association as the talks progressed.[37]

All this lay ahead, however, and despite disadvantages and divisions, there was an upbeat mood among Irish people when the negotiations opened on 11 October. The first week of negotiations went well, and there were 'grounds for high hopes of a satisfactory outcome'. Public opinion in Ireland demanded that internees should be released, and the Catholic hierarchy made an appeal, urging 'the immediate liberation of all internees'. However, despite this stumbling block, the 'tone and temper of the meetings [were] extremely pleasant ... a happy augury for future meetings'.[38] Initial optimism waned, however, as the negotiations became protracted and dragged on into November. The present work is not the place to re-tell the story of the treaty negotiations, and there is no need to do so. Pakenham's *Peace by Ordeal* and Macardle's *The Irish Republic* both provide detailed accounts, and much ink has been used in more modern works providing commentary and analysis on every aspect of the talks and their outcomes. However, Barton's place in Irish history is defined – rightly or wrongly – by the fact that he signed the treaty. His participation was integral to the negotiation process, and there were some key moments when his contributions and actions had significant effects on events. Any study of Barton must examine these, and endeavour to evaluate their cause, course and consequences as the talks progressed. Thus, the approach taken here is to focus on the part played by Barton and to follow his thread through the wider tapestry of negotiations between the delegations – and his impact on events as they unfolded.

Conferences and Sub-conferences
(Early October–Early November 1921)

Like the other plenipotentiaries, Barton had left Dublin with two con-
tradictory and conflicting pieces of paper – his credentials and his
instructions. Barton's copy of his instructions has survived, perhaps
indicating the value he placed on them.[1] The two documents read
as follows:[2]

In virtue of the authority vested in me by Dáil Éireann, I hereby
appoint Arthur Griffith, T.D., Minister for Foreign Affairs;
Michael Collins, T.D., Minister for Finance; Robert C. Barton,
T.D., Minister for Economic Affairs; Edmund J. Duggan, T.D.
and George Gavan Duffy, T.D., as Envoys Plenipotentiary from
the elected Government of the Republic of Ireland to negotiate
and conclude on behalf of Ireland, with the representatives of His
Majesty George V, a treaty or treaties of settlement, association and
accommodation between Ireland and the community of nations
known as the British Commonwealth. In witness whereof I hereun-
der subscribe my name as President.
Eamon de Valera.

1. The Plenipotentiaries have full powers as defined in their credentials.
2. It is understood before decisions are finally reached on a main
   question, that a despatch notifying the intention to make these
   decisions will be sent to members of the Cabinet in Dublin, and

that a reply will be awaited by the Plenipotentiaries before final decision is made.

3. It is also understood that the complete text of the draft treaty about to be signed will be similarly submitted to Dublin, and reply awaited.

4. In case of a break, the text of the final proposals from our side will be similarly submitted.

5. It is understood the Cabinet in Dublin will be kept regularly informed of the progress of the negotiations.

In addition, the delegates had been instructed to ensure that, if the talks were to break down, they should do so over the question of partition (which was likely to garner international approval) rather than on the question of Irish status inside or outside of the Commonwealth or Empire.[3] Barton had been reluctant to travel, but arrived in London with a determination to do his best as a delegate. Griffith and Collins (a reluctant delegate himself), had endorsed Barton's inclusion in the delegation. Indeed, Collins had suggested that both Barton and Childers should travel with the delegation.[4] Lord Birkenhead recorded pen pictures of all the Irish delegates at the beginning of the negotiations. Appearing to be detached, single-minded and aloof, Barton did not make a good first impression, and Birkenhead noted that he 'has no outstanding quality'.[5] Therefore, once the talks began, the British team, who also perceived Barton to be the head of the de Valera-Childers faction,[6] and viewed him as de Valera's puppet,[7] opted for exclusion as the best policy. They tried to marginalise him from many aspects of the negotiations by setting up a series of sub-conferences after the seventh plenary session on 24 October, on which date the precedent was set.[8] Eamon Duggan was asked to relay a request for Griffith and Collins to meet Lloyd George and Chamberlain separately for 'ten minutes private conference' either before or after the full conference. Although Barton was a little uneasy about this, the suggestion seemed innocuous enough so he could find no real grounds for objection, and the private meeting went ahead after the main one.[9]

Barton later recalled:

It was a suggestion of Lloyd George's that Michael Collins and Arthur Griffith only should meet him in private conferences at a fairly early stage in the course of the proceedings. It was a specious argument of Lloyd George's that he was leader of a coalition government and that many of his colleagues – some of them, at any rate – were difficult to deal with, that they held different political views from his and that a smaller delegation on his side would be likely to make better progress and, therefore, there should be a smaller delegation on our side. Possibly Lloyd George also felt that he could make more progress with Griffith and Collins than he had made with a full delegation. That is supposition on my part ... I am merely speculating as to why Lloyd George made this proposal of small meetings, but it would seem to be a reasonably good tactical move, and I think it was quite successful too. Once smaller delegation meetings had been agreed, then other private meetings followed when Griffith alone met Lloyd George, or Collins alone met Birkenhead.[10]

However, Barton, who was, according to Mais, a man of 'absolute integrity',[11] went on to clarify that it was not his intention to cast aspersions on the characters of Griffith and Collins. In an apparent effort to be scrupulously fair regarding the sub-conference model of progressing the negotiations, and to clarify his feelings towards his fellow delegates, in whom he had full confidence at the time that the 'private conferences' were proposed and introduced, Barton continued:

Obviously, you can get a better idea of what is in another person's mind when talking privately than when talking to five. People might be more nervous of stating precise views if they were more or less publicly expressed before four or five than would be the case when two talk confidentially. I think we all thought more progress might be made in this way, and Gavan Duffy and I had not at that stage lost confidence in our colleagues ... I think Gavan Duffy and I did at the time express some diffidence. I would have to refer back to papers to confirm. But we did not put in a direct negative.[12]

Prior to the introduction of the private sub-conference model, the full delegations had met on a number of occasions. Barton provided Pakenham with a sketch of the seating arrangements (below).[13]

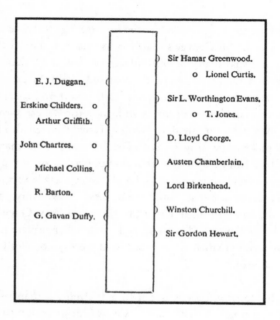

E. J. Duggan.

Erskine Childers. o

Arthur Griffith.

John Chartres. o

Michael Collins.

R. Barton.

G. Gavan Duffy.

Sir Hamar Greenwood.

o Lionel Curtis.

Sir L. Worthington Evans.

o T. Jones.

D. Lloyd George.

Austen Chamberlain.

Lord Birkenhead.

Winston Churchill.

Sir Gordon Hewart.

From the outset of the talks, the British were focussing on Crown, Empire and defence,[14] the latter of which included the question of British naval access to Irish ports. The first plenary session of the talks opened in 10 Downing Street at 11 a.m. on Tuesday, 11 October. The question of the ports soon reared its head, and it led to a revealing intervention on Barton's part. Lloyd George maintained that access to Irish ports was essential for defence, and Churchill elaborated by using the exemplar of British naval rights at a South African port. However, when asked directly, Churchill had to admit that the port itself was under South African control. The point was won, but Barton intervened, trying to distance the proposed British naval presence at Irish ports further from the South African reality, while tying it into the arena of sovereignty over foreign policy by recalling that South Africa need not join in a British war. This immediately drew an icy rebuff from Birkenhead, who retorted with the words: 'That is not conceded.'[15] Although insignificant both of itself and in the bigger picture of the negotiations and their outcome, Barton's contribution at this early stage provides a tantalising glimpse of his mindset. It was not enough for Barton that Churchill had conceded the point about control of the port, he wished to

88

press home his advantage. In addition, being probably the most doctrinaire republican among the Irish delegates, he also wished to link the discussion to Irish foreign policy, specifically Ireland's position if the British were at war – an area of sovereignty that would be integral to the whole question of external association. It was also a reminder of his single-mindedness – and a certain degree of inflexibility – regarding the republic, which needed external association if it were to exist and be recognised. The alternative would be dominion status, which was not an option at this stage for the Irish team, particularly the inflexible Barton.

The next day, Wednesday, 12 October, saw a meeting of the sub-committee that had been formed in London to deal with the observance of the truce. Given Barton's prominent role in negotiating the terms and implementation of the truce, it was unsurprising that he was a member of the Irish team. He was joined by Michael Collins, Eamon Duggan and Art O'Brien, with Erskine Childers as secretary. The British side consisted of Sir Laming Worthington Evans and Sir Hamar Greenwood, assisted by Sir J. Anderson, Alfred William Cope, General Sir Nevil Macready and General Tudor, with Tom Jones and Lionel Curtis as secretaries. In addition to any violent incidents that were alleged to have breached the terms of the truce, the committee also discussed issues such as I.R.A. drilling and the alleged stockpiling of arms.[16] Barton remained ignorant in relation to the latter, as he reminisced in his witness statement:

> As for any discussion in the Dáil on collecting arms for a continuation of the fight, that was rather *sub rosa* business all the time and was carried on by Michael Collins and Cathal Brugha outside the Dáil. It was not a fixed plan of the Cabinet, as far as I remember, to take advantage of the Truce period to rearm.[17]

Barton's time in prison had distanced him from military operations during much of 1921, so that by the October negotiations he was out of the loop, and not as *au fait* as he might have liked with the up-to-date situation regarding arms and ammunition. Nonetheless, while he was not directly involved, there certainly were attempts by the I.R.A. to import arms, as evidenced by the landing of weapons from the *Frieda* at Waterford the following month.[18] Despite a degree of mutual distrust, however, the committee for the observance of the truce drew up an agreement that covered the disputed points on the second day of negotiations, and the committee continued to meet at intervals throughout the process. The agreement concluded with the words: 'notice of termination of the truce: seventy-two hours to be given'.[19] Barton's participation in this committee meant that he was keenly aware of the threat of the renewal of hostilities. While the threat of war may have been a bluff, Barton could not take that risk, and he had first-hand knowledge of how little time was needed for hostilities to resume. This committee and the agreement regarding seventy-two hours' notice would be a crucial factor when the time came in December for Barton to make a decision about signing the treaty. However, that eventuality could not be foreseen during the first meeting of the committee on 12 October.

During the third plenary session, which began at noon the following day, Thursday, 13 October, much of the discussion centred on trade. According to F. S. L. Lyons, by the early twentieth century, 'the [Irish] economy was in a permanently subservient position, overshadowed by the wealth and sophistication of its formidable neighbour'.[20] This was Barton's specialist area, and he was forceful in his quest for full fiscal autonomy, putting his case clearly and concisely to his listeners. Using Lloyd George's own figures, Barton skilfully demonstrated that full fiscal autonomy posed no threat to English trade. In response to Barton's argument of inequality, the Prime Minister tried to show that England's autonomy would be affected by Barton's proposals, but he became confused while trying to demonstrate that tariffs were unnecessary for Irish economic development. He then changed tack, telling Barton that: 'your real protection is cheap labour'. Barton retorted: 'Our railwaymen will not accept your wages.' Lloyd George switched his approach again, leading with: 'Your cost of living is lower, and Irish workers accept wages that Englishmen would not look at.' Barton countered: 'The cost of living in Ireland is higher, and ... cheap labour is of little value for industries like spinning etc.'[21] This type of cut and thrust continued throughout the session, but by the end of the day Barton seemed to convince the English side that Ireland did not have any aggressive trade intentions that would seek to penalise England. Chamberlain even suggested that England should find a way to ensure that Irish industries 'would not be strangled in their cradle' by their English counterparts. Lloyd George also promised to investigate the matter.[22] Barton's first foray into the area of economic and trade talks had been a success, and provided a forum where he demonstrated his expertise of the subject matter in his own field.

As the month of October progressed, so did the negotiations. After ten days the Irish team submitted the first ever set of Sinn Féin proposals to the English side. This was known as Draft Treaty A, and in its conspicuously few pages the idea of external association was unveiled.[23] De Valera had given the plenipotentiaries a copy of Draft Treaty A – of necessity, in incomplete form – which outlined external association.[24] However, a good deal of vagueness still surrounded the concept, and there was a complete dearth of detail about how it might work in practice. Moreover, the articles on finance, trade and the Ulster question (articles six, seven and eight) were not completed and were to be drafted by the relevant ministers at a later stage. As Minister for Economic Affairs, Barton was to undertake responsibility for drafting article seven. In fact, Barton had fought long and hard to include a section in the draft treaty making a specific claim for full fiscal autonomy, knowing that some concession would be necessary if the claim were to be accepted. Barton proposed to soften the blow with a trade convention giving Britain 'most favoured nation status'. Despite Barton's efforts, however, the claim was not inserted into the Irish proposals as Barton's colleagues did not have the same zeal for full fiscal autonomy as he did.[25] Barton championed the idea zealously throughout the negotiations though, and he was determined in his quest to obtain full fiscal autonomy, pursuing the claim doggedly until the bitter end of the talks.

Barton's zeal was also evident in his pursuit of external association as the negotiations unfolded. His single-mindedness, inflexibility and tenacious insistence on de Valera's formula in discussions on Irish foreign affairs never faltered, and his constant harping on the subject during the talks began to infuriate some of the other negotiators. Barton's intransigent attitude enraged Lloyd George, who scathingly referred to the Irish Minister for Economic Affairs as a 'pipsqueak'.[26] Annoying the British Prime Minister was one thing, but Barton's obdurate attitude also irritated Griffith, his own chairman. Griffith was suspicious of Barton's vocal insistence on external association, which he regarded as pushing de Valera's agenda, and which he felt was frustratingly impeding the progress of the negotiations. Griffith was also suspicious of the Englishman, Erskine Childers, and the familial relationship between Childers and Barton was one reason why Griffith tarred the cousins with the same brush, perceiving them as de Valera's champions – and moles – within the delegation. Moreover, Griffith disliked the Annamoe cousins because he was jealous of their educational status, which probably made him feel inferior to them in some ways. Coming from a background of privilege and wealth, the cousins' Oxbridge education was a cause of envy to Griffith, whose formal education ended before he was aged 13, when he went to work as a messenger boy.[27] Though fate, circumstance and politics had thrown them together as plenipotentiaries, they came from different worlds, and Griffith came to share the British side's antipathy to Barton. Griffith's antipathy also extended to Gavan Duffy, whom he perceived as Barton's satellite in the negotiating team, and the chairman criticised both his fellow plenipotentiaries as 'being too emphatic and creating the wrong atmosphere' in talks concerning trade and neutrality.[28] However, Griffith preserved the greatest share of his dislike and distrust for Childers. In 1954, Barton recalled the enmity between the two men, demonstrating a mature understanding of the relationship between them and an acute, insightful understanding of how Griffith as chairman, and Collins as his assistant, may have felt intellectually inferior to one of the delegation's secretaries who was nominally far below them in the hierarchy of the group:

> Griffith had made Childers' position very difficult and, no doubt, he was diffident of tendering advice unless specifically asked for it. On more than one occasion Griffith had been very insulting to him. Erskine had always been very good on paper. He drafted the memoranda in which he put up arguments for us to study. He knew what was the relationship within the Commonwealth. He knew what words meant and how far the powers which they were offering us were curtailed in practice. He was always emphasising the difference between the law and the practice. He knew what the law appeared to mean and how differently it could work in practice. I think that Collins and Griffith felt they were in a position of inferiority to Childers. Their minds were confused because they lacked the knowledge he possessed. He had superior intelligence and knowledge. He pointed out to them that what they thought they had got, they had not necessarily got in practice because terms could be differently interpreted. On one occasion Collins complained that he was being confused by 'pettifogging lawyers'; by this he meant Gavan Duffy and Childers.[29]

There is little doubt that similar arguments could be made in relation to Griffith's attitude to the educated Barton who, being a full member of the delegation, was higher than his cousin in the delegation's pecking order.

This situation created a fault line in the Irish delegation – one along which it would eventually split.[30]

It was against this background that the negotiations began to break into sub-conferences. The initial 'ten minutes private conference' between Griffith and Collins on the Irish side and Lloyd George and Chamberlain on the English set a precedent. It became the first of many such meetings that excluded Barton and his adherent, Gavan Duffy, as plenipotentiaries, and Childers as secretary. Barton believed that their exclusion was at the behest of the British. He later stated: 'The suggestion came from Lloyd George. I think it was proposed to us by Tom Jones, Secretary to the British Cabinet, who stressed Lloyd George's difficulties with the members of his own Coalition Government.'[31] However, there may have been more to the move than Barton suspected. Both Coogan and Ryle Dwyer maintain that the idea actually emanated from Griffith and Collins, who were frustrated at the lack of progress and felt hamstrung by Barton's and Gavan Duffy's obdurate negotiating stance.[32] The British were quick to comply with the suggestion, facilitating it by allowing people to assume that it had come from their side. Whatever the truth about the origin of the sub-conference idea, it certainly seemed that more progress was made in the smaller meetings and on Sunday, 30 October, a hugely significant talk took place. At 9.30 that night, Griffith met Lloyd George alone at Churchill's house. The Welsh Wizard assured Griffith that he would strongly recommend peace with Ireland if the British were certain of real goodwill from the Irish side, particularly regarding Crown, Empire and naval access to ports. Griffith told the Prime Minister that he would recommend recognition of the Crown if the Irish delegation was satisfied with the other points at issue.

Lloyd George wanted Griffith's personal assurance on the matters in question and he asked for some documentary evidence to show to an upcoming Unionist party meeting in Liverpool on 17 November. Therefore, on Tuesday, 1 November, Griffith showed the Irish delegation a draft of a personal letter to Lloyd George. In it, Griffith stated that he would recommend recognition of the Crown, provided he was satisfied on every point (including the essential unity of Ireland), and that he would also recommend free partnership with the British Commonwealth. However, Griffith's authority was contested for the first time at this juncture. Both Barton and Gavan Duffy voiced strong opposition to the idea of sending such a personal letter, and were vehement in their objections to the tone and contents of the document. Childers supported this opposition with no less vehemence, but with less effect as he was not a delegate. According to Barton: [The letter] 'was in our opinion stating a false case. Going much further than either we or the Cabinet at home were prepared to go.'[33] The tone of the meeting turned vitriolic, and Griffith was very sharp in his admonition of Barton, Childers and Gavan Duffy in particular. Afterwards, Barton, Gavan Duffy and Childers had a meeting of their own. They would not allow Griffith's personal letter to be sent, maintaining that they could never support its contents in their existing form.[34] According to Barton: 'We [Barton, Gavan Duffy and Childers] decided that in no circumstances would we permit this letter to be sent as a personal letter, or in the form submitted to us.'[35] From this point onward, the covert fault line in the delegation became an overt battle line, and one that was clearly drawn, with Griffith and Barton leading forces from opposing camps.

The following day, Wednesday, 2 November, there were two sub-conferences discussing the substantive issues of partition and Ireland's future relationship with the British Empire and/or Commonwealth, but without much progress. Barton took minutes of both meetings.[36] Griffith also took steps to surmount the obstacle of Barton-led opposition, which maintained that the original draft of the contested letter would undermine the stand the delegation had taken in its memorandum on the form of recognition of the Crown that they were willing to recommend. The chairman redrafted his letter to the Prime Minister, making subtle changes such as 'free partnership with the other states associated within the British Commonwealth' instead of 'with the British Commonwealth'. Griffith would sign the altered document in his capacity as chairman of the delegation. Collins and Duggan approved the redrafted letter, and the hesitant and suspicious Barton and Gavan Duffy reluctantly gave it their grudging consent.[37] Griffith sent a copy to de Valera in Dublin, together with an upbeat report of the progress that had been made. De Valera responded to the jubilant Griffith with a congratulatory reply.[38] Notwithstanding the apparent progress, the Barton camp was worried about the turn that developments were taking. Barton actually saw the events of these four days, 30 October–2 November, as pivotal in the whole saga of the negotiations. He would later muse: 'In my opinion, these conferences between the English and Griffith and Collins on 30 October, 1 November and 2 November sealed the doom of the republic.'[39] In retrospect, it seemed that the die had been cast.

Twists, Turns – and Tensions
(3 November–3 December 1921)

Barton was anxious about the continued use of sub-conferences as the month of November progressed. He and his acolytes had not objected when the idea of private conferences was mooted, but once these meetings came into play their suspicions were aroused. Barton recalled that:

> It was not until later that Gavan Duffy, Childers and I realised that Griffith and Collins were prepared to settle for less than we thought it possible to obtain. We had trusted them fully. We had complete confidence in them up to a time. Griffith fought magnificent actions during the full conferences. We had no reason to suppose at the time that he would agree in private to anything which he had not been agreeing to with five of us present. Therefore, we had little or no reason to suspect anything.[1]

As the negotiations progressed, Barton and Gavan Duffy became more and more worried about the direction in which they were moving. They thought that Griffith was giving Lloyd George the impression that if he proceeded strongly against the Ulster Unionists, the Irish delegation would accept a dominion status settlement, but such a settlement was out of the question. Barton felt that Griffith knew full well the impossibility of such a settlement, and he was stringing the English along. This went against Barton's finely honed sense of honour, and he went as far as to tell Griffith that his tactics were not fair.[2] According to Macardle:

The line which Griffith and Collins were pursuing with the English had troubled Barton greatly for some time. Griffith, he felt now, was permitting the English to delude the Ulstermen with the idea that there was a possibility of the Delegation's agreeing to a settlement bringing Ireland within the Empire, while no such settlement was, in reality, possible. Gavan Duffy shared [Barton's] anxiety. They would have seriously considered resigning but they believed – as did Erskine Childers – that the final decision would rest with the Cabinet in Dublin, and that nothing that happened in London could constitute a fatal surrender of Ireland's claim.[3]

They were anxious about the developments within the sub-conferences – from most of which they were excluded as the to-ing and fro-ing continued through the autumn and into the winter. The final tally of attendances at the sub-conferences demonstrates the levels of exclusion of the Barton camp. Collins and Griffith (whether separately or together) were present at all twenty-four sub-conferences. On the other hand, Barton attended four, Gavan Duffy three and Childers one.[4] As their exclusion and isolation from the decision-making process increased, the Barton camp became alarmed and decided to alert the Cabinet in Dublin to the situation. This extraordinary move was a gamble on their part, but they evidently felt that it was a necessary step to take. Barton deferred to Gavan Duffy's legal expertise, probably feeling that the lawyer could explain the situation to those in Dublin better and in more detail and depth than he could. Macardle again takes up the tale:

> Gavan Duffy went to Dublin to impress on the President the dangers which seemed to him to exist in the policy that was being followed in London of dividing the Delegation, only Griffith and Collins negotiating with the British; the President, however, preferred not to interfere with the arrangements so long as in all formal actions the Delegation acted as a whole.[5]

Barton's own recollection of Gavan Duffy's trip to Dublin and the circumstances surrounding it makes interesting reading. He was in his seventies when he provided this account in his witness statement, and it shows a level of acceptance and wisdom that came with his mature years. His empathy with the personalities involved – his refusal to blame Griffith and

Collins for anything more than under-reporting the private conferences, his understanding that the Cabinet were not privy to the daily round of the negotiations and did not act because their suspicions were not aroused, and his referencing the humanity of the problem at the end – all point to degrees of resignation and self-knowledge that he may not have possessed in 1921:

> After these private conferences – it was then we began to get suspicious, and it was then we decided that one of us must go to Dublin to acquaint the Cabinet and de Valera that we were not at all sure that the reports given us of what transpired at private conferences were comprehensive and feared that the general position was being undermined. But when Gavan Duffy got here and expressed these views to the other members of the Cabinet in Dublin who had not had their suspicions aroused, they possibly thought we were taking an exaggerated view. It was a very human problem.[6]

The Barton camp's last throw of the dice to warn de Valera and his colleagues in Dublin had failed. Gavan Duffy's exhortations to the Cabinet had fallen on deaf ears; they had dismissed his concerns. From this point forward, Barton's position and that of his allies in the Irish delegation became almost untenable. Barton, who had strong beliefs about honour and duty, would not countenance resigning. Such a course would be a dereliction of his duty to Ireland, and could bring dishonour to his country now that it was thrust on the international stage through its role in the negotiations. Moreover, he drew comfort from his belief that the final decision would rest with the Cabinet and the Dáil. Notwithstanding this crumb of comfort, he continued to be excluded from conferences as negotiations continued. As plenipotentiaries, Barton and Gavan Duffy's minority roles now resembled those of a perpetual parliamentary opposition. They were listened to by the others, but their rhetoric was completely ineffectual. Pakenham likened them to Cassandra, the Greek prophetess whose prophesies were never believed. It was an apt comparison. Pakenham's paragraph provides a good summary of the new reality in the delegation, and it is worth quoting here:

> [Following his unsuccessful mission to Dublin, Gavan Duffy's] position and Barton's became in consequence unenviable. They

saw courses adopted which they despised and feared. But they were always in a minority, and they had been originally selected as likely to 'work in well with Griffith and Collins'. With the rejection of Duffy's warning their main positive function was frustrated ... In relation, however, to the main drift of the struggle, the pair lingered, embarrassed, Cassandra-like, inevitable victims of the tragedy which eventually overtook them on the evening of the 5th. It is true that they could have cut the knot by resigning, but to have done so was to present England with a heaven-sent opportunity for driving home the wedge, and to discredit their country in its first international trial.[7]

The isolated Barton was also acutely aware that Griffith and Collins were the leaders of the delegation. He respected Griffith' role as chairman, and he had long been a warm admirer of Collins.[8] Despite not being given an actual brief by de Valera before he travelled, Barton was expected to assist and support them on economic, fiscal and trade matters, while Gavan Duffy was expected to contribute to the field of drafting and constitutional law. It was not up to them (and certainly not to Childers in his capacity as secretary) to develop policies and create counter-proposals that flew in the face of the progress made by the leaders of the delegation. Notwithstanding (or perhaps due to) their stubbornness, the Barton camp had failed to progress the talks in any way, shape or form. The Griffith camp had, and they probably felt it was a bit rich that Barton and his cronies should try to take the moral high ground in the delegation, given the fact that, unlike Griffith and Collins, they had made no impression whatsoever on the British negotiators.[9]

The talks continued their tortuous progress. By 11 November, Griffith had led Lloyd George to believe that Ireland would be prepared to accept allegiance to the throne and membership of the Commonwealth if the question of the essential unity of Ireland could be solved. The Prime Minister informed the Unionist leader, James Craig, that Sinn Féin had contingently undertaken to recommend agreement on association, Crown and defence, if an all-Ireland parliament were established. Craig would have none of it, but when the Irish delegates saw Lloyd George's letter a few days later, it led to another tempestuous scene. Barton and Gavan Duffy called for instant repudiation of a dominion status settlement, but they were overruled, with Griffith arguing that 'though our goal is not

Dominion Home Rule, we must explore their avenues if we want them to explore ours'.[10] Unhappy but impotent, the Barton camp once again yielded to the inevitable. Craig's blunt refusal to consider the possibility of an all-Ireland parliament moved the discussions between the British and Irish delegates on to the concept of a boundary commission. The Irish were under the impression that such a body would allot large swathes of the six counties to the twenty-six.[11] The Irish delegates were ready to accept partition and trust that the findings of a future boundary commission would solve the problem by convincing the Unionists that unity would be the only option for their (hopefully) significantly reduced territory. Griffith, in particular, placed his trust in such a solution, believing that what would be left of the northern statelet would not be viable, and so would opt for unity with the rest of the island. A decade later, in a speech made in Enniscorthy, Barton averred that:

> Arthur Griffith, after the conversations which he and Michael Collins used to have with Mr Lloyd George, Mr Chamberlain and Lord Birkenhead, used to return to our house in Hans Place and, standing in front of the fireplace, over and over again declared: 'If they do not come in, they will lose half their territory and they can't stay out.' Not once, but many times, he reiterated this.[12]

The mud was clearing around many aspects of the negotiations by mid-month, and on 16 November the British side delivered a draft of their proposed terms, including a boundary commission, to the Irish side. Ireland was to be a self-governing dominion, but the Crown was not mentioned, so the idea of an externally associated republic was not negated.[13] The British drafted their offer in the form of treaty proposals and, having read the draft, de Valera wrote to Griffith on 17 November advising the delegation to prepare their counter-proposals, modifying Draft Treaty A as required.[14] On the following Tuesday, 22 November, the delegation met to discuss their reply to the British proposals. The Barton-led triumvirate had drafted a memorandum, chiefly authored by Childers. However, Griffith had shown such antipathy to previous proposals suggested by Childers that they decided to pass the document off as coming from Barton, which Griffith might regard as the lesser of two evils. The draft memorandum was modified at the meeting, and a toned-down version was adopted and presented to the British. Awaiting a reply, Barton, Gavan

Duffy and Childers complained that all the concessions were coming from the Irish side. Childers drew up a memorandum to prove the truth of their argument. This document infuriated Griffith, who accused Childers (and, by association, Barton and Gavan Duffy) of working against a settlement. Another unsavoury scene ensued, deepening the divisions within the Irish delegation. The series of clashes within the Irish delegation – the disagreement regarding Griffith's personal letter of 2 November, the denouncement of Lloyd George's letter to Craig in mid-month, and now the open hostility surrounding the Childers memorandum – had fractured relationships between the Griffith and Barton camps beyond repair. By the last week in November, Barton cut a sad figure, all too well aware of the cleavage wrought within the group, but powerless to do anything about it.

Unsurprisingly, the Irish counter-proposals, despite being watered down, did not meet with British approval. Barton noted that the British negotiators were 'bitterly disappointed' with the Irish memorandum, and that they had 'the dogs of war ready to unleash' should the talks break down.[15] It appeared as if the talks had reached a stalemate and were deadlocked. Nevertheless, efforts persisted to keep the embers of negotiation burning. Another conference to explore the possibility of finding some common ground was arranged for 23 November. Griffith, Collins and – unusually – Barton (described as 'a noteworthy addition')[16] attended this meeting as the Irish representatives. The meeting was acrimonious as the Irish trio covered every angle with Lloyd George, Birkenhead and Chamberlain without making headway.[17] Barton's presence as the economic expert of the team may have been responsible for some minor British concessions regarding trade. Minor progress was also made on the question of defence.[18] However, these were no longer the substantive issues – the real sticking points were Crown (and Irish allegiance to it) and Empire (and Ireland's status as a dominion rather than a republic). Another impasse loomed, but Griffith and Collins agreed to meet Birkenhead (at the Earl's suggestion) the following day. Birkenhead's proposal was not as innocent as it seemed, as it effectively eliminated Barton, the leader of the intransigent faction in the Irish delegation, once more.[19] The next day's meeting yielded little or no fruit. The Irish offered to recognise the king as 'head of the associated states' of the Empire, and John Chartres suggested that Ireland might vote an annual donation to the king's personal revenue.[20] Collins and Griffith raised no real objection to this suggestion, and travelled back to Dublin with Barton to confer with de Valera and his colleagues at a Cabinet meeting on Friday, 25 November.[21]

Two decisions resulted from the Cabinet meeting held on that Friday. The Crown, it was agreed, should be recognised as head of an association of states and Ireland should donate annually to the Civil List.[22] There was nothing new in the first decision, but the second one was controversial. According to Austin Stack:

> [There] was a memo prepared by Mr Chartris (sic), Mr Collins said. It came before us at a specially convened meeting towards the end of November. Mr Collins was over, and in attendance. There was reference in the document to a contribution towards the King's household, or something of the kind. Cathal Brugha at once objected, and said he would never consent to anything of the kind. Mr Collins said that was a pity, as he feared the document had by this time – looking at his watch – been handed into Downing Street. Cathal Brugha became very angry and I did my best to throw oil on the troubled waters.[23]

This meeting was the first time that Griffith had returned to Dublin.[24] The other delegates had been back and forth, but the chairman's presence in the Irish capital was the first indication of the London talks nearing their climactic stage. In Stack's opinion, this meeting was also the first indication of something more sinister. In relation to the decision to contribute to the Civil List, he opined: 'This was the first instance of the *fait accompli* succeeding in the game, but we did not see this at the time. We trusted our colleagues in London implicitly.'[25]

Back in London, the plenipotentiaries handed another memorandum proposing and justifying external association to the British on Monday, 28 November. The next day, Griffith, Collins and Duggan met the British at 10 Downing Street, but Barton and Gavan Duffy were once again relegated to the bench, where they were out in the cold.[26] On that day, Griffith was informed that the British would have their final proposals ready by 6 December. He managed to obtain a promise that the Irish delegation would receive a copy of these proposals by Thursday, 1 December, so he asked de Valera to hold another Cabinet meeting on Saturday, 3 December.[27] De Valera was actually away from Dublin at the time. Stack recalled, 'About the end of November, the President left

Dublin for the South and West on a tour of Army Inspection, accompanied by the Minister of Defence and the Chief of Staff.'[28] On receipt of Griffith's urgent missive, Stack had to telegraph de Valera and Brugha to summon them to Dublin. Meanwhile, in London, the 'Proposed Articles of Agreement' duly arrived on 1 December and Barton was immediately despatched to Dublin to show them to de Valera and the other Cabinet members in Ireland.[29] The Wicklow man was an interesting choice – his hard-line republican stance made little difference to the Cabinet members in Dublin since, in de Valera, Brugha and Stack, he would be preaching to the converted. However, his absence from London meant that he was not available for any last-minute tweaking that might produce a revised draft. This was perhaps a little strange, as such tweaking would invariably involve economic matters, which was Barton's field. In the event, Griffith and Collins discussed such changes, which led to some amendments and a revised draft being produced and sent to the Irish delegation about 1.30 a.m. Griffith departed for Dublin on the morning of 2 December. Collins, Duffy and Childers sailed later on and were delayed by a nautical collision, which meant that the mail boat only docked at 10.15 a.m. The Cabinet meeting was scheduled for eleven o'clock.[30]

The gathering at the Mansion House was a tempestuous affair. In the morning, the Cabinet's numbers were swollen by the addition of the non-ministerial delegates, Erskine Childers and Kevin O'Higgins. Griffith put the case for acceptance of the suggested terms, emphasising that this was Britain's best offer. Barton, however, rejected Griffith's argument, stating his belief that Britain's last word had not been reached. He thought that full fiscal autonomy – his principal objective in relation to trade – could still be won. He opined that Britain would not renew the War of Independence over the question of allegiance to the Crown. He thought better terms could be achieved – as things stood, Barton reminded his listeners, the terms neither secured dominion status nor guaranteed anything definite about the Ulster question. Barton let it be known that he would vote against acceptance of the proposed terms. Gavan Duffy supported Barton in his stance.[31] When consulted, Childers also supported his cousin, pointing out that the terms did not give national status to Ireland, thus negating the possibility of neutrality in wartime.[32] The debate continued, with Griffith 'still persisting that the document should be signed',[33] and eventually Brugha asked who was responsible for the implementation of the sub-conference model and the splitting of the delegation so that most of the work fell to Griffith and Collins? On hearing the reply 'the British government', Brugha remarked pointedly: 'The British government selected their men.' It was an ugly moment – the suspicion and mistrust of the Minister for Defence (and others in his camp) were laid bare – and the atmosphere was charged with tension. Collins retorted: 'If you are not satisfied with us, get another five to go over.'[34] Griffith rose from his seat, strode across to Brugha, and demanded that he retract his allegation. It seemed as if the Cabinet meeting might have to be abandoned over the impasse.

Barton, however, saved the day. In what turned out to be a vital intervention, he managed to diffuse the unpleasant situation. A man of honour himself, Barton knew that Griffith valued his own honour very highly and that the chairman of the delegation was extremely sensitive whenever it was impugned. Thus, although he had reservations about the sub-conferences when they were introduced, and he continued to disapprove of them, Barton interposed to say that he refused to have the private proceedings of the delegates discussed. He reminded the gathering that Griffith and Collins had attended the sub-conferences with the full knowledge and consent of the whole delegation. The oppressive silence had been broken, and Duggan intervened to support Barton, stating that there had been meetings of the full delegation after the sub-conferences, and their proceedings had been reported to the whole delegation. No one contradicted this, either from the delegation or from the Dublin-based cohort within the room. After a pregnant pause, Brugha asked that his remark be withdrawn.[35] Thanks to Barton and his sense of honour the crisis had passed, but the rift within the delegation, the Cabinet and the wider membership of the Dáil was widening visibly as the discussions resumed and the first session of the day continued.

The second session that day saw the withdrawal of non-Cabinet members from proceedings, leaving the Cabinet members alone to discuss the proposals on offer. The majority of the Cabinet rejected the terms, and de Valera spoke at length regarding the merits of external association as opposed to dominion status.[36] Griffith was unmoved, trying to persuade the others to accept the British offer. Collins said little; Brugha and Stack were opposed to signing. It was all very predictable, and at this point Barton interjected, urging de Valera to reconsider his decision to stay in Dublin. Resorting to the use of emotional blackmail, he exhorted the president to go to London to join the delegation, asking him whether it was fair to force Griffith, who was trying desperately to avoid a resumption of hostilities with Britain, to pursue terms that would only be secured if the country was prepared to go to war?[37] De Valera seemed to waver in the face of Barton's impassioned appeal, perhaps of a mind that it would actually be wiser to travel.[38] However, Brugha interpolated at this critical juncture, sombrely asking Griffith whether he realised that accepting the British offer would split Ireland in two? Stack has left a retrospective record of the incident:

> Then Cathal Brugha turned to him, saying: 'Don't you realise that, if you sign this thing, you will split Ireland from top to bottom'? The truth seemed to strike Griffith very forcibly and he said: 'I suppose that's so. I'll tell you what I'll do. I'll go back to London. I'll not sign the document but I'll bring it back and submit it to the Dáil and, if necessary, to the people.' That was quite satisfactory to everybody, and there was no necessity, in face of the pledge thus given, to substitute delegates to go over for the purpose of breaking off the negotiations.[39]

Brugha's question and Stack's answer therefore meant that de Valera would not travel to London. He may have decided against it anyway, but the Brugha–Griffith exchange acted as a catalyst, cementing his position regarding staying in Dublin. According to Barton:

> I pressed de Valera to return with us to London on the score that it would be impossible for us to get the maximum terms without his being present and that it was unfair to expect us to get the best terms without his assistance. He was, however, unwilling to move from the decision [to stay in Dublin] which he had made earlier.[40]

Thus, Barton's appeal came to nought and discussions continued, becoming hurried as the time drew near for the delegates to embark on the mail boat back to Britain. Before the delegates left, de Valera let it be known that he was opposed to any form of oath of allegiance, but when he was told that the British would insist on an oath, he conceded that, if an oath had to be included, 'it should be in conformity with our status of external association'.[41] Barton tried to write down de Valera's actual words, but the Long Fellow was speaking rapidly and there is some doubt as to the actual wording that he used. According to de Valera, the formula that he used was as follows:

> I do swear true faith and allegiance to the Constitution of Ireland and to the Treaty of Association of Ireland with the British Commonwealth of Nations and to recognise the King of Great Britain as head of the association.[42]

Barton agreed with de Valera's recollection but, in an ironic twist, he could not be sure of the President's words because he had abbreviated the end of the oath's wording to 'Assoc'. The next day, in London, Griffith, Collins and Duggan thought that de Valera had said 'associated states'. Barton thought that the word used had been 'association', but he was uncertain, so he yielded to the majority opinion. The phrase 'associated states' was included in the final draft of Irish terms presented to the British. This was significant as 'head of the association' could mean that Ireland's relationship with the Crown was external, whereas 'head of the associated states' would be taken to mean that the king was head of Ireland for all purposes, including domestic ones.[43] However, that dilemma would be faced later. As it was, on the night of 3 December, the delegates left the Cabinet meeting and rushed to catch their sailings. It was a mark of just how acrimonious and divisive the proceedings of that day had been that the delegation returned to Britain on two separate sailings – Barton, Gavan Duffy and Childers left from Dublin's North Wall, while Griffith and Collins departed from Dun Laoghaire.[44] More ominous than the physical division of the delegates was their mental division – they travelled back to London with different ideas regarding what they should do next as they did not know what the Cabinet had actually decided was to be their bottom line.[45]

While *en route* to London, Barton happened to meet with Tim Healy,[46] who was perceived as one of the elder statesmen of Irish politics at this time.[47] They fell into conversation and, when Barton outlined the current state of play in the negotiations to him, Healy strongly advised acceptance of the terms on offer. He was appalled by the prospect of the renewal of war. Healy's incredulity at the possibility was probably accentuated by the fact that the risk of war now hinged on the wording of the oath. He could probably have understood the Ulster question being central to the resumption of hostilities. An enthusiastic supporter of Home Rule, Healy could comprehend a break on Ulster – after all, the Irish Volunteer Force had been founded to defend Home Rule in response to the establishment of the Ulster Volunteers almost a decade earlier. Partition was enacted and was a reality by this time, but it was fragile and there were questions regarding its permanence. However, to break on the wording of the oath would probably be viewed by Healy as the height of folly. Healy also told Barton that he had had a long interview with Michael Collins, informing him that, in Healy's view, Collins was 'the only sensible man amongst us'.[48] Barton had much on which to reflect on his return to the oppressive atmosphere of Hans Place in the wake of the fraught, discordant, indecisive Cabinet meeting in Dublin.

12

From Plenipotentiary
to Signatory
(4–6 December 1921)

It was evident that the negotiations were now entering a crucial, and possibly final, stage. On the morning of Sunday 4 December, Barton, Gavan Duffy and Childers convened to draft counter-proposals. Having done so, they were flabbergasted to learn that Griffith, Collins and Duggan had not drawn up, nor did they intend to present, counter-proposals to the British, with Collins going so far as to say that only those who wanted to break off negotiations should do so.[1] The Barton faction's counter-proposals were eventually perused, and a number of changes (including substituting 'associated states' for 'association') were made. The altered document still hinged on external association, however, and Collins had such a feeling of *déjà vu* that he refused to accompany the delegation to hand over the document. So did Griffith, who could only see the prospect of another rejection ahead. However, *déjà vu* or not, and whether rejection was a *fait accompli* or not, Barton was going to do what his sense of duty demanded and deliver the counter-proposals in accordance with the wishes of the Cabinet meeting the previous day. Only when Barton and Gavan Duffy were preparing to undertake this mission by themselves did Griffith relent; he joined them to try to preserve the appearance of unity within the Irish group.[2] Barton remembered: 'That meeting consisted of Griffith, myself and Gavan Duffy. At it a definite rupture took place. Collins and Duggan refused to go.'[3] During the meeting that followed,

Stack suggested that Griffith was only going through the motions. Stack's account reads as follows:

> It was after much hesitation that Mr Griffith accompanied Messrs. Barton and Gavan Duffy to present them to Lloyd George. Mr Griffith, by accounts, did not put his heart into the argument. Negotiations were broken off, and our Delegates prepared for return home.[4]

Barton, however, who was actually present at the meeting, debating with Chamberlain on trade,[5] and emphasising the necessity of a peace settlement based on goodwill,[6] had a very different recollection of events:

> There was a difference of opinion between us as to what the British would agree to, and Collins objected to our going back again with proposals which he claimed the British had already turned down. Gavan Duffy and I thought more could be gained if we pressed further. Griffith agreed to accompany us, but Collins refused. Duggan also refused. Whatever Collins decided, Duggan always agreed with. Failure was foredoomed. To succeed, our case would have to have been pressed with vigour by all five of us ...[7]
>
> Griffith played up like a man and fought as hard as we did. [It was] one of his greatest efforts in debate. Considering that a few minutes before he had been refusing to come at all, his force and conviction were astounding ...[8]
>
> I feel sure that de Valera would agree with me that up to the time when he received information that the Treaty had been signed − up to that time − he had confidence in Griffith. I think he had, and I think he would agree that he had ...[9]

Griffith's sterling performance floundered, however, when Gavan Duffy told the British team that Ireland's difficulty was 'coming into the empire'. The British walked out and it seemed as if the negotiations had broken down irretrievably. Press reports on the morrow would confirm the gravity of the situation, reporting 'Irish conference fails [due to] Sinn Féin's refusal ...',[10] which caused a 'Grave Irish outlook [with] little hope of settlement now entertained'.[11] On the way back to Hans Place, Barton congratulated Griffith on his verbal *tour de force*, particularly his tenacity regarding the Ulster question. However, the Wicklow man's attempt to pour oil on troubled waters meant little as the break had come, not on Ulster, but on Crown and Empire. The dejected Griffith could not contain himself – he lambasted Gavan Duffy soundly, realising that his decision to accompany Barton and the lawyer had brought about the loss of his objective on breaking off negotiations – should they need to be broken off – on Ulster. Settlement prospects were looking bleak on the night of 4 December.

All was not lost, however. Collins' absence from the Irish team provided a loophole, which led to an invitation for him to meet Lloyd George alone the following day. Collins duly met the Prime Minister in the morning and reported back to the rest of the Irish delegation after his private meeting. Collins, it seems, had been persuaded that a boundary commission would prevent partition becoming permanent. In 1933, Barton recalled in his speech at Enniscorthy that Collins recorded that the Prime Minister had reminded him:

> that I myself [Collins] pointed out on a previous occasion that the North would be forced economically to come in. I assented, but I said that the position was so serious that I was anxious to secure a definite reply from Craig and his colleagues and that I was as agreeable to a reply rejecting as accepting. In view of the former we would save Tyrone, Fermanagh and parts of Derry, Armagh and Down by the Boundary Commission.[12]

In the event, Collins asked his fellow plenipotentiaries to meet Lloyd George that afternoon. Griffith supported this development and persuaded the others to agree as well. Significantly Barton, the leader of the intransigent wing of the delegation, accompanied Griffith and Collins to this meeting. In addition to Barton's ideological status at the hard-line republican end of the delegation's spectrum, he was, like Griffith and Collins, a full Cabinet minister, so the Irish trio represented the political heavyweights on the Irish side. They faced a British team consisting of Lloyd George, Chamberlain, Birkenhead and Churchill.[13] After the opening salvos, including a discussion on Ulster during which Griffith indicated that he wanted a letter from Craig either accepting or rejecting the idea of Irish unity, and Collins pointed out that the Irish position would be undermined if they agreed to sign without Craig first agreeing the principle of the essential unity of Ireland,[14] the British delegates withdrew. In their absence, Barton and his colleagues resolved to press for the document from Craig.[15] However, when Lloyd George eventually returned, he reminded Griffith of a previous letter, which the Prime Minister had been shown on 13 November. Barton and Collins were clueless about the missive, with Barton asking the Big Fellow *sotto voce* 'What is this letter?' Collins' reply, 'I don't know what the hell it is' did not augur well. It transpired that Griffith had previously agreed that if Ulster did not accept an all-Ireland parliament, he would not break off negotiations and there would be a boundary commission established later. Griffith had essentially promised Lloyd George not to break on the Ulster question. The Irish chairman told the Prime Minister that he would not let him down, and this incident ended his attempts to focus on Ulster, leaving Barton (and Collins) taken aback.[16] This personal commitment isolated Griffith from the rest of the delegation and he eventually agreed to sign the agreement, even if his colleagues would not.[17] This meant, in effect, that the delegation was now further split, and that the other delegates would have to oppose the chairman if they refused to sign the document.[18]

Lloyd George seized the moment, and sought to press home his advantage in a move that would appeal specifically to Barton. Knowing that the Wicklow man would be the hardest to convince, the Welsh Wizard now dangled a carrot that he would find hard to refuse. He offered Ireland full fiscal autonomy.[19] Gavan Duffy had wanted Barton to continue to press for more gains in the economic sphere. This pressing had borne fruit for Barton. Here was the economic holy grail – the primary objective that he had set out to achieve as the economics expert at the very outset of negotiations. It actually meant that out of all the plenipotentiaries, he was the only one to achieve his principal stated goal – the concession for which he had argued throughout the negotiations and from which he had never wavered. There is no doubt that from the perspectives of finance, trade and economy, this concession made it more difficult for Barton not to accept the agreement now on offer. With Griffith having agreed to sign, Lloyd George tried to elicit acceptance from Collins and Barton, but Griffith prevented him from doing so. The Welsh Wizard changed tack, saying that he understood that Griffith, as chairman, spoke for the Irish delegation – and that this was peace or war.[20] To the carrot of full fiscal autonomy had been added to stick of an immediate renewal of warfare.

The Prime Minister then made an emotional appeal, which he directed specifically at Barton, informing him that those who were not for peace must take the full responsibility for the war that would immediately follow. The weight of responsibility on Barton's shoulders was enormous. Coogan (and others) have gone on record opining that Lloyd George was bluffing at this point.[21] Whether he was or not is a moot point. What was important was that Barton evidently did not think that he was. The Wicklow man's dilemma deepened. His incarceration during the War of Independence had put him out of step with developments in the republican movement, leaving him uncertain of what exactly the grassroots feeling on the ground was like in Dublin. The lack of clarity surrounding the Cabinet meeting on 3 December had not helped matters, and Barton was reluctant to plough a lone furrow, or take a strong line or go out on a limb, since the leadership of the delegation was in the hands of Griffith and Collins. The lure of full fiscal autonomy provided another incentive for Barton to acquiesce to Lloyd George's appeal. Barton was under mounting pressure, which he later described to the Dáil:

> On Monday at 3 p.m., Arthur Griffith, Michael Collins, and myself met the English representatives. In the struggle that ensued, Arthur Griffith sought repeatedly to have the decision between war and peace on the terms of the Treaty referred back to this assembly. This proposal Mr Lloyd George directly negatived. He claimed that we were plenipotentiaries and that we must either accept or reject. Speaking for himself and his colleagues, the English Prime Minister with all the solemnity and the power of conviction that he alone, of all men I met, can impart by word and gesture – the vehicles by which the mind of one man oppresses and impresses the mind of another – declared that the signature and recommendation of every member of our delegation was necessary or war would follow immediately.[22]

The British ultimatum meant that the moment of truth had arrived. In effect, Lloyd George's ultimatum had come with a time limit: it seemed that the treaty had to be signed that night or not at all. It was by then quite late in the evening; Griffith told the British negotiators that the Irish reply would be delivered later that night. As the Irish delegates were returning to Hans Place, Collins wearily informed his colleagues that he would sign the agreement. The Big Fellow's bombshell astounded Barton, who never imagined for a moment that Collins would adopt such a course. Anne Dolan and William Murphy highlight Barton's astonishment at Collins' decision as one exemplar to remind us not to be dogmatic about our understanding of the plenipotentiaries' and other key actors' motivations and choices during this period.[23] Up to that day, Barton and Collins were described as 'real friends, for all the gulf that separated their circumstances'.[24] Barton's reaction to Collins' decision revealed the depth of the rift in the Irish delegation, but the Wicklow man later recognised the reasoning behind Collins' choice when he wrote: 'He [Collins] knew that physical resistance, if resumed, would collapse, and he was not going to be the leader of a forlorn hope.'[25] There is no doubt that the I.R.A. was pitifully short of manpower, arms and ammunition, which was probably one of the factors that prompted Collins to support Griffith's decision to sign the agreement. Back in Hans Place, Eamon Duggan supported Griffith and Collins, adding his weight to the 'Ayes'. These three let it be known that they would sign the document whether Barton and Gavan Duffy did or not.[26]

The hours that followed were agonising for Barton. This was one of the most dramatic and significant nights in Irish history, and one in which Barton was to be a pivotal figure with a principal role. Lloyd George's ultimatum may have been a bluff, but could Barton take that gamble? The Prime Minister's 'solemnity and power of conviction' had evidently made a huge impression on the Wicklow man. Even Gavan Duffy, who had thought that the Welsh Wizard was bluffing, changed his mind when confronted with the credibility of the threat in the minds of the other four plenipotentiaries. The lawyer wavered, eventually letting it be known that he would allow himself to be guided by Barton's decision.[27] This was significant – as Pakenham noted: 'If Barton signed, Gavan Duffy could hardly stand out.'[28] Thus, it transpired that, in effect, Barton had the casting vote among the Irish delegates, for they all had to sign the document in order for it to be accepted.[29] Griffith, Collins and Duggan now piled pressure on the angst-ridden Barton, as he fretted about betraying the Republic. Griffith spoke almost passionately for signing; Collins highlighted the lack of I.R.A. manpower, asking Barton if he wanted to send out the few remaining volunteers to be slaughtered; Duggan added to this by telling Barton that he would be hanged from a lamppost in Dublin if his refusal to sign caused a new war in Ireland.[30] Barton was strengthened by Childers' tacit support for his hard-line stance, but Childers' encouragement remained tacit as he did not have a vote, being a secretary rather than a delegate. Barton later referred to this fact:

> Childers, as secretary, was present during this discussion, but only principals took an active part in it ... Childers was active all the time, but he took no part in the final dispute. He was never referred to. I don't remember his entering into the discussions at all at that last meeting, but I was well aware that he agreed with the arguments stated by Gavan Duffy and myself. It was a dispute amongst the five delegates. I don't think Childers could have taken any active part, because I know that it was a surprise to Collins that Childers took such a very determined stand afterwards.[31]

Being pressurised was only one facet of the quandary in which Barton found himself that night. He also doubted his judgement in terms of the mood and militarisation in Ireland. Was the country in a mood to accept and support another war? Could Irish military resources sustain another war? Surely, Collins was in a better position to judge than he – the economics expert of the team who had been incarcerated for much of the recent war? In the words of Pakenham:

> Griffith and Collins did not mince their words. Lloyd George had pictured Irish homes laid waste and the youth of Ireland butchered. They left Barton in no doubt on whom future generations would fix the blame. For every drop of blood shed in Ireland he, and he alone, would be responsible. But Barton's dilemma lay deeper than they knew. War embraced by a united Ireland he was ready to face. But supposing he brought war on a country whose chief Plenipotentiaries had already thrown in their hands? How many men would be found to sustain it at all? What chance would they have? What good would they do? Was it for him, a technical expert, outside the movement these last fifteen months of the struggle, to renew by single fiat a war repudiated by the soldier who had hitherto done most to wage it? With Collins seeking peace, what sort of claim had he, Barton, to decide that war was the people's will?[32]

Barton was painfully aware that any gains made in the negotiations were in danger of being lost if the war-weary and weakened people of Ireland were plunged into a new conflict.[33] However, he was also painfully aware of his oath to the Republic, to him 'the most sacred bond on earth'.[34] As Barton agonised over his republican principles, Griffith, Collins, and Duggan donned their hats and coats to leave for Downing Street. They had reached the landing by the time Barton called them back. This was the first of three times that night when Barton stopped the three other members of the delegation from going to Downing Street.[35] Barton sought and was granted permission for a private conversation with Childers, following which 'he came back with the suggestion that, if signature there must be, it should be accompanied with the explicit reservation that it was being performed under duress'. However, the British side was hardly likely to accept such a signature or allow the addendum to be included in the document or appended after it. Hence, 'the idea presented advantages at first, but it did not survive long. All attempts to tone down the sharpness of the decision had now failed.'[36]

As the to-ing and fro-ing continued, Duggan made a passionate appeal to Barton, which may have played a part in helping to persuade him to sign the agreement.[37] Pakenham takes up the tale:

Suddenly Duggan broke down; his mind went back to Richmond Barracks and Kilmainham Gaol, 'to that morning in Mountjoy when I saw the hangman who was to hang our young lads there'. He lived again his conversations with some of those who had been executed for Ireland from 1916 to 1921. He poured out an appeal to Barton not to cast away the chance for which these simple martyrs had died, and plunge once more in blood the country they loved so well. Unsophisticated, from the heart, utterly unlike the preceding exhortations, it touched some chord in Barton, not far from breaking down himself.[38]

Childers recorded in his diary: 'There was a long and hot argument about committing our young men to die. Die for nothing. What could Gavan Duffy get better? G.D. assented quietly. Bob was shaken. Asked me out and I said it was principle ... and I felt Molly was with us.'[39] Molly was Childers' wife, described by Dulcibella Barton as being 'always an invalid'.[40] Seemingly, this reference to Molly Childers inadvertently tipped the balance of decision in Barton's mind. He replied: 'Well, I suppose I must sign.' Coogan suggests that the idea of resolving his tumult of conscience on the basis of what Childers' American wife had to say about the situation angered Barton.[41] This is probably true, but it is also possible that the honourable and chivalrous Barton was appalled by contemplating the spectre of war and what it might mean for vulnerable, weak, infirm and sickly people – especially women such as Molly and innocent children. Barton capitulated, and the battle of wills ended with him reluctantly agreeing to accept the treaty document as a means of averting more bloodshed.[42] Gavan Duffy, as indicated, followed suit within minutes. His objections to signing were dead in the water once Barton had decided to sign. Barton's own account of that night, given more than three decades later, captures some of the inner conflict which he experienced at the time, and lays bare the position of the plenipotentiaries, and the divisions within the Irish delegation during those fateful hours:

> In London, Gavan Duffy was in very much the same position as I was in. First of all, Collins and Griffith and Duggan were going to sign whether Gavan Duffy or I did, or not, and Lloyd George had said all five must sign, or war would follow. Gavan Duffy and I were in this position. Neither of us knew what de Valera or the Dáil would do if Collins, Griffith and Duggan signed. If we refused to sign and war was resumed immediately, the Dáil would have no option of accepting. If war was made on the country, we should have to carry the responsibility; and neither of us knew whether we would have de Valera, or anyone, behind us. We might well be asked, 'Why did you commit us to war without consulting us'? Three leaders had committed themselves; that was a new situation, one never at any time considered in Dublin. In Dublin, Griffith had stated to de Valera that he would not sign without referring the terms back. In London he, Collins and Duggan were determined to sign, whether we did or not. We could not tell what de Valera would do in new circumstances. You must remember that for three hours we had a most frightful battle in the delegation, among ourselves, at which the most terrific things were said to Gavan Duffy and to me by Collins and Griffith and Duggan. They called us murderers, stated that we would be hanged from lamp-posts, that we would destroy all they had fought for. The most terrible prospect was held out by Collins and Griffith to us.[43]

Amazingly, during all of this time, none of the plenipotentiaries thought to telephone Dublin.[44] Barton, reminiscing in 1970, recalled that: 'None of us even thought of using the phone to try to resolve the difficulty.'[45] It was probably an indication of the stress under which they laboured, of the isolation that they felt, and of the urgency and immediacy of their situation. Dublin was across the Irish Sea, but the British delegates were awaiting them in Downing Street, and beginning to doubt whether they would see the Irish again.[46] Finally, Griffith, Collins and Barton departed together for Downing Street, arriving well after midnight.[47] Following a few minor changes (some of which involved Ulster, but none of which were substantive),[48] the document was signed in the small hours of the morning of Tuesday, 6 December. Barton recalled that 'the only members of the Delegation who signed the Articles of Agreement in Downing Street were Griffith, Collins and myself. Duggan and Gavan Duffy were not present at the last conference at which the Articles of Agreement were signed by us three.'[49] That day would prove to be a watershed in Irish political history, and Barton's decision to sign made the Irish Free State a reality, paved the way for an Irish Republic and shaped the twenty-six-county Ireland that we know today.[50] However, these consequences lay far into the future. On the morning of 6 December, as Barton and the other delegates made their weary way back to Hans Place, their minds were probably focussed on the more immediate results of their decision, as they wondered what headlines would be generated by their actions, and what reactions would be forthcoming from various quarters – not least back in Dublin.

The signatories arrived back at Hans place at about 2.45 a.m. One of the secretaries to the delegation, Kathleen Napoli McKenna,[51] described the scene as the men entered:

> Diarmuid O'Hegarty was holding the Treaty document rolled round, scroll-like in both hands. He moved towards the telephone table, unrolled it and displayed it with the ink signatures fresh, almost still damp, on it. The others stood nearby gazing at the two columns of signatures. Slowly, Duggan, his eyes fixed on the document, a cigarette between his lips, unscrewed the cap of his fountain pen and in a bold calligraphy, added his signature, E. S. O Dugain. Gavan Duffy was the last of the delegates to sign, in his miniature handwriting, Seórsa Ghabhain Uí Dhubhthaigh.[52]

All five plenipotentiaries had now signed the treaty, and according to Barton, 'Griffith and Collins decided that the Articles, as signed, must be transmitted immediately to de Valera. It was agreed that Duggan should take the earliest possible transport to Dublin with the document.'[53] Duggan's early departure gave rise to a minor, but revealing controversary, regarding his signature on the treaty document – and one in which Barton played a leading role. The contention was that Duggan had left Hans Place before he had actually signed the document, and that his signature had to be pasted on afterwards. The allegation appeared in print in the 1920s,[54] and resurfaced in 1944 (eight years after Duggan's death). The story seemingly originally emanated from Barton, who confirmed its veracity when he was contacted. He stated that the document that was signed merely contained 'articles of agreement and nothing more'. He claimed that Duggan had signed a different version of the document which had the word 'treaty' added into the title, but that his signature had to be pasted in place in the early hours of the treaty morning.[55] A decade later, Barton reasserted his memory of the incident in his witness statement:

> The original of the Articles of Agreement had not reached Hans Place when Duggan left. The original document was brought to Hans Place next morning to be signed by Duggan and Gavan Duffy, but Duggan had already left for Dublin. Somebody suggested – I don't know who it was – that the best thing to be done was to cut Duggan's signature from some other document. His signature was cut from a menu card and pasted on to the original document and, if you look at a reproduction which appeared in the press the following day, you will see that Duggan's signature stands out clearly as having been pasted on ... Gavan Duffy signed the document when it came around next morning, but Duggan had gone to Ireland. Duggan may have signed another copy here in Dublin, but he did not sign the original while in London.[56]

However, McKenna's account of the signing in Hans Place gives the lie to Barton's version of events. Moreover, her account was supported by Dan MacCarthy, who stated:

> The true facts of the matter are that immediately the Treaty was signed, Eamon Duggan and Desmond Fitzgerald left for Ireland by

the morning Mail taking the copy of the Treaty with them. Later in the day Mr Jones, Lloyd George's Private Secretary, called at Hans Place and asked for another signed copy of the Treaty. Whether that copy was to be used as the British Copy of the Treaty or as a second British Copy for the purposes of photographic record, I cannot say. Griffith was just going to sign the copy per pro Duggan when I remembered that I had a copy of his signature in the house which was a copy of a Special Programme of Celebrations which were held in the Albert Hall. I mentioned this fact to Arthur Griffith and suggested to him the pasting of the signature on the copy and both he and Mr Jones agreed. There was obviously no intention to deceive anybody. The fact that Mr Duggan's signature was pasted down on a copy of the Treaty could not interfere with its validity.[57]

The reason behind Barton's unreliable memory of the event may be partially answered by the final line in MacCarthy's account. Barton eventually took the anti-treaty side in the Civil War, and his assertions around this incident seem designed to cast doubts regarding Duggan's signature, hence calling the validity of the treaty (or, as Barton maintained, 'articles of agreement') into question. Such doubts supported the arguments of the anti-treatyites that the document that arrived into Dublin with the plenipotentiaries on their return from London was not an actual treaty, and so lacked legitimacy. Barton's memory of Duggan's emotional outburst in Hans Place on the fateful night, which one suspects instigated a turning point in Barton's thought processes, causing him to rethink his position, soften his ultra-republican stance and sign the document, probably rankled in the back of his mind. He may have been antagonistic towards Duggan, whom he perceived as instrumental in persuading him to sign, given that he subsequently regretted doing so.

It is possible, of course, that Barton's false memory regarding the pasted signature was a genuine mistake, rather than a deliberate attempt to provide misleading information that might help to justify the anti-treaty position in the ensuing Civil War. Possible – but implausible. Barton's memory of all the other key events surrounding the signing of the treaty seems to be excellent, both in Pakenham's book and in his own later witness statement. The evidence appears to show that Barton's false memory was deliberate and mischievous, driven perhaps by anti-treaty and anti-Duggan sentiments. Barton also appeared to be very lucid and completely *compos mentis* in his 1969 television interview. On the balance of probability, this is a (seemingly rare) instance of both political and personal bias on Barton's part, and a timely reminder that even eyewitness accounts must be treated with caution as historical sources. Tellingly, there is no mention of the pasted signature in *Peace by Ordeal*, but there is a record of an exchange between Stack and Duggan in Dublin the following day, when Duggan was delivering the document to de Valera, in which Stack asked Duggan, 'Why did ye sign – How could ye?' to which Duggan replied, 'It was war in five minutes unless we signed.'[58] This indicates that Duggan did sign in London, and the Irish delegation began preparations to leave that city and return to Dublin.

Debating the Issue
(December 1921–January 1922)

The treaty had been signed by all five plenipotentiaries in the early hours of 6 December, and a press report on the following day spoke of a 'feeling of relief' in Dublin, adding that 'those who have maintained the spirit of optimism which widely prevailed, even when the outlook seemed darkest, appear to have bßeen justified'.[1] A few days later, the 'historic pact closing a 700-year-old war between Britain and Ireland' was hailed as 'Ireland's Magna Carta'.[2] However, such adulation in the press was at odds with the mood of the plenipotentiaries as they prepared to return to Dublin.

Duggan arrived in the Irish capital on the evening of Tuesday, 6 December, and proceeded to the Mansion House, where he met Stack and de Valera. Stack left the following account of the encounter:

> Duggan reached (sic) the President an envelope which the President ignored. Duggan asked him to read the contents. 'What should I read it for?' 'Oh,' said Duggan, 'it is arranged that the thing be published in London and Dublin simultaneously at 8 o'clock, and it is near that hour now.' 'What,' said the President, 'to be published whether I have seen it or not?' 'Oh well, that's the arrangement', Duggan replied. The President took up the envelope, opened it, glanced over the contents. Then he came over to where I was leaning on the mantelpiece and, putting his back to the fire, said – looking down at his Professor's gown – 'I see myself in three weeks, back in these, teaching.' At the moment he appeared to me to be an

Fig 9. Barton (between Gavan Duffy and Griffith) returns to Dublin, 8 December 1921. (Image (HOG_3) courtesy of the National Library of Ireland)

almost broken man ... before de Valera opened the dispatch, I said to Duggan: 'Surely ye didn't make that settlement.' 'That settlement?' he asked. 'Is such and such an oath in it?' I asked. 'Oh, yes.' 'And recognition of the Crown?' 'Yes.'[3]

Knowing the terms of the agreement, de Valera called a Cabinet meeting for the following day. Brugha, Stack, Cosgrave and O'Higgins all attended. None of them spoke in favour of the agreement but, presciently, Cosgrave urged the President not to take action against the plenipotentiaries until he had heard their version of events, thus allowing them to explain their position.[4] The delegates, meanwhile, were sailing back to Dublin. The atmosphere on board was sombre and more than a little tense. Barton recalled, 'I think the whole of the rest of the Delegation came back on the night of the 7th, arriving here in the morning of the 8th ... I don't think we were very friendly towards each other. I think we were a little distraught.'[5] There had been another Cabinet meeting called for that day. Stack's account of events provided the full line-up:

'The Plenipotentiaries all returned in time for Thursday's Cabinet meeting. The attendance was complete: President [de Valera], Griffith, Brugha, Collins, Cosgrave, Barton and myself, of the Cabinet; Gavan Duffy and Duggan – Plenipotentiaries – O'Higgins, whilst Erskine Childers had also been asked to attend.' In his notes, Stack continued:

> The meeting lasted the whole day and late into the night. Strangely enough, we were not unfriendly towards one another. The merits and demerits of the Agreement were gone into, but not in detail to any extent. The main thing was how they came to sign. Mr Griffith, if I remember aright, would not admit duress by the British; Mr Collins said, if there was duress, it was only 'the duress of the facts', whatever he meant by that; but both Barton and Gavan Duffy were candid and said that they had been forced to sign. On and on dragged the discussion … [Eventually] a division was taken – Griffith, Collins, Cosgrave and Barton voting one way and the President, Cathal and myself the other. Barton explained that he thought he was bound to vote for the document, having signed it and undertaken to recommend it.[6]

Barton's account of this meeting confirms Stack's assertion that the atmosphere was neither unfriendly nor uncivil. It was, however, an extremely frank and very tense affair. Although he had great personal loyalty to de Valera, Barton uncharacteristically turned on the President, holding him responsible for the mess in which the Cabinet now found itself. He blamed de Valera for turning down requests to go to London from all three Cabinet ministers in the delegation, in addition to rejecting similar appeals from Gavan Duffy and Childers. Barton's attitude at this Cabinet meeting is revealing. It demonstrated that, although he was and would remain a political ally and personal friend of de Valera, he was no mere 'yes man'. Barton's relationship with his chief was not a sycophantic one, and he was not afraid to criticise the President to his face when he thought the situation merited such action. The fact that he chose to do so now was indicative of his state of mind, and his disquietude regarding his part in the drama surrounding the signing of the agreement in London. Rounding on de Valera, Barton also reminded him that he had been instrumental in conferring full plenipotentiary powers to negotiate a settlement on people that he knew were more moderate than himself, while he remained in

Dublin. Ruefully, Barton concluded thoughtfully with the words: 'The disaster was we were not a fighting delegation.'[7] Barton later recalled that:

> As soon as we arrived in Dublin, I think we drove straight to the Mansion House. We had a Cabinet meeting at which explanations were made. Griffith and Collins explained their views. They were surprised, I think, that a suggestion had been made, by Cathal Brugha perhaps – by someone anyway – that all the Delegate members should be arrested at Dún Laoghaire on arrival, and I think de Valera negatived it. I think there was a very free expression of disagreement at the Cabinet meeting. I don't think there were any insults hurled about, not as far as I remember. I think it was a very tense meeting, with very visible efforts at restraint.[8]

The meeting ended with a vote being taken. Predictably, de Valera, Brugha and Stack voted against, while Griffith and Collins voted for acceptance. Less predictably perhaps, given that he had not spoken in favour of the agreement the previous day, Cosgrave joined the 'Ayes'. He had, however, wanted to hear the explanations and arguments put forward by the returning plenipotentiaries and, having done so, he evidently decided that there were enough reasons to support the leaders of the delegation in voting for the agreement. That left Barton. Once again, fate had decreed that his would be the casting vote on the treaty. With a single vote majority of course, all the votes were, in effect, casting votes, but it was by no means certain which side Barton would choose. He had not been in favour of the agreement, and he had held out for hours on the final night in London before he agreed to sign the document. He made it clear earlier in the Cabinet meeting that he had acted under duress and had been forced to sign. The threat of immediate war by Britain had been held over him, and Barton said later that Collins also threatened him.[9] Moreover, the document went against his republican beliefs. Against all that, however, was the fact that he had actually signed it. The document bore his signature, so he saw it as his duty to recommend it. The internal battle between Barton's political principles and his sense of honour must have been one of epic proportions, but in the end, he chose to vote with the 'Ayes'. Barton's decision was in line with his thinking in Hans Place before he decided to sign the document. The question then had been, 'What sort of claim had he – without reference to the Dáil – to decide that war was the people's will?'[10] Barton was a republican, but he was also a democrat, and he believed in the democratic process whereby the government would be given a chance to debate the issue. Barton later mused: 'The Articles of Agreement had to be referred to the Dáil. The Dáil would decide. Commitments had been entered into and had been signed by the Delegation, but they had to be confirmed by the Dáil. And that was the agreement with the British also, that they must be confirmed by both Parliaments.'[11] The final say, he believed, should rest with the Dáil and not the Cabinet. The agreement had overcome its first hurdle – the Cabinet had accepted it by four votes to three – and the decision regarding its acceptance or rejection would now move to the Dáil.[12]

The switching of arenas from the Cabinet to the Dáil opened up a new phase in the politics surrounding the Anglo-Irish treaty. On 11 December 1921, Barton was informed that the West Wicklow branch of Sinn Féin had unanimously declared their acceptance of the treaty, a decision that must have caused him to have mixed feelings.[13] Fresh from the angst of Hans Place and the tension of the recent Cabinet meeting, Barton now hurtled headlong into the drama that was to unfold in University College Dublin, Earlsfort Terrace, the location of the Dáil during the treaty debates. This series of discussions began on Wednesday, 14 December.[14] The early sessions were held in private. De Valera tried to reintroduce Document Number 2 and external association as an alternative to the treaty, but the assembly repudiated this idea since the British had already rejected it, so de Valera withdrew it.[15] However, these private sessions were acrimonious, and Barton later remembered Collins and Childers arguing in a corridor after one of them – an argument that signalled a final parting of the ways between the two former colleagues.[16] The veil of secrecy surrounding these opening sessions was blown away on Monday, 19 December, when the debates (and the acrimony) became public, meaning that they could be closely followed by newspaper readers throughout Ireland. The treaty debates were intense – a strange mixture of raw emotional pleas and well-reasoned arguments, with sentiments ranging from noble appeal to vitriolic invective contained in the speeches. They were the battleground in the struggle for the hearts and minds of the T.D.s and, from 19 December, of the populace at large. They have been called 'the most crucial, heart-wrenching exchanges in modern Irish politics'.[17] It had become evident that Griffith was prepared to lead a party for acceptance and de Valera one against.[18] As the debates progressed in the Dáil, deputy after deputy rose to speak. On Monday, 19 December, Collins made a speech in which he invoked the republican dead but concluded: 'I think the decision ought to be a clear decision on the documents as they are before us ... On that we shall be judged as to whether he have done the right thing in our own conscience or not ... Let us take that responsibility ourselves and let us in God's name abide by the decision.'[19]

Barton's speech on the treaty, delivered to the Dail the same day, was also hugely significant. It was not long – in fact, when judged against many of the other treaty speeches, it was very short – but it was evidently heartfelt. Calton Younger put it very well when he claimed that, 'Robert Barton almost tore himself apart, so agonising was his admission that he had broken his oath to the Republic in choosing the lesser of the outrages forced upon him.'[20] In an emotional address to the Dáil, Barton began with the admission, 'I do not seek to shield myself from the charge of having broken my oath of allegiance to the Republic – my signature is proof of that fact.' He then informed the assembly of how, during the Monday afternoon meeting in London, Griffith tried to have the choice of war or peace referred back to the Dáil, but Lloyd George would have none of it. He impressed upon his audience, emphasising the Prime Minister's 'power and conviction', that immediate war would follow if all Irish plenipotentiaries failed to sign the document. He described the drama that unfolded in Hans Place, emphasising that three delegates were in favour of accepting the proposals, so the responsibility for war fell squarely on Gavan Duffy and himself. He continued, 'I preferred war ... but for the nation, without consultation, I dared not accept responsibility.' He stated that signing 'seemed to me the lesser outrage', and in doing so he had given the Dáil the opportunity to debate the issue. Having done his duty, he closed by recommending the treaty that he had signed to the House.[21] It came across as the speech of an honest man who was faced with a horrendous dilemma and a nearly impossible choice. The Dáil record shows that the oration was greeted with applause; there was no dissent or disrespect from either side of the House, which was now dividing rapidly along pro- and anti-treaty lines.[22]

According to Diarmaid Ferriter, Barton's contribution to the treaty debates was striking.[23] One measure of the veracity of Ferriter's assessment was the rapid reaction of the British government, who moved expeditiously via the Press Association to issue a denial of

Barton's allegation of duress being applied by Lloyd George. The piece read as follows:

> The statement by Mr Robert Barton, one of the Irish Peace Treaty signatories, that the agreement was signed under duress, and that Mr Lloyd George 'threatened' war in the event of a refusal occasioned no undue surprise in authoritative quarters in London to-day. It was pointed out that the Irish Envoys, who, it must be remembered, were Plenipotentiaries, had negotiated during the preceding weeks with full knowledge of the alternative in the event of a final rejection of the terms. 'They accepted the proposals under duress of circumstances or duress of their own minds and not because of any eleventh-hour declaration on the part of the Prime Minister,' declared an authority this [Tuesday] evening.[24]

The British Cabinet members were jittery following Barton's speech, and Dublin Castle (who had been economically advised by the Bank of Ireland), urged them not to postpone, cancel or threaten the plans for British military withdrawal and the forthcoming release of Irish political prisoners. The advice suggested that to do so would be to 'play into the hands of Barton' by breaking – or appearing to break – the truce.[25]

Another measure of the veracity of Ferriter's assessment was the number of T.D.s who referred to Barton's oration during their own speeches. Intriguingly, both pro- and anti-treatyites made references to the address, and even though Barton had recommended the treaty to the House, the anti-treatyites seemed to find more ammunition than their opponents in the Wicklow man's words. Without actually mentioning the word, Barton made it clear that he had signed the document under duress. It was evident that he didn't actually approve of the final articles of agreement even though he had signed the document. However, as he would later claim, he was not acting in a personal capacity, and Barton's recommendation had been, at best, lukewarm. Later that day, Sean Etchingham told the House: 'You must remember this statement made by the Minister of Economics (Ríobárd Bartún). That statement will be recorded in history as one of the most momentous ever made. It was a human address, but it told a terrible tale.' Kathleen O'Callaghan thought Barton had explained why the document had been signed without referral to Dublin, stating: 'The Minister for Economics explained that last night. The delegates were ... bluffed by the threat of war into signing that Treaty. Well, it cannot be helped; they did their best.' Dr Patrick MacCartan also referenced Barton and acknowledged the Wicklow deputy's moral dilemma in his own emotional speech:

We had a bird in the hand and a bird in the bush. Let those of you who can conscientiously do as Robert Barton has done boldly – be false to your oath. Let you vote for a bird in the hand. I tell you that the bird in the bush that we have seen is not worth going after, thorny though the bush may be. I feel myself in the position of a man landed on an island without any means of escape, who was asked to vote if he will remain or vote if he would leave it. You have no means of leaving, there is no escape from the Treaty that has been signed, because, as I said, you have not a united people, you have not a united Dáil – I question if you have a united Army.[26]

The next day, the pro-treaty William T. Cosgrave also referred to Barton, but in an argument for averting war, he concentrated on what the Wicklow T.D. did not say: 'The Minister for Economics ... had not ... up to this referred to the economic situation in bringing about war. Here in the capital of Ireland there are something like 20,000 families living in single-room tenement dwellings, and are these the people you are going to ask to fight for you? It is not fair, I submit.' Gavan Duffy made his reservations about the agreement clear when he stated: 'At the risk of reiterating a good deal that Deputy Barton has said ... I am going to recommend this Treaty to you very reluctantly, but very sincerely, because I see no alternative.' Later, he claimed:

The complaint is not that the alternative to signing a Treaty was war; the complaint is that the alternative to our signing that particular Treaty was immediate war; that we who were sent to London as the apostles of peace – the qualified apostles of peace – were suddenly to be transformed into the unqualified arbiters of war.

Professor William Stockley admitted: 'The remarks of the last speaker have added to the impression we had, and which I felt deeply, and I think everybody felt it deeply, after the speech of Mr Barton.' Professor Joseph Whelehan confided that: 'The two speeches that weighed most with me are the expression of the sincere convictions of Mr Gavan Duffy and Mr Barton.' P. J. Ruttledge opined: 'We have Deputy Barton's explanation, and what can I or any man deduce from it but that there was force, the threat of a terrible and immediate war?' Mary MacSwiney was clear in her interpretation of Barton's contribution when she said:

> Mr Barton has made a statement about this, and his attitude to it, which has moved our admiration, but the sentence in his statement which stands out is this: 'The Irish Republic, to which I swore allegiance and which is my faith.' Mr Gavan Duffy has agreed with Mr Barton as to the signing of the Treaty and the duress under which it was signed.[27]

Barton had certainly captured the attention of the House with his telling contribution. On Thursday, 22 December, the final day of the debates before the Dáil broke for Christmas recess, further references were made to Barton's remarkable treaty speech. Sean T. O'Kelly was the first speaker to bring Barton's words to the attention of the House when he said:

> Before I heard Deputy Barton's story of Lloyd George's big stick, corroborated by Mr Gavan Duffy, I had been wondering what wizard's wand, what druidic draught so confounded our trusted Delegates in London, that they could have been oblivious even for one moment of the position in which this ignoble settlement to which they had put their hands would place us.

However, surely the most telling, and the most poignant, reference to Barton's address that was made that day came from an unlikely source. Kathleen Clarke was the widow of the executed 1916 leader Tom Clarke, in many respects the mastermind behind the Easter Rising. She had been extremely impressed by Barton's speech, telling the Dáil:

> I was deeply moved by the statement of the Minister for Economics on Monday. Listening to him I realised more clearly than ever before the very grave decision put up to our plenipotentiaries. My sympathy went out to them. I only wish other members of the Delegation had taken the same course, having signed the document, bring it home and let An Dáil reject or ratify it on its merits.[28]

Having heard Barton's speech, far from expressing any desire to punish the plenipotentiary signatories, Clarke, who would be expected to take a hard line in her rejection of the treaty, was actually expressing sympathy for their unenviable plight. Perhaps it was the spirit of Christmas, as the Dáil rose and the members returned to their constituencies at the close of the day's business.

In constituencies around the country, people had followed the Dáil debates with avid interest. The general populace was divided on the issue: some of those who had been active in the War of Independence wanted to reject the treaty, but most people simply wanted peace. To them, tackling the daily tasks involved in rebuilding an economy on its knees was more important than whether or not that economy operated in a dominion or a republic, or whether their T.D.s would have to take an oath. The national press urged acceptance of the treaty, and most local newspapers followed suit. The mood in the constituencies favoured peace over war. In the heartland of Barton's Kildare-Wicklow constituency, Dunlavin, a Wicklow village on the Kildare border, was probably as good a barometer as any other microcosm of the nation at this time. Everyday events continued in Dunlavin during December, with the village fair going ahead on the 14th, an I.T.G.W.U. meeting the week before Christmas, the Kildare Hounds' meeting in the village on Thursday 22nd, Dunlavin representation at a Farmers' Union meeting just after Christmas and the local Napper Tandy branch of the Foresters advertising a New Year's dance in the hall.[29] However, despite the normality of village life on the surface, as 1921 melded into 1922, there was evident and palpable tension in the Dunlavin air. The principal topic of conversation at Dunlavin G.A.A. club's football tournament and the Kildare Hounds' meeting in the village in January 1922 probably centred around the resumption of the treaty debates in the Dáil. An editorial in the local press opined that 'ninety per cent of the people in these parts want the settlement as submitted by the five plenipotentiaries', and hoped that 'no matter what the result, there will be no split in the national ranks, and that if the treaty is accepted by a majority, no matter how small, the opponents will co-operate with the national government in building up the nation'.[30]

The Christmas break had allowed the Dáil deputies to gauge the overwhelmingly pro-treaty mood of the country. Away from the cauldron of the Dáil chamber, most ordinary people were primarily concerned with ending the violence. The composition of the Dáil meant that it was a Sinn Féin arena, and those voted into office were usually chosen because of

their hard-line and often ultra-republican beliefs. Both the Cabinet and
the Dáil were quite evenly split on the issue of the treaty, but the division was not as even among the more moderate general populace. While
some anti-treaty T.D.s would vote according to their personal principles no matter what the majority of their constituents wanted, other
deputies listed to their electorates and took their views on board, changing their minds in line with popular support for the treaty. When the
debates resumed on 3 January 1922, it was not long before Barton's treaty
speech was mentioned in the chamber once again. Anti-treaty T.D. Brian
O'Higgins praised Barton when he told the House:

> I should like to pay a tribute to one Deputy in particular who has
> spoken here, Deputy Robert Barton. He admitted he was weak
> in London, and broke his oath to the Republic ... If Mr Barton
> was weak in London he has been strong here. He has revealed the
> strength of a true man. And his statement will be the most thought-
> compelling page in the history of these proceedings.

Pro-treaty Ernest Blythe, on the other hand, gave a much harsher verdict
on Barton's words. It is worth quoting it in full here:

> A reference has been made to Mr Barton. I do not want to be offen-
> sive at all, but it is as well that I should say what I have to say. I
> believe that the plenipotentiaries should have realised all along that
> a break might, and probably would, mean immediate war, and the
> plenipotentiaries should have made up their minds as to the exact
> point to which they would go rather than face immediate war. And
> I think if any plenipotentiary was put in a hole by the short time
> for making up their minds that was given on that last night by Mr
> Lloyd George, that plenipotentiary was in a difficulty only because
> of his own negligence in making up his mind as to the distance to
> which it would be right for him to go, and the place at which he
> was prepared to choose war. [At this point Michael Collins called
> out 'Hear, Hear'.] Again, I say I do not want to be offensive, but it
> was either that or the plenipotentiary was so impressionable as to
> make him by temperament unfitted to bear the responsibility of a
> plenipotentiary. That is really how the matter stands, and I think the
> circumstances under which this Treaty was signed, except in so far as

all the plenipotentiaries were convinced that the alternative was war, and no more was to be got, have no bearing on it at all.[31]

Blythe's interpretation was also greeted with applause in the chamber. The angst-ridden Barton may have almost torn himself apart in his speech, but Blythe's accusation basically boiled down to the fact that he should have known better. He should have been prepared for the threat of immediate war if what were essentially talks to hammer out a peace settlement failed. Griffith had told de Valera that he couldn't bring back a republic and the delegates were handed a nigh-impossible task by the President, but Blythe was questioning Barton's temperament and suitability to act as a plenipotentiary. Barton was certainly acting under strain and the threat of war must have added to his stress levels, but perhaps his background, political beliefs and inflexible personality also meant that he was naïve in his expectations. His reserved and somewhat aloof nature may have isolated him when he alone was carrying the weight of a decision on war or peace on his shoulders. Pakenham's verdict on Barton hints at the possibility that Blythe's accusation might have contained at least some truth:

> And if it was left to him to save the Republic, and if his spirit, intelligence, and utter disinterestedness seemed to fit him peculiarly for the task, his isolation made his gifts of no avail. Education and final adherence to a Republic aligned him with Gavan Duffy, but Gavan Duffy was not a Cabinet Minister and special affinity was lacking. Childers, his great friend, could co-operate, but only from the outside. Barton, come to London as economic expert, would find it his function to thwart his leaders' plans. He would have to act in ignorance of the determining undercurrents, and when ultimate responsibility was reached, quite alone. Before him lay confusion and embarrassment, beyond them the tragedy of dilemma.[32]

That dilemma was laid bare as Barton bared his soul while speaking in the Dáil on Monday, 19 December 1921. His speech stood out for many deputies as the Dáil continued to debate the treaty during the first week of January 1922. The impact of Barton's contribution was summed up by James Murphy, who informed the assembled deputies that, 'I desire to carry away with me only one memory from this session of An Dáil and that is a remembrance of two very honest speeches delivered; one of them delivered by Deputy Barton, and the other delivered by Deputy Dr MacCartan, whose speech expressed my own thoughts and feelings.'[33] The debates were well advanced by then, and the all-important vote was drawing close. On Saturday, 7 January, the Dáil accepted the treaty by sixty-four votes to fifty-seven. Unlike Griffith, who had recommended and voted for the treaty on the basis of merit, Barton did so on the basis of signature. Despite this not-so-subtle means of letting it be known that he did not approve of the document, Barton did his duty and voted for acceptance. The result was close, but the treaty had overcome its second hurdle and had been passed in the Dáil. A minority of deputies, however, refused to accept the document, and the anti-treatyite leader de Valera and his followers withdrew in protest. Their thoughts were encapsulated in Deputy Mary MacSwiney's parting tirade. She called the acceptance of the treaty 'the grossest act of betrayal that Ireland ever endured', finishing her polemic with the ominous words: 'I tell you here, there can be no union between the representatives of the Irish Republic and the so-called Free State.'[34] The political and military drift towards civil war had begun.

14

Uncivil Recriminations and Civil War
(January 1922–December 1923)

According to Barton, 'the post-treaty situation was a very nebulous affair'.[1] The situation was strange, tense and filled with foreboding. The anti-treaty side had rejected the democratic vote of the Dáil. At a deeper level, this amounted to a rejection of democracy itself. These circumstances prompted Eoin MacNeill to suggest that, 'Deputies who are against the will of their constituents should be called on to resign – publicly, insistently, repeatedly.'[2] The general populace had split into two opposing camps once the terms of the treaty were known, and the rift widened when the anti-treaty T.D.s walked out of the Dáil after the vote. Barton's Dáil speech, and the many references to it by other T.D.s during the debates, meant that the general populace now focussed their own arguments on how they would have acted had they been in the shoes of the plenipotentiaries. This had the unfortunate effect of focussing people's attention on the personalities involved rather than the issues at stake.[3] The treaty was divisive and the I.R.A., which had always been characterised by a strong localism, also separated into two factions, but many factors (including local peer pressure) determined the sides taken by its members. Perhaps veteran Seán Harling summed it up best when he said: 'It all depended on which crowd you got into.'[4] In Barton's case, having honourably carried out his duty by recommending the treaty to the Dáil and voting for its acceptance, he lost little time in switching his allegiance to the other crowd. Once he had done what he had promised to do, he felt that he was now in a position to support de Valera in opposing the treaty. Barton had come into the anti-treaty camp as a penitent plenipotentiary.

The early months of 1922 were characterised by a propaganda war fought between the proponents and opponents of the treaty, both of whom used the pages of the press to make their cases.[5] Once he had switched allegiances, Barton busied himself by working with Childers in promoting the anti-treaty propaganda campaign.[6] Barton published newspaper articles, many of which he compiled into the pamphlet *The Truth about the Treaty and Document No. 2* in February. The sub-title of the pamphlet was 'A reply to Michael Collins' and in it he took Collins to task for 'not for the first time yielding to British duress when he [Collins] signed the treaty'.[7] Collins had maintained that he did not think that 'the British would have declared terrible and immediate war upon us', and Barton questioned why, if this were the case, Collins did not support Gavan Duffy and himself in refusing to sign.[8] Barton also accused Collins of 'refusing to face the issue', opining that 'he refused to attend the meeting on 4 December because he refused to break'. Barton continued his attack: 'What duress prompted him then? I challenge him to reply.'[9] The paths of Barton and Collins had diverged and there was a coolness between the former friends. According to Barton, 'We spoke after we returned from London and we spoke occasionally during the debates but, once the vote had been taken, as far as I remember, I went home and took no further part.'[10] In his pamphlet, Barton also pilloried Collins regarding Document No. 2, accusing him of 'distorting the truth'.[11] He portrayed Collins as inconsistent, advocating external association to the British in London and now discarding it in favour of the terms of the treaty, and finished his attack on the Cork man with a stinging rebuke: 'He has no right to use the world-wide publicity which his present position gives him in order to distort the truth and discredit our National Leader.'[12] While mutual respect between the two men remained, by the spring of 1922 Barton and Collins were in opposite camps. Barton later recalled that: 'Our relations were completely severed after the Dáil debates. I never spoke to him and never saw him again.'[13]

The treaty split meant that the country was on a knife edge. The majority of the population were pro-treaty, but the majority of active republicans were not. Cumann na mBan voted overwhelmingly to

Fig 10. Barton's pamphlet
*The Truth about the Treaty and
Document No. 2* (February,
1922). (Image taken from
author's collection)

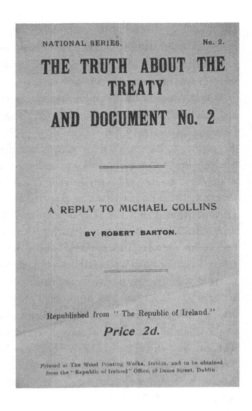

reaffirm allegiance to the Irish Republic and reject the treaty on Sunday, 5 February 1922.[14] The Cumann was the first republican organisation to formally reject the treaty, but the majority of the I.R.A. also opposed it.[15] According to Peter Hart: 'the guerrillas thought of themselves as sovereign ... they had brought the republic into being [and] nobody else had the right to give it away'.[16] Matters deteriorated on 26 March, when the I.R.A. held an army convention, and leaders Liam Mellows and Rory O'Connor rejected the authority of the Dáil, with O'Connor stating that they now recognised their own newly formed I.R.A. executive as the only government in Ireland.[17] One pro-treaty newspaper reported that 'the I.R.A. Sectional Convention' had 'repudiated the Dáil', with a rival anti-treaty broadsheet calling Michael Collins 'reckless' and accusing him of 'disreputable misrepresentation', before informing its readers that this latest development 'raised a serious position'.[18] As the pro- and anti-treaty I.R.A.

faced off, occasional violent incidents occurred even before the 'formal' outbreak of hostilities in late June. Then, on 14 April, anti-treatyite Rory O'Connor and his supporters occupied the Four Courts in Dublin, and the tension was ratcheted up a notch.

The prospect of a forthcoming election delayed the inevitable move against O'Connor's Four Courts garrison. Both sides, pro-treaty Sinn Féin and anti-treaty Sinn Féin, now prepared themselves for the vote. According to Barton: 'There were very definite efforts made to jockey for position and to prevent civil war and yet save all faces. Document No. 2, which Erskine devised with de Valera, was a terrible bone of contention'.[19] There is little doubt that the document was central to the anti-treaty argument, and that the idea of external association was still (however unrealistically) being mooted as the election drew closer. Despite having their own agendas, independents and smaller parties also lined out along treaty lines. For example, Labour took a pro-treaty stance in the election. Barton, standing as an anti-treaty candidate in the Kildare-Wicklow constituency, was targeted by pro-treaty propagandists in May. A copy of an article ridiculing his political position has survived, in which the author jibed: 'First he signed the Treaty. Then he voted for its acceptance by Dáil Éireann, and since, he has been doing everything he can ... to smash the Treaty and to stultify the action of Dáil Éireann in approving the Treaty.' A handwritten note on the script revealed that Michael Collins felt that focussing on Barton's political inconsistency, 'May be useful for a paragraph in *Free State* or *Young Ireland* or for leaflet.'[20] The Collins–Barton friendship was evidently but a distant memory as Ireland prepared to go to the polls.

The situation was volatile, but Collins and de Valera met to work out a deal, and on 20 May the announcement of a pact between the two leaders shocked the British government.[21] Pro- and anti-treaty Sinn Féin would fight the election as one party and, if elected, would form a coalition government afterwards. Barton's name headed the list of pact candidates on posters displayed throughout the constituency of Kildare-Wicklow.[22] However, the pact was fragile, and Barton would later muse: 'I suppose the Pact Election was really another effort to stave off civil war without committing ourselves to anything – again jockeying.'[23] Barton himself was not above such jockeying, delivering a speech on 5 June in his constituency at Naas, County Kildare, in which he spoke in favour of the pact.[24] However, Collins advised the electorate to 'vote for the candidates you think best of',[25] and the revised Free State constitution was only published in the press the following day, allowing de Valera to claim that people did not have time to consider its terms before voting.[26] The much-anticipated election was eventually held on 16 June, resulting in a landslide victory for the pro-treatyites.[27] Barton was elected, though, as the last candidate across the line in the Kildare-Wicklow constituency, but with a mere 8.23 per cent of first preference votes.[28] He was the only anti-treaty Sinn Féin candidate (from four) elected in the constituency.[29] Despite the Collins–De Valera pact and its ultimate fate, the electorate of the time should be credited with knowledge of what they were voting for. These voters were very politically aware, and the Irish electorate had been following the whole saga of the treaty and its fallout, and digesting the arguments regarding the pros and cons of acceptance in press reports for weeks – and months in the case of the text of the treaty document and the other paperwork it generated – and they had spoken at the polls.

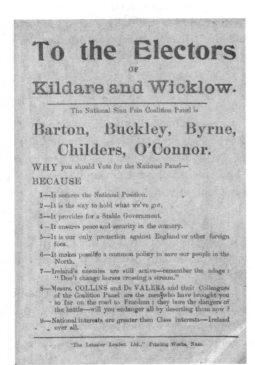

Fig 11. Robert Barton's name on a pact election poster, June 1922. (Image (being re-catalogued) courtesy of Kildare County Archives and Local Studies)

However, the anti-treatyites did not recognise the mandate given to the pro-treatyites in the election. As far back as Saint Patrick's Day in a speech at Thurles, de Valera had spoken of 'wading through Irish blood' if the treaty was accepted,[30] but Barton was at pains to point out that: 'De Valera was struggling to keep the peace. He made one effort after another to prevent civil war.'[31] However, tension continued in the wake of the election and, following the assassination of Sir Henry Wilson in London on 22 June and the kidnap of pro-treaty General J. J. O'Connell in Dublin on 27 June, Arthur Griffith, Michael Collins and their pro-treaty colleagues in government felt that they had to act. Collins agonised, but the order was reluctantly given, and pro-treaty forces shelled the Four Courts on 28 June.[32] In his recollection of events, Barton was at pains to exonerate de Valera from any responsibility for the attack on the Four Courts, stating: 'The army took matters out of his [de Valera's] hands. They took over the Four Courts. It wasn't de Valera who took over the Four Courts.'[33] This may be true – neither de Valera nor Collins actually wanted hostilities to begin – but once the decision to shell the Four Courts was taken, as one recent work on Collins observes: '[He] may well have started the Civil War he had done so much not to fight.'[34] Barton suspected British involvement in the attack on the Four Courts:

> With regard to the attack on the Four Courts, I should imagine it was done at the instigation of the British Government. That would seem to be the obvious explanation. I should imagine the English would have said that the Provisional Government should show that they were able to govern. Why wouldn't it? Wasn't this open obstruction defiance? They could not possibly hand over to a Government under Griffith and Collins which could not keep control even of the Four Courts.[35]

Whoever was behind the fatal decision to bombard the Four Courts, the Civil War had begun, and heavy fighting initially occurred in Dublin, but within a week it spread beyond the city.

Barton's account of his activities during the Civil War is noticeably short on detail. In his own words, he stated that he went home after the treaty debates, but admitted to being 'drawn into the Civil War'.[36] Barton's use of the passive voice is significant – he seems to imply that he was overtaken by events and had no choice in the matter, being powerless to resist the rising tide of violence in the capital in late June 1922. Following the initial attack on the Four Courts, the combat zone shifted to Sackville Street.[37] Barton was there, having been 'drawn into the Civil War' ... by making a conscious decision to travel to Dublin and join up with other anti-treaty leaders! Perhaps his use of language was somewhat disingenuous when he stated he was drawn in. Barton later recollected:

> When the Civil War had started, I came in to Dublin and saw de Valera – he was in a state of distress but his sympathies were with the Republican Army, although he was not in control of it – and, as far as I remember, I joined with de Valera and Stack and Cathal Brugha, and I went down to the Hammam Hotel which they were holding. Seán T. [O'Kelly] was there too. I slept beside Seán T.[38]

The hotel was among the buildings attacked by the Free State army as Dublin's principal thoroughfare once again became a war zone. According to Todd Andrews, who had escaped from the battered Four Courts, he found de Valera, Brugha, Austin Stack, Oscar Traynor, Art O'Connor, Countess Markievicz and Barton all together, 'all apparently without purpose'.[39] This concentration of anti-treaty leaders in one place constituted a tactical blunder, but most of them managed to escape from Sackville Street.[40] The most notable exception was Brugha, who remained behind with a small rearguard to cover the retreat of the others – and who refused to surrender. Barton recalled: 'Early one morning we were all instructed to leave. Everyone was told to evacuate and it was soon after that Cathal Brugha was killed. The rest of us evacuated.'[41] In Barton's constituency of Kildare-Wicklow, Brugha's death was reported under the headline 'Great Irishman falls fighting', in a regional broadsheet on 8 July.[42]

Meanwhile, Barton, having escaped from Sackville Street, made his way to the house of Erskine and Molly Childers at 12 Bushy Park Road. Erskine was not at home, but Barton met Molly and was just sitting down to breakfast when the house was raided by members of the National Army. Barton darted out into the back garden and endeavoured to effect an escape, but the house was surrounded and he was captured. Ironically, the soldiers were actually looking for the absent Childers when they found Barton, who was taken as a prisoner to Portobello Barracks. In his witness statement, Barton stated simply: 'I was taken to Portobello Barracks, and I escaped from there with Joe MacDonagh and others.'[43] In contrast to the wealth of detail in the account of his capture, time spent in prison and escape during the War of Independence, Barton's reticence to provide any details in relation to a similar experience during the Civil War is striking. It becomes even more remarkable when one takes into account that Barton's escape on 14 July 1922 in the company of Joseph MacDonagh,[44] Noel Lemass,[45] and about forty other prisoners was part of a successful mass breakout that embarrassed the Free State authorities.[46] This reticence was possibly due to a consideration that did not apply to the War of Independence – a desire not to remember, or at least, not to publicly mention the Civil War – a desire often (rightly or wrongly) attributed to many veterans who had fought in both conflicts. However, there may have been deeper reasons behind Barton's comparative silence.

In 1928, Patrick Horan, also known as Pádraig Ó Horan,[47] bitterly denounced the fact that he and seven other young anti-treatyites had been ordered to risk their lives 'to keep the [Free] Staters back' while Barton and the other republican leaders made good their escape from the battered Hammam Hotel.[48] Even more damningly, later the same year Horan also accused Barton of suppressing a planned prison coup (instigated by Horan) because it endangered the Wicklow man's chances of an escape, which was due to happen on the same night.[49]

Given Barton's wish to identify with his tenants (or employees, as he called them) and his perception that his sympathies lay with the heroes of 1798 rather than the Hugo family who had occupied the house formerly on the site of his home, it is probable that Barton would have reacted badly to Horan's accusation. Michael Farry has suggested that those who had done badly out of the Irish revolution such as rural smallholders, landless labourers and the unskilled urban proletariat and lumpenproletariat were more likely to support the anti-treaty side.[50] Barton's background, family circumstances, education and lifestyle marked him out as different from the rank and file of the anti-treaty side. However, the anti-treaty T.D. did not want to be perceived as different to those who were now on the same side as he was, and accusations such as Horan's assertion that he suppressed a rank and file prison coup to enhance his own chances of escaping while leaving others behind as prisoners in Portobello Barracks would probably have rankled the Wicklow man. Barton's reticence regarding his escape from Portobello may have been due to something more than a desire to forget his Civil War experience – it may have been because of his desire to forget his role in placing young men's lives in danger so that he and others could escape from the Hammam Hotel, and to overlook his part in halting a potential prison revolt so that he and others could escape from Portobello. This is one of the very few occasions where Barton was accused of having selfish motivations for his actions – most accounts of his contribution to the Irish Revolution actually stress his detachment, his single-mindedness and his selflessness – and Barton may have harboured a guilty conscience regarding his time in Portobello and his escape if there was any truth in Horan's assertions.

Barton's incarceration in Portobello had not lasted long, but his freedom was also short-lived. Following his escape, he sought sanctuary in Áine Ceannt's house on Oakley Road, from which, according to his noticeably vague recollection, he was 'more or less in touch with de Valera and the rest of the Republican members'.[51] Barton was once again 'on the run' and he remained at large for a little over three months. However, on Sunday, 22 October, a pastoral from the Irish bishops was read at all Masses, and it proved to have serious consequences for Barton. The document condemned the anti-treatyites' resistance to the Free State government as having 'no legitimate authority to justify it'.[52] This prompted de Valera to establish an 'Emergency Government' on 25 October, to act as a rival to the Free State government and to provide some (arguably dubious) legitimacy to the anti-treaty forces.[53] De Valera acted as president of this shadowy body, and he appointed Barton to his Cabinet as Minister for Economic Affairs.[54] The position carried no power as de Valera's 'Council of State' was not in charge of the country, but Barton received a call to attend a 'Cabinet' meeting. He cycled away from Oakley Road to answer de Valera's summons, but he was recognised by two National Army soldiers in a passing car, one of whom knew him well. They stopped and arrested the rival 'Minister for Economic Affairs', taking him to Wellington Barracks, from where he was sent to Mountjoy Jail and, later, to Hare Park Camp on the Curragh.[55]

Barton was already incarcerated in November 1922 when his family home, Glendalough House, was raided by members of the National Army. Dulcibella was again providing a safe house (now for anti-treatyites) as the Civil War progressed. She later reminisced about some incidents connected with this in her witness statement:

I had one mysterious visitor during the Civil War period. He came dressed in clerical garb and said his name was Father Murphy from

Wexford. He said he was 'on the run', but did not say who sent him
... There was something about him that I did not like ... So when
... Paddy Ruttledge came I asked him to send him away ... and very
shortly after he went away on his bicycle. I felt uncomfortable the
whole time he was there, as I had the idea that he might be a spy.

During the Civil War one morning two priests ... came to the
door and said I could expect ... Mr De Valera, the following day
to stay in the house, if I could have him. I said I could. They asked
me to provide an escort to bring him back to Dublin. That was not
so simple. Dev came very early and spent certainly a night. I sent
somebody with him to bring him to a house on the way to Dublin
and from this he was brought safely into the city ...[56]

At the time of the November raid by Free State forces, Barton's cousin
Erskine Childers was staying in Glendalough House. Though he was
imprisoned, Barton had left instructions that if Childers sought sanctuary
in Annamoe, he was to be hidden in the cellars of the house. Childers,
however, slept in his old room, much to the consternation of the servants.[57] Events proved that they were right to be uneasy. When Childers
came out of his bedroom, the raid was in progress and there were soldiers on the stairs, so he drew a revolver. However, an old family servant
quickly placed himself between Childers and the troops and shouted,
'You'll not shoot Mr Childers.' Following this heroic intervention,
Childers was captured peacefully in possession of the small pearl-handled
revolver.[58] Ironically, Childers was the last in a long line of republicans
who had come to Glendalough House while 'on the run' during both
the War of Independence and the Civil War, and the only one to be captured.[59] Even more ironically, the pistol in Childers' possession had been a
gift from Michael Collins,[60] whose death in an ambush at Béal na mBláth
on 22 August 1922 had acted as a catalyst for the introduction of a strict
new Public Safety Act by the Free State government.[61] Childers was put
on trial for possession of a firearm, an offence punishable by death under
the new law. Animosity towards Childers was evident when he was publicly denounced in both the Irish parliament by Kevin O'Higgins and the
English parliament by Winston Churchill. Unpopular on both sides of
the Irish Sea and with a vengeful personal vendetta waged against him,
the Childers verdict was a foregone conclusion. Childers was philosophi-
cal about his sentence, and he bade farewell to some of those close to

him before his execution was carried out. In a letter to Ivor Lloyd Jones he wrote, 'Dearest Ivor, It doesn't matter what you *think* of me. I know you love me – the first friendship in my life and indestructible ... from my heart and soul God bless you and Gwladys and her daughter and give you great happiness. Erskine.'[62] On 24 November 1922 he was executed by an Irish firing squad in Beggars Bush Barracks.[63] Probate was granted on Childers' will on 9 March 1923 and his estate was valued at £9,772 14s 8d.[64] Although he did not reveal it publicly, there is little doubt that Childers' execution had a profound effect on Barton, both at the time and in later life. He was disillusioned by the death of his first cousin, and other Civil War deaths.[65] His non-display of overt emotion, however, was in keeping with the course of action that he pursued at other times of stress and strain, that of 'keeping a stiff upper lip'. Though it is something of a generalisation, this was also the course of action encouraged by his class, the landed elite, and the idea of the 'stiff upper lip' would have been drummed into Barton from an early age, as were his devotion to duty and his sense of honour.

Barton remained in Hare Park Camp for the duration of the Civil War. The anti-treaty military leader Liam Lynch was killed in action in County Tipperary on 10 April 1923.[66] His death effectively ended anti-treatyite resistance. On 24 May, both Éamon de Valera and Frank Aiken ordered the anti-treatyites to cease hostilities.[67] However, Barton had to wait for freedom until December, when he was eventually released as part of the general release of political prisoners.[68] He had again contested his Dáil seat in August, while still imprisoned. He stood on a republican ticket in the three-seat constituency of Wicklow, which had an electorate of 36,753, but he narrowly missed out on securing the third seat. In the event, both Christopher Byrne of Cumann na nGaedheal and Labour's James Everett were elected, with Richard Wilson of the Farmers' Party scraping past Barton to take the third seat. Wilson polled 4,281 first-preference votes, with Barton gleaning 4,218 – the relative share of the votes was 18.7 per cent for Wilson and 18.42 per cent for Barton.[69] The defeat had been narrow, but Barton had lost his Dáil seat, and with it his mandate to represent County Wicklow at national level. With the pro-treaty party, Cumann na nGaedheal, now in power and his Dáil seat lost, Barton decided to retire from the arena of national politics. He returned to farm at Annamoe and never stood for election to the Dáil again.[70]

A Return to a Life
of Public Service
(January 1924–August 1975)

The second half of 1923 witnessed the emergence of a (relatively) peaceful Free State. For a polity born out of the throes of a bitter civil war, the I.R.A. order to dump arms and cease operations was surprisingly well received and, in the main, respected. The government could finally get on with the business of governing and the people in the countryside, villages and towns could begin a process of rebuilding. In County Wicklow, as elsewhere, this was as relevant to trust and relationships as it was to physical buildings and infrastructure. In 1923, Kevin O'Higgins, the Minister for Justice in the Free State, reflected: 'We were probably the most conservative-minded revolutionaries that ever put through a successful revolution.'[1] This statement telegraphed O'Higgins' intention, in the wake of victory in the Civil War, to govern the infant state 'according to conventional parliamentary principles' now that conflict had ended.[2] Even with this conservative mindset however, there were changes across the country from 1923 onwards. Some of these were evident in Annamoe. Painting the post boxes green may have been a minor change, but it represented a huge political shift, on a par with flying the tricolour instead of the union flag. From September 1923 the Irish flag was also flown at the League of Nations. At county level, county councils acquired some additional responsibilities; county health districts and county homes were introduced. There was still a police presence throughout the county, but the unarmed Civic Guard had replaced the former armed R.I.C. men. Their numbers dwindled as the memory of the Civil War began to recede into the background of the collective mindset. Local courts still sat, but from 1924 they were district courts, where district justices replaced magistrates and justices of the peace as judges. Circuit courts also replaced the old assizes as a new legal system took shape. When Barton was finally released from prison in December 1923, a new Ireland was gradually emerging.[3]

Following his release, Barton's disillusionment with the futility of the Civil War and, in particular, the loss of his cousin Erskine Childers, had an impact on his health. His sister, Dulcibella, was similarly affected. On 8 June 1924, the West Wicklow branch of Sinn Féin wrote to Barton to try to persuade him to reverse his decision to retire from the political arena. The letter referred to both Childers' execution and the Barton siblings' ill-health:

> Your own record, and the memory of your noble kinsman, who sacrificed himself for the Irish Republic are an inspiration to the people of Wicklow, and will strengthen them in the final stages of the long drawn-out struggle. Knowing the faithfulness and the suffering endured by you and yours, we believe that your resignation would bring joy to the upholders of the Free State, and would be used by them as propaganda to injure the Republican cause ... We are truly sorry that your health has become impaired, and we realize that the mental and physical strain of the last few years made it inevitable that this should be so. We pray that you may shortly be restored to your former vigour. Our sympathies too are with Miss Barton. She has indeed had a double burden to bear, and nobly has she fulfilled the responsibilities of both private and national affairs. May God grant her the blessing of renewed health, and may He strengthen both you and her for whatever work lies before you ...

The letter also provides revealing insights about the Ireland that was emerging from the trauma of the Civil War, and about how Barton was regarded in the new state. The writers assured Barton that they knew that he was 'actuated by the purest and highest ideals for the ultimate good of the Irish people' when he signed the treaty. They also informed him that they appreciated how he acted afterwards 'to rectify the decision which was forced upon you'. Tellingly, they also suggested to Barton that 'most people (whether republican or Free State) now admit that if your example had been followed by the other delegates, the country would have been spared the agony and bitterness of the past two years'.[4] Although the letter lays bare the open wounds left festering in the wake of civil war, there is a tantalising suggestion that both sides regretted the 'agony and bitterness' and, like Barton, the disillusionment caused by the recent conflict. Barton occupied a singular position within the political perspectives of the fledgling state. As a signatory who voted for the treaty, he was an acceptable figure to many on the pro-treaty side, but by renouncing his decision and joining de Valera and his followers immediately prior to and during the Civil War, he was also acceptable to many on the anti-treaty side. His actions and his emotional performance during the treaty debates meant that, strangely and perhaps uniquely, he was respected by all but the most diehard elements within the erstwhile opposing camps as the infant Free State grappled with the many teething problems associated with trying to move forward in the brave new world of everyday life in post-Civil War Ireland. Though progress was slow, the peacetime Free State was starting to recover after a decade of revolution, which had ended in civil war.

As formal administrative state services returned to normal, or melded into a 'new normal' format, informal leisure activities also re-emerged as part of the daily round. Following the establishment of the Free State, local G.A.A. clubs often involved the whole community in organising teams for the love of the parish, town or village. County Wicklow's G.A.A. clubs flourished and in parts of the county other games such as hockey, rugby (and, later, soccer) also became part of daily life again during the mid-1920s.[5] Nationally, these games have often been perceived as attracting more Protestants than the G.A.A., and Gaelic games were rarely played in Protestant schools. However, there was some level of Protestant involvement in the organisation throughout the G.A.A.'s history, which was probably pleasing to Barton. A number of Church of Ireland players may have used aliases to circumvent the ban on playing rugby and soccer or to avoid being identified as participants in sport on Sundays, but overall, Protestant involvement in the G.A.A. benefitted both parties, as it allowed Protestants to participate in community life and helped to prevent discrimination within the G.A.A. itself.[6]

Nationally, the educational system was also overhauled. The fledgling Free State operated a nationalistic agenda and nowhere was this to become more apparent than in the field of education. The new state regarded the teaching of the Irish language and of Irish history, poetry, culture, drama and games in its schools among its prime objectives. National schools now taught the new curriculum, with a greater emphasis on the Irish language. Professor Eoin McNeil had become the Free State's Minister for Education and one of his first priorities was changing the curriculum. The type of nationalistic education provided by the Irish Christian Brothers was an obvious model to follow, as they had educated many of the leaders of the Irish revolution.[7] The order rapidly became a pillar of the new educational crusade. For most young people, school ended in adolescence with the primary cert, and then they had to face an introduction to the harsh reality of the world of work. Despite some initiatives by the new departments of industry and commerce, agriculture and finance,[8] jobs remained stubbornly scarce. In County Wicklow, as elsewhere throughout the new state, the populace was discovering that political independence was not a silver bullet that would usher in economic independence and prosperity. Many County Wicklow residents continued to out-migrate and to emigrate as the 1920s progressed. Those that remained often found only casual labour, but they were at least guaranteed certain freedoms under the constitution of the Irish Free State (passed in October 1922),[9] which stated that all citizens without distinction of sex now had freedom of speech, freedom of assembly and freedom of religion.[10]

The religious breakdown of the populations of many Wicklow settlements was little altered from the pre-revolutionary period a decade or so beforehand. Wicklow's Catholics had predominantly made up the numbers in the county's I.R.A. companies. The Catholic population was bitterly divided in the aftermath of the Civil War in County Wicklow, but religion was a unifying factor as Catholics settled back into a semblance of normality in the wake of the period known as the 'Irish Troubles'. For many, Catholicism provided a sense of shared identity and cohesion clearly distinct from Protestant England,[11] so both the old pro- and anti-treaty factions returned to Masses and the celebration of the sacraments in the churches of County Wicklow. Protestants, on the other hand, adopted a more reserved role in local society as the twentieth century progressed. Before partition, Protestants had accounted for 27 per cent of the population of Ireland, but the 1926 census revealed that they only accounted for 7 per cent of the population in the new Free State,[12] so it was unsurprising that they shunned the limelight in uncertain and potentially hostile new surroundings. However, for many Protestants, 'keeping the head down was not done out of a sense of unease, but because things were just fine and it suited'.[13] They fitted in and lived in harmony with their Catholic neighbours. This had always been true in Barton's case, and he spent the next decade or so living quietly in the fledgling Free State, tending to day-to-day agricultural matters in the tranquil surroundings of his estate at Annamoe.

Although his retirement from active politics remained permanent, political developments during the 1920s ensured that Barton returned to public life in the 1930s. Anti-treaty Sinn Féin continued to abstain from taking seats in the Dáil, but de Valera was softening his position on this stance. At the Árd Fheis of March 1926, he proposed that 'once the admission oaths of the twenty-six and six county assemblies are removed, it becomes a question not of principle but of policy whether or not Republican representatives should attend these assemblies'.[14] However, de Valera's proposal was defeated and the party reinforced this hard-line position, resolving 'that it is incompatible with the fundamental principles of Sinn Féin, as it is injurious to the honour of Ireland, to send representatives into any usurping legislature set up by English law in Ireland'.[15] De Valera resigned as party leader and, two months later, he set up a new party, Fianna Fáil (meaning 'the soldiers of destiny'). The party grew at a 'quite phenomenal' speed,[16] and in August the following year (1927), Fianna Fáil decided to take the oath and enter the Dáil. On 11 August the party's Executive issued a statement declaring that the oath was meaningless and calling it 'merely an empty political formula'.[17] The party members took the oath – or, at least, uttered the words – and in the words of J. J. Lee: 'Thus, seeing no oath, hearing no oath, speaking no oath and signing no oath, the Soldiers of Destiny shuffled into Dáil Éireann.'[18]

One cannot help but wonder how the course of the history of the formative years of the Irish state might have been different if de Valera and his followers had taken the pragmatic 'empty formula' approach to the oath in 1921 and 1922. Diarmaid Ferriter has suggested that 'the tragedy, perhaps, was that what divided Sinn Fein was so little, in practice at least'. He goes on to quote Barton's treaty debate speech in which the Wicklow man told the House: '... for the nation, without consultation, I dared not accept that responsibility ... I signed'. Ferriter wryly observed that 'de Valera and his followers were to sign too, though belatedly and with fingers crossed'.[19] In 1954, with the benefit of hindsight, Barton mused: 'It would have been reasonable to accept the position as it was and combine (both pro- and anti-treaty sides) to get more as time went by.'[20] Barton, who was still loyal to and friendly with de Valera, may have been coming to the conclusion that it would have been better for the pro- and anti-treaty sides to work together as early as the late 1920s or the early 1930s. Despite the close relationship between the two, Barton could be critical of the Fianna Fáil leader on occasion.[21] However, he supported Fianna Fáil (although from the outside, as he did not actually join)[22] when the party mounted general election campaigns in 1927, 1932 and 1933. Cumann na nGaedheal were returned in 1927, but Fianna Fáil were victorious in 1932 and, following a peaceful handover of power, the party triumphed again in the snap election of 1933.

Barton campaigned energetically for Fianna Fáil during the 1933 election campaign in particular, claiming that Collins and Griffith had been duped on the issue of the boundary commission (which had been established in 1924 but collapsed the following year with no changes made to the border) during the treaty negotiations.[23] It is interesting that Barton concentrated on the border issue during his political campaigning, as this approach is somewhat at odds with the views expressed in his later witness statement. In that document, Barton admitted that everyone expected the boundary commission to reduce the size of Northern Ireland, and he offered the opinion that both Collins and Griffith were 'no partitionists'.[24] The expected boundary commission changes meant that the North was not a sticking point for most people, including many republican supporters in the Free State, in the early 1920s. Indeed, despite later events in Northern Ireland, one cannot ascribe partition as a principal cause of the Civil War – only one speaker, Sean MacEntee, mentioned it in the treaty debates.[25] Issues such as the oath of allegiance, Commonwealth membership or external association were much more central to contemporary consciousness in the early 1920s. A decade later, however, following the failure of the boundary commission, the electoral politics of the early 1930s had again placed the border in the spotlight, and Barton did not shy away from embracing the views expressed in Fianna Fáil propaganda during the campaign, which ended in another victory for the party.

Though Barton continued to take an interest in farming his estate, and in such matters as 'shooting, hunting, coursing, and taking game and wild fowl' on his lands, including those at Drummin,[26] de Valera's return to government meant that Barton's secluded life in Annamoe changed beyond all recognition. To counteract the pro-government *Irish*

Independent, de Valera founded the *Irish Press* in 1931. According to the Fianna Fáil leader, it was 'a people's paper pledged to honesty and truth without bias'. One letter writer to the new broadsheet suggested that it was better for a newspaper 'to have a soul and be propagandist than to have no soul and still be propagandist'. In addition to social and economic matters, the *Press* had a culturally nationalistic agenda – the first issue, for example, contained an article by Douglas Hyde encouraging the everyday use of the Irish language.[27] During the run-up to the 1932 election, the Cosgrave government prosecuted the *Press* for seditious libel before a military tribunal – a move that produced disdain for Cumann na nGaedheal and increased support for Fianna Fáil.[28] Perhaps as a reward for his loyalty, de Valera appointed his close ally Barton as a company director of the new newspaper.[29] Barton had the educational background and experience for this and other positions that he was offered, and accepted, during Fianna Fáil's time in office, but perhaps there was also an element of cronyism. Either way (and the one does not preclude the other), Barton worked hard and achieved a lot in his new public roles. The *Irish Press* would go on to become an Irish institution, and rivalled the *Irish Independent* for most of the twentieth century, before its collapse 'amidst much recrimination' in 1995 – some twenty years after Barton's death.[30]

Barton was also appointed to the board of the Agricultural Credit Corporation (A.C.C.) by Sean MacEntee in 1932, and he became its chairman in 1933, serving in that capacity until 1959.[31] The A.C.C. position was tailored to suit the education, background, experience and talents of the former Minister for Agriculture, who had been instrumental in establishing the Land Bank during his term in the first Dáil. In a bold new departure, a decision was made to make long-term loans available to farmers for productive purposes on reasonable terms. The 1927 Agricultural Credit Act provided for setting up the A.C.C. as a limited company with a nominal share capital of £500,000. This sum increased significantly as its operations expanded later on. A.C.C. finances were state guaranteed. By 1936 the A.C.C. had advanced loans of just over £1,250,000. However, individual transactions were usually small – the average loan was £82. Despite the paucity of this sum, reflecting small farm size in rural Ireland, almost £30,000 of bad debts had had to be written off by 1936. The Economic War of the 1930s was a major factor in increasing rural poverty. However, despite this unpromising first decade, the A.C.C. had huge significance. Along with the Electricity Supply Board

(E.S.B.), it was the first of a number of similar organisations involving state intervention in various sectors of the economy previously devoid of capital.[32] Barton steered the organisation through the stormy waters of the Economic War of the 1930s, the Emergency years of the 1940s and the economic stagnation of the 1950s, and many farmers derived positive benefits from its operations in rural Ireland during these decades.

Barton was also a central figure in another organisation that arguably had an even greater effect on rural Ireland in the 1930s, '40s and '50s. In 1934 he became chairman of the Turf Development Board.[33] The position was part-time and unpaid, but Barton brought vision and energy to the role. Ireland was well supplied with peat bogs – but Barton had a huge task ahead of him. Despite the existence of copious amounts of peat, extraction using basic technology such as hand tools meant that there was no possibility of getting turf of the required standard in any quantities. Bogs vary in quality too much to yield turf of uniform density.[34] Two types of peat bogs are found in Ireland: blanket bogs and raised bogs. Blanket bogs occur in mountainous areas with high precipitation levels, and are usually small and shallow, with an average depth of 1 – 3m. Raised bogs, on the other hand, occur in lowland areas with lower (but still ample) precipitation, and are large and deep, with an average depth of 7 – 8m.[35] They cover much of a huge area of the midlands across a roughly triangular zone stretching from Lullymore in County Kildare to Littleton in County Tipperary to Lanesboro in County Longford.[36] Barton recognised the potential of the raised bogs, and he brought a new efficiency to the Turf Development Board's planning for the peat industry. According to Todd Andrews, from the moment Barton made a minute of the board's decisions (during his first meeting), 'Neither he nor any of the minutes he made was ever questioned. Without his prestige in government circles and in the country generally our plans for turf development would never have been brought to fruition in the face of the opposition stemming from the Department of Finance.'[37] Despite some progress, the shortcomings of the outdated system of turf extraction by manual labour were brutally exposed during the years of the Emergency (1939–45), when the supply of British coal to Ireland all but dried up as the vital fuel was needed in Britain for the war effort.

Barton rose to the challenge of fuel scarcity, and oversaw a massive effort to organise the cutting of turf on the midland bogs and transport it to urban centres. In the five-year period 1942–47, more than half a million tons of hand-cut turf was transported to Dublin by canal, by train and by army lorries. The turf was stored in mounds up to 30ft, on the Fifteen Acres and along Chesterfield Avenue in the Phoenix Park, earning it the nickname of 'the new bog road'.[38] The war had shown the potential of the raised bogs and in 1946 the Turf Development Board was replaced by a new body, Bord na Móna. Barton remained at the head of the new organisation and he spearheaded a drive to introduce modern technology to the production of turf. Special drainage machines were developed with wide caterpillar tracks to create a network of drains criss-crossing the bogs. Surplus water was allowed to run off, in some cases for up to seven years. Peat strippers were developed to remove vegetation and bulldozers and tractors were introduced to level the bog surface. Once the peat was ready to be harvested, sod peat was cut by special machines known as baggers. Milled peat (for use in power stations) was harvested by specially adapted milling machines, turned with large harrows and gathered by other specialised machines called ridgers. Crucially, all the turf extracted from the bogs was transported along a newly built network of bog railways, radiating back from the production areas to central points or directly to power stations and peat briquette factories. Bord na Móna also diversified its markets, with moss peat (for the improvement of soil quality) being exported to many countries. All these developments had a hugely positive impact on the economy of the midlands, and by the time Barton retired from the post in 1960, Bord na Móna had altered the landscape of the region, provided much-needed employment and revolutionised the production of turf for domestic and industrial purposes.[39]

Barton was nearly 80 years of age when he retired from Bord na Móna. In addition to his roles in the Irish Press, the A.C.C. and Bord na Móna, his other public appointments had included membership of the banking, currency, and credit commission (1934–38), of a special committee to advise on post-war agricultural policy (1942–45), and of the Hospitals Trust board in the 1940s.[40] All these high-profile positions ensured that he was a well-known and respected public figure. In 1947, as Barton was driving Stuart Mais through the streets of Bray, Mais noticed that 'a considerable number of people we passed recognised and saluted Barton. He is obviously a very popular public figure.' However, Mais had also noted that 'the years of martyrdom have left their mark on his refined, ascetic face. He looks frail physically, but spiritually agile.'[41] Frail or not, four years later, on 21 July 1951, at the age of 69, Barton married Rachel

Warren Lothrop, a niece of Molly Childers (the widow of his executed cousin Erskine) in Boston, Massachusetts.[42] Barton continued his work with Bord na Móna for another decade, and resumed his quiet agricultural life in Annamoe upon his retirement. He retired from farming his estate in 1970, and invited his nephew, Robert (Bobby) Childers, over from England to take control of the farm. At that time, the farm was prosperous and the gardens of Glendalough House were still looking particularly well, with azaleas and rhododendrons planted on terraces, and a sequoia tree, which had been planted in the middle of the lawn in 1881 to mark Barton's birth, towering over everything.[43]

However, Barton's health was beginning to fail in the early 1970s, and he was admitted to hospital in 1974.[44] Poor health notwithstanding, Barton continued to be a well-respected figure up to his final days with, for example, one local builder described as having 'a rustic reverence for Barton, and in his presence never spoke unless he was spoken to'. Barton's old friend and ally, de Valera, continued to visit him at Annamoe during the early 1970s.[45] Now in his twilight years, Barton brooded over his role in the signing of the treaty and in the disastrous Civil War that followed. So consumed was he by his momentous decision to sign the document that he later wrote that he often wished that he had died in Portland prison rather than lived to take part in 'those cursed negotiations' that had cost so many lives.[46] Barton lived to the ripe old age of 94, eventually dying on 10 August 1975, three years after the death of his wife. His former chief, de Valera, died nineteen days later.[47] Their passing, as the last of the 'treaty generation' to die, marked the end of an era. The last signatory of the Anglo-Irish treaty to die, to the very end of his life Robert Barton was haunted by his decision to sign the agreement. By 1980, Glendalough House had been altered beyond all recognition by the demolition of the old Gothic pile, and Barton's birth tree had been felled.[48] Like Bob Barton, the sequoia had been consigned to the pages of history.

Conclusion

The decade of revolution in Ireland from 1913–23 produced some remarkable figures, and by any standards, Robert Barton was one of them. His background, his education and his religion set him apart from many of his contemporaries. Barton came from an elite, landed background and his family was a wealthy one. This was not the case for many of the Irish rebels, although Constance Markievicz also comes to mind as an exception. It was probably no accident that Barton's sister, Dulcibella, was on very friendly terms with the countess, as they shared both privileged backgrounds and political beliefs. Dulcibella often looked after Constance's cocker spaniel, Poppet, during the countess' frequent sojourns in prison from 1919 to 1923.[1] They shared a wealthy lifestyle about which many rank and file rebels of the period could only dream. Barton's background provided him with excellent educational opportunities, and his time at Rugby, Cirencester and Oxford meant that, in addition to receiving a well-rounded education, he was well-versed in both agriculture and economics. His knowledge and understanding of both subjects were factors in his inclusion in both Irish delegations sent to London in 1921. He attained an educational level far above most other revolutionaries of the time, sparking envy and suspicion, particularly within Arthur Griffith. In many ways the polemicist of the Irish Revolution in print, Griffith had left school at 12 years of age and worked his way up within journalistic circles. Barton's education engendered unease within the treaty delegation.

Barton's Anglican religion also set him apart from many of his revolutionary comrades. Irish Catholicism was growing in confidence and advancing steadily during the late nineteenth and early twentieth

Fig 12. Dulcibella Barton pictured with Countess Markievicz's cocker spaniel, Poppet. (Image [KMGLM.2021.0020] courtesy of Kilmainham Gaol)

centuries.[2] The identification of Catholicism with nationalism in Ireland also occasioned the Catholic faith to be perceived by some as a badge of nationalist identity. This was particularly true of the movement known as Irish-Irelandism. The leader most associated with this movement was D. P. Moran, a Catholic nationalist supporter of Home Rule, who maintained that the real struggle was between Catholicism and Protestantism, rather than between Britain and Ireland *per se*. For Moran, the benefit of implementing Home Rule was that it would allow Catholic values to develop and dominate within Ireland.[3] This Irish-Ireland mindset was also present in some of the participants in the Easter Rising, and when nationalist Ireland abandoned Home Rule in favour of more militant republicanism, Moran's ideas still permeated the thinking of many of the revolutionary generation. It was all the more remarkable, then, that the Protestant Barton supported the Irish nationalist cause at a time when many of his co-religionists felt threatened by it. He was not, of course, the only revolutionary Protestant of this era – there were others, but they were in the minority.

Barton was not the first Protestant nationalist from County Wicklow. It has been suggested that there is a revolutionary thread running through Wicklow Protestantism.[4] The 1798 rebel leader, General Joseph Holt, was possibly the first 'modern' republican Protestant to emerge within the county.[5] However, Holt was not from the same social class as Barton – he was a comfortably-off tenant farmer – and during his life he was dogged by suspicions that his sympathies actually lay with the authorities.[6] During the late nineteenth century, the Protestant Charles Stewart Parnell and his sisters, Anna and Fanny, were leaders of the Land League and Ladies' Land League. In addition to land reform, Charles led the Home Rule movement until his fall from grace because of the Katharine O'Shea divorce case. The Parnells were members of the landed elite, and Barton's father, Charles, fell out with his neighbours because of their nationalist leanings. A pillar of the local Anglican community, Charles Barton was staunchly Unionist, so it was surprising that his children Robert and Dulcibella adopted strong nationalist, and later republican, beliefs aligning themselves with the Parnells and Holt in the ranks of County Wicklow Protestant nationalists and/or republicans.

However, before one accepts the proposition of such a thread running through Wicklow Protestantism, it is important to realise that Robert and Dulcibella Barton were in the political minority even within their own family, not to mention in their own social class or their own religion. Holt, the Parnells and the Bartons were vastly outnumbered by their Unionist peers and co-religionists during the whole period from the 1790s to the 1920s. These people were studied, written about and well known because they were the exceptions rather than the rule, and perhaps because the independent Irish state wanted to provide Protestant nationalist and republican role models to show that Protestants too had a part to play in the new Ireland. However, the majority of Protestants' loyalties lay with Unionism during the revolutionary period. This is particularly true of wealthier Protestants of the landed elite class. Protestants were disproportionately represented in Irish land ownership circles in the eighteenth and nineteenth centuries, which led to the coining of the phrase 'Protestant Ascendancy'. Despite some Catholic advancement in land owning in the post-Famine period, there was still a large proportion of landed Protestants both nationally and in County Wicklow. The majority of them were loyal to King and Country, and many occupied positions in the colonial services or in the armed forces. The military tradition in

Barton's own family saw some of its members serving in the British army in Africa and in Europe, and two of his brothers lost their lives during the First World War.

Barton also joined the British army in 1915. Given his background, his upbringing and his character, he probably took this course of action to do his duty honourably. This had also been the case when he joined the Irish Volunteers to defend Home Rule. Barton had been interested in the cause of Home Rule even in his student days at Oxford, and he became utterly convinced of the necessity of its implementation during a tour of the west of Ireland in 1908. However, when the First World War erupted in Europe, Barton chose to support the war effort. He may have done so (as did many of the National Volunteers, whose side he took when the Volunteer movement split) in the hope of getting Home Rule implemented after the war, but his background, education and the social circles in which he moved meant that he was also well aware of German militarism. His deep, thoughtful character probably aided his decision, and he may have seen it as his duty to do the honourable thing and leave the Volunteers to join the British army and play his part in trying to stop German expansion. Duty and honour had led him into the O.T.C., and Captain Erskine Booth's recommendation letter for Barton touched on his depth of character when he wrote, 'Whatever he does, he does really well, putting his whole soul into it.'[7] This trait of absolute commitment, leading to dogged determination and a certain level of inflexibility, would be characteristic of Barton throughout his life and political career. Commitment, duty and honour all weighed heavily with the newly commissioned second lieutenant, who still supported the cause of Home Rule when he landed in Dublin during Easter Week 1916.

All the evidence points to Barton's spell in charge of prisoners' effects in Dublin from 1916–18 being a transformative time in his life, and one during which his political views matured. It was not an overnight conversion, but it was rapid nonetheless. Barton backed the Irish Convention, a last-ditch effort to salvage Home Rule, but when it collapsed in April 1918 he threw in his lot with Sinn Féin. Clearly, the republican prisoners with whom he associated made an impression on him and on his thought processes. Thus, two years or so after his arrival in Richmond Barracks, he found himself standing as a Sinn Féin candidate for West Wicklow. He won the seat handsomely, and was appointed as Director of Agriculture in the first Dáil, but spent much of the War of Independence in prison, being recaptured after his daring escape from Mountjoy Gaol. He was released to help negotiate the truce of 1921, and played a key part in that process, which saw a cessation of the conflict and an Irish delegation under de Valera travelling to London in July of that year. By then Barton, who was an ardent supporter of de Valera, and who had done much good work as Director of Agriculture, had been promoted to Minister for Economic Affairs, so he was a natural choice to be one of the delegates. That first attempt at political agreement came to naught, but both sides agreed to keep in contact after the Irish delegates returned empty-handed.

Crucially, Barton also travelled to London with the second Irish delegation of 1921, this time led by Arthur Griffith in the self-imposed absence of de Valera. Also crucially, he and the other delegates were given plenipotentiary status, so they could accept an agreement on behalf of the Irish government. De Valera tried to counterbalance this by giving the delegates instructions to refer any proposed agreement back to Dublin before signing it. He also tried to balance the members of the delegation between inflexible republicans like Barton and those, such as Griffith and Collins, who might be more moderate. Cleavage was inevitable, and the resulting fracture was disastrous for the delegation, with Barton and Gavan Duffy finding themselves in a minority, powerless to influence events. They had support from Childers, but being a secretary rather than a delegate, he had no vote. The Barton camp was excluded from sub-conferences; the camps polarised and split and Barton cut a wretched figure as the talks progressed. Their progression was slow and painful for Barton, who was labouring under the strain of the situation, and matters came to a head in early December. A tense and tetchy Cabinet meeting in Dublin was followed by a return to London – and a realisation that the talks were now in their climactic phase. The stage was set for Lloyd George's ultimatum. It came with a plea from the Welsh Wizard that seemed to be addressed specifically to Barton, on whose decision acceptance or rejection of the document would hinge, and who would become the key player in the whole drama.

At that moment, the weight of responsibility on Barton's shoulders was enormous. The other delegates – Griffith, Collins and Duggan – had all agreed to sign the document, and Gavan Duffy made it clear that he would be guided by Barton and follow his example. The burden of Ireland's expectations, intense pressure from three other plenipotentiaries (including the leader and deputy leader of the delegation) and, above all, the threat of imminent war all told on Barton. Despite Childers' exhortations, Barton, still mentally agonising over breaking his sacred oath to the Republic, eventually and reluctantly agreed to sign the document. Given the depth of Barton's character and his attitude to duty and honour, the internal struggle being played out in the mind of the Wicklow man must have been enormous at that moment. The mental struggle remained immense during the ensuing treaty debates, in which Barton made it clear that he was acting on behalf of the nation – 'For myself, I preferred war ... but the for the nation, without consultation, I dared not accept responsibility.'[8] He upbraided de Valera for putting the delegates in a near-impossible situation. However, having signed the treaty, the honourable Barton felt duty-bound to vote for its acceptance. In the event, the majority of the Dáil accepted the Anglo-Irish treaty, but the minority did not accept the result of the vote.

As the drift towards civil war began, Barton did not waste any time in switching over to the anti-treaty side. He had done his duty in the Dáil, so he felt that he was now free to give his support to de Valera and the anti-treatyites. He attacked Collins in his pamphlet *The Truth about the Treaty and Document No. 2*, and he travelled to Dublin as the Civil War began. He was stationed with other anti-treatyites in the Hammam Hotel at the outbreak of hostilities and escaped from there, only to be arrested almost straight away. He was imprisoned in Portobello Barracks, but escaped, allegedly scuppering a planned prison coup in the process. This allegation by Patrick Horan is one of the few instances when Barton was accused of putting his own good above the good of the cause he served. (The only comparable instance may be his mischievous and perhaps vindictive suggestion that Duggan's signature had to be pasted on to the original treaty document.) Barton's freedom was short-lived – he was recaptured and spent the remainder of the Civil War in captivity, eventually being released in December 1923. Barton lost his Dáil seat while he was imprisoned, so he retired from politics and public life generally, returning to Annamoe to manage his estate and concentrate on agriculture.

Barton re-entered public life in the early 1930s, by which time de Valera's new Fianna Fáil Party had come to power. Barton supported but never joined the party, and de Valera appointed him to some very prominent positions of public service. His transformative work with the Agricultural Credit Corporation and, in particular, with Bord na Móna did much to improve life in rural Ireland. Ironically, this was when much of Barton's most effective work was done, creating long-term change in rural Ireland, particularly across the midlands, but it has been overshadowed in popular and historical memory by his role in the Irish Revolution, and in particular, his role during the treaty negotiations and the treaty debates. He married late in life, retired even later and died at the advanced age of 94 in a changed Ireland, an independent republic within both the United Nations and the Common Market – an Ireland in whose formation he had played a major part.

When one comes to assess the role played by Robert Barton in the Irish Revolution, the thoughts he nurtured, the words he spoke, the stances he took, the actions he performed and the role he played in bringing the new state into being, we begin to glimpse the complexities of his life and of the times in which he lived. A myriad of influences was at play within his young mind as he shifted his political ideals from the paternal Unionism of his boyhood through Home Rule and republicanism to the anti-treaty agenda that he adopted during the Civil War. His background and upbringing were different to the majority of his revolutionary contemporaries. His 1969 television interview was shared with both James Ryan and Ernest Blythe, and Barton's Oxbridge accent is at odds with the soft Wexford tones of the former and the slightly harsher Northern tones of the latter. Roy Foster reflects on the demise of 'the Protestant accent' in the preface of *Protestant and Irish*,[9] but Barton's Oxbridge intonation went beyond Protestantism – it was evidently an Anglo-Irish 'Ascendancy' intonation. In fact, Barton's accent probably epitomised the reasons for Griffith's envy and distrust of the better-educated Wicklow man who hailed from a privileged world. However, Barton's ideas about honour and duty learned in that world and, above all the steely determination of his character meant that, once converted, he gave his all to the cause of Irish freedom. This determination ensured that Barton was fully focussed on any project in which he engaged, and was evident during the treaty negotiations, where Barton was stubborn to the point of intransigence as a negotiator. The intense nature of his character meant that half-measures were not in Barton's repertoire, and he whole-heartedly involved himself in any cause that he chose to support.

The circumstances of his early life meant that Barton was, in many ways, a remarkable revolutionary. He has left a fairly detailed witness statement outlining his activities during the Irish revolution. As with all witness statements – indeed, as with all memoirs – one must be aware of

Barton's biases and personal opinions when reading the document. One must also take into account what is not said or included. There is also a certain reticence in parts of Barton's statement. Perhaps pointedly, Barton made it clear that, in relation to signing the treaty, he had 'very little to add to the information in Lord Pakenham's book'. He also provides no details of his time as a prisoner during the Civil War, and his admission that, 'I can understand that it might be claimed now that the position having been given away by the signature of the Treaty, it would have been reasonable to accept the position as it was and combine (both pro- and anti-treaty sides) to get more as time went by' may hint at remorse on his part for supporting the anti-treatyites.[10] Despite its shortcomings, Barton's own account provides unique insights into the thoughts and activities of this remarkable revolutionary.

It is appropriate to leave the final word to Stuart Mais, Barton's university friend, who wrote of him:

> He struck me as a quiet but forceful leader of absolute integrity, who had devoted his whole life to the Irish cause, without ostentation or thought of recognition or reward. Through him I caught a glimpse of the spirit that was actuating the rulers of the new Ireland. He gave me confidence in the ultimate destiny of [its] people.[11]

Mais' tribute would be a fitting epitaph for Bob Barton, who now rests in the remote mountain cemetery of Derrylossary, deep in the countryside of his boyhood, where he first came to reflect on the cause of Irish independence.

Appendix 1

Recommendation from Captain Booth for Robert Childers Barton, 17 December 1915

Curragh Camp,
Dec 17th 1915.

I have known Robert Childers Barton all his life, and can conscientiously say that I know no man more suitable for a commission. His character, ability and his thoroughness, thoroughly fit him for the position of a leader of men. Whatever he does, he does really well, putting his whole soul into it. He is 34 years of age and has given up a very large house and farm so that he may do his duty to his country.

Erskine Booth Capt.
CRE, Curragh.

Appendix 2

Lloyd George–De Valera Correspondence, 7 and 12 September 1921

LLOYD GEORGE TO DE VALERA, 7 SEPTEMBER 1921

Town Hall,
Inverness,
September 7th, 1921.

Sir,

His Majesty's Government have considered your letter of August 30th, and have to make the following observations upon it.

The principle of government by consent of the governed is the foundation of British constitutional development, but we cannot accept as a basis of practical conference an interpretation of that principle which would commit us to any demands which you might present – even to the extent of setting up a republic and repudiating the Crown. You must be aware that conference on such a basis is impossible. So applied, the principle of government by consent of the governed would undermine the fabric of every democratic State and drive the civilised world back into tribalism.

On the other hand, we have invited you to discuss our proposals on their merits, in order that you may have no doubt as to the scope and sincerity of our intentions. It would be open to you in such a conference to raise the subject of guarantees on any points in which you may consider Irish freedom prejudiced by these proposals.

His Majesty's Government are loth to believe that you will insist upon rejecting their proposals without examining them in conference. To decline to discuss a settlement which would bestow upon the Irish people the fullest freedom of national development within the Empire can only mean that you repudiate all allegiance to the Crown and all membership of the British Commonwealth. If we were to draw this inference from your letter then further discussion between us could serve no useful purpose, and all conference would be vain. If, however, we are mistaken in this inference, as we still hope, and if your real objection to our proposals is that they offer Ireland less than the liberty which we have described, that objection can be explored at a Conference.

You will agree that this correspondence has lasted long enough. His Majesty's Government must therefore ask for a definite reply as to whether you are prepared to enter a Conference to ascertain how the association of Ireland with the community of nations known as the British Empire can best be reconciled with Irish national aspirations. If, as we hope, your answer is in the affirmative, I suggest that the Conference should meet at Inverness on the 20th instant.

I am, Sir,
Yours faithfully,
D. Lloyd George.

DE VALERA TO LLOYD GEORGE, 12 SEPTEMBER 1921

Mansion House,
Dublin,
Sept. 12th, 1921.

Sir,

We have no hesitation in declaring our willingness 'to enter a Conference to ascertain how the association of Ireland with the community of nations known as the British Empire can best be reconciled with Irish national aspirations.' Our readiness to contemplate such an association was indicated in our letter of August 10th. We have accordingly summoned Dáil Éireann that we may submit to it for ratification the names of the representatives it is our intention to propose. We hope that these representatives will find it possible to be at Inverness on the date you suggest, September 20th.

In this final note we deem it our duty to reaffirm that our position is and can only be as we have defined it throughout this correspondence. Our nation has formally declared its independence and recognises itself as a sovereign State. It is only as the representatives of that State and as its chosen guardians that we have any authority or powers to act on behalf of our people.

As regards the principle of 'government by consent of the governed,' in the very nature of things it must be the basis of any agreement that will achieve the purpose we have at heart, that is, the final reconciliation of our nation with yours. We have suggested no interpretation of that principle save its every-day interpretation, the sense, for example in which it was understood by the plain men and women of the world when on January 5th, 1918, you said:

'The settlement of the new Europe must be based on such grounds of reason and justice as will give some promise of stability. Therefore it is that we feel that government with the consent of the governed must be the basis of any territorial settlement in this war.'

These words are the true answer to the criticism of our position which your last letter puts forward. The principle was understood then to mean the right of nations that had been annexed to empires against their will to free themselves from the grappling hook. That is the sense in which we understand it. In reality it is your Government, when it seeks to rend our ancient nation and to partition its territory, that would give to the principle an interpretation that 'would undermine the fabric of every democratic state and drive the civilised world back into tribalism.'

I am, Sir,
Faithfully yours,
Éamon de Valera.

Appendix 3

Robert Barton's Treaty Debate Speech,
19 December 1921

I am going to make plain to you the circumstances under which I find myself in honour bound to recommend the acceptance of the Treaty. In making that statement I have one object only in view, and that is to enable you to become intimately acquainted with the circumstances leading up to the signing of the Treaty and the responsibility forced on me had I refused to sign. I do not seek to shield myself from the charge of having broken my oath of allegiance to the Republic – my signature is proof of that fact [hear, hear]. That oath was, and still is to me, the most sacred bond on earth. I broke my oath because I judged that violation to be the lesser of alternative outrages forced upon me, and between which I was compelled to choose. On Sunday, December 4th, the Conference had precipitately and definitely broken down. An intermediary effected contact next day, and on Monday at 3 p.m., Arthur Griffith, Michael Collins, and myself met the English representatives. In the struggle that ensued Arthur Griffith sought, repeatedly to have the decision between war and peace on the terms of the Treaty referred back to this assembly.

This proposal Mr Lloyd George directly negatived. He claimed that we were plenipotentiaries and that we must either accept or reject. Speaking for himself and his colleagues, the English Prime Minister with all the solemnity and the power of conviction that he alone, of all men I met, can impart by word and gesture – the vehicles by which the mind of one man oppresses and impresses the mind of another — declared that the signature and recommendation of every member of our delegation was necessary or war would follow immediately. He gave us until 10 o'clock to make up our minds, and it was then about 8.30.

We returned to our house to decide upon our answer. The issue before us was whether we should stand behind our proposals for external association, face war and maintain the Republic, or whether we should accept inclusion in the British Empire and take peace.

Arthur Griffith, Michael Collins, and Eamonn Duggan were for acceptance and peace; Gavan Duffy and myself were for refusal — war or no war. An answer that was not unanimous committed you to immediate war, and the responsibility for that was to rest directly upon those two delegates who refused to sign.

For myself, I preferred war. I told my colleagues so, but for the nation, without consultation, I dared not accept that responsibility. The alternative which I sought to avoid seemed to me a lesser outrage than the violation of what is my faith. So that I myself, and of my own choice, must commit my nation to immediate war, without you, Mr President, or the Members of the Dáil, or the nation having an opportunity to examine the terms upon which war could be avoided. I signed, and now I have fulfilled my undertaking I recommend to you the Treaty I signed in London [applause].

Appendix 4

West Wicklow Comhairle Ceanntair of Sinn Féin to Robert Barton, 8 June 1924

Comhairle Ceanntair, West Wicklow
8 June 1924.

Dear Mr Barton,

It was with feelings of the deepest regret we read your letter announcing your intention of retiring from public life. While we understand and sympathize with the considerations which moved you to take this decision, we are not without hopes that we may be able to dissuade you from such a step.

It is true that there are not many on the Comhairle Ceanntair today when you were chosen as representative and afterwards as Dáil candidate, but the Wicklow people well remember that it was only after pressure was brought to bear on you that you, with much reluctance, accepted the responsibility entailed. How heavy those responsibilities proved to be, none of us could then foretell, but as time went on, and the conflict became more severe, we knew that we had chosen rightly when we appointed you as the standard bearer of our liberties.

As regards the Irish Delegation of 1921, no republican has any delusions as to the part you took in those deliberations, and the subsequent signing of the Treaty. We are not in a position to judge the motives which prompted the signatories to the Treaty, but we are well aware that in the action you took you were actuated by the purest and highest ideals for the ultimate good of the Irish people. We honour and appreciate the steps you afterwards took to rectify the decision which was forced upon you then: and most people (whether republican or Free State) now admit that if your example had been followed by the other delegates, the country would have been spared the agony and bitterness of the past two years.

We are convinced that no worthier or more loyal representative could be found to fill your place either in the Comhairle Ceanntair, or as prospective candidate at a future election, and we would earnestly urge you to reconsider your decision to retire into private life. Your own record, and the memory of your noble kinsman, who sacrificed himself for the Irish Republic are an inspiration to the people of Wicklow, and will strengthen them in the final stages of the long drawn-out struggle. Knowing the faithfulness and the suffering endured by you and yours, we believe that your resignation would bring joy to the upholders of the Free State, and would be used by them as propaganda to injure the republican cause. Ireland cannot afford to lose any of her faithful sons, and it is for these reasons we wish you to remain with us, and work with us for the fruition of our hopes.

We are truly sorry that your health has become impaired, and we realize that the mental and physical strain of the last few years made it inevitable that this should be so. We pray that you may shortly be restored to your former vigour. Our sympathies too are with Miss Barton. She has indeed had a double burden to bear, and nobly has she fulfilled the responsibilities of both private and national affairs. May God grant her the blessing of renewed health, and may He strengthen both you and her for whatever work lies before you!

In conclusion, may we perhaps hope that these our earnest wishes will in some measure weigh with you, and induce you to continue with us, even though we know that by doing so it may entail further sacrifices on your part. Ireland will be the poorer should you now withdraw.

We have sown in tears — stay with us and help us to reap the harvest of joy.

Seán Mac Domhnaill
John Rogers
James Doyle
Murtagh Corrigan
Daniel J. Kehoe
Liam Ó Góróg (?)
John Cunningham
Thomas M. Lynch (?)
Andrew Kinsella M.C.C.

Bibliography

PRIMARY SOURCES

Manuscript and Document Sources

<u>Dublin</u>
Irish Military Archives
Bureau of Military History, witness statements
I.R.A. brigade activity reports
Military Service Pensions Collection

National Archives of Ireland
Dáil Éireann papers
Department of the Taoiseach papers
Records of the courts services in Ireland
Robert Barton papers

National Library of Ireland
Department of Ephemera
Dulcibella Barton Papers
McGarrity Papers

T.C.D. Manuscripts and Archives Library
Papers of Robert Erskine and Mary Childers

U.C.D. Archive
Papers of Desmond and Mabel Fitzgerald

<u>Kildare</u>
Kildare County Archive
Local Studies collection

Wicklow
Wicklow County Archive
Barton papers
Wicklow County Council Minute Book 1916

Location Unknown
Untitled collection of documents compiled by Robert Barton, loaned to Tim Pat
 Coogan by Dr T. P. O'Neill (quoted in Coogan, *Michael Collins*)

United Kingdom
Imperial War Museum
First World War Portraits Collection

Parliamentary Archives
The Representation of the People Act (1918), C. 64.

University of Cambridge, Churchill Archives
Winston Churchill papers

Newspapers and Periodicals

Cork Examiner
Daily Chronicle
Daily Express
Drogheda Independent
Evening Herald
Evening Telegraph
Freeman's Journal
Irish Independent
Irish Press
Irish Weekly Independent
Leinster Leader
Nationalist and Leinster Times
Nationality
Poblacht na h-Eireann/The Republic of Ireland
Sinn Féin Weekly
The Irish Nation
The Irish Times
The Irish World and American Industrial Liberator
The Times
The Weekly Freeman
Weekly Irish Times
Wicklow News-Letter
Wicklow People

Contemporary Publications

Anonymous, *Supplement to the London Gazette*, 7 June 1918.
Barton, Robert, *The Truth about the Treaty and Document No. 2* (Dublin, 1922).
Beaslaí, Piaras, *Michael Collins and the Making of a New Ireland* (2 vols, London, 1926).
Childers, Erskine, *The Riddle of the Sands* (London, 1903; reprint, London, 1979).
Griffith, Arthur, *The Resurrection of Hungary: A Parallel for Ireland* (Dublin, 1904).
Horan, P. K., 'Prisoners in Portobello', in *Methodist Magazine* (1928), pp.434–8.
Horan, P. K., 'Thro' red days', in *Irish Christian Advocate*, 9 March 1928.
MacNeill, Eoin, 'The North Began', *An Claidheamh Soluis*, 1 November 1913.
Macready, Nevil, *Annals of an Active Life* (2 vols, London, 1924).
O'Hegarty, P. S., *The Victory of Sinn Féin* (Dublin, 1924).

SECONDARY SOURCES

Printed Sources

Aldous, Richard (ed), *Great Irish Speeches* (London, 2007).
Andrews, C. S. (Tod), *Dublin Made Me* (Cork, 1979).
Idem, *Man of No Property* (Dublin, 1982; reprint, 2001).
Beckett, J. C., *The Making of Modern Ireland 1603–1923* (London, reprint, 1973).
Bence Jones, Mark, *Burke's Guide to Country Houses: Ireland* (London, 1978).
Bennett, Richard, *The Black and Tans* (London, revised ed., 1970).
Bunbury, Turtle, 'Barton and Childers of Glendalough House', in *The Landed Gentry and Aristocracy of County Wicklow*, vol. 1 (Dublin, 2005), pp.107–27.
Cairns, Henry and Gallagher, Owen, *Aspects of the War of Independence and Civil War in Wicklow 1913–1923* (Bray, 2009).
Cairns, Henry (ed), *Wicklow in Revolt: A History of County Wicklow from 1913–1923* (Bray, 2016).
Coldrey, Barry, *Faith and fatherland: the Christian Brothers and the Development of Irish Nationalism 1838–1921* (Dublin, 1988).
Coleman, Marie, 'Women activists during the Civil War', in Gannon, Darragh and McGarry, Fearghal (eds), *Ireland 1922: independence, partition, civil war* (Dublin, 2022), pp.54–60.
Connell, Joseph E. A. Jr., 'The executions after the Easter Rising', in *History Ireland*, vol. 24, no. 3, (May/June 2016), editorial.
Idem, 'The burning of the Custom House, 25 May 1921', in *History Ireland*, vol. 29, no. 3 (May–June, 2021), pp.29–31.
Connell, Peter (in association with Hayes, Mary), *Eamon Duggan: Counsel to the Revolution* (Meath County Council, 2021).
Connolly, Ross M., 'A rightful place in the sun – the struggle of the farm and rural labourers in County Wicklow', in Ken Hannigan and William Nolan (eds), *Wicklow History and Society* (Dublin, 1994), pp.917–24.

Bibliography

Coogan, Tim Pat, *Michael Collins: A Biography* (London, 2nd ed., 1991).

Idem, *De Valera: Long Fellow, Long Shadow* (London, 1993).

Corish, Patrick J., *The Irish Catholic Experience: A Historical Survey* (Dublin, reprint, 1986).

Idem, 'The Cromwellian regime, 1650–1660', in T. W. Moody, F. X. Martin and F. J. Byrne (eds), *A New History of Ireland: Early Modern Ireland 1534–1691*, vol. iii (Oxford, 1976), pp.353–86.

Cullen, Kevin, 'The R.I.C. and the I.R.A. in Wicklow's War of Independence', in *Journal of the West Wicklow Historical Society*, vii (Naas, 2013) pp.62-72.

Daly, Dominic, *The Young Douglas Hyde* (Dublin, 1974).

Dolan, Anne and Murphy, William, *Michael Collins: The Man and the Revolution* (Cork, 2018).

Donnelly, Brian, *For the Betterment of the People: A History of Wicklow County Council* (Wicklow, 1999).

Dooley, Terence, *Burning the Big House: The Story of the Irish Country House in a Time of War and Revolution* (Yale, 2022).

Idem, 'Irish land questions, 1879–1923', in Thomas Bartlett (ed), *The Cambridge History of Ireland*, iv (4 vols, Cambridge, 2018), pp.117–44.

Durney, James, *The Civil War in Kildare* (Cork, 2011).

Fanning, Ronan, *Fatal Path: the British Government and the Irish Revolution* (London, 2013).

Farry, Michael, *The Aftermath of Revolution: Sligo 1921–23* (Dublin, 2000).

Feehan, John M., *The Shooting of Michael Collins* (Cork, reprint, 1987).

Feeney, Tom, *Seán McEntee: A Political Life* (Dublin, 2009).

Ferriter, Diarmaid, *A Nation and Not a Rabble: The Irish Revolution 1913–1923* (London, 2015).

Idem, *Between Two Hells: the Irish Civil War* (London, 2022).

Idem, *The Transformation of Ireland 1900–2000* (London, 2005).

Fewer, Michael, 'R.C. Barton and Glendalough House', in *Roundwood and District Historical and Folklore Journal*, no. 19 (Greystones, 2008), pp.1–7.

Foster, R. F., *Modern Ireland 1600–1972* (London, 1988).

Idem, *Vivid Faces: The Revolutionary Generation in Ireland* (London, 2014).

Idem., 'Parnell and his neighbours', in Ken Hannigan and William Nolan (eds), *Wicklow History and Society* (Dublin, 1994).

Furneaux Smith, Frederick Winston, *Frederick Edwin, Earl of Birkenhead: The Last Phase* (London, 1933).

Gorry, Paul, *Baltinglass Chronicles 1851–2001* (Dublin, 2006).

Griffith, Kenneth and O'Grady, Timothy, *Curious Journey: An Oral History of Ireland's Unfinished Revolution* (Cork, 1988).

Hart, Peter, *The I.R.A. and its Enemies: Violence and Community in Cork, 1916–1923* (London, 1998).

Henry, William, *Éamonn Ceannt: Supreme Sacrifice* (Cork, 2nd ed, 2012).

Holt, Edgar, *Protest in Arms: The Irish Troubles 1916–1923* (New York, 1960).

Irish Peatland Conservation Council, *Bogs: A New Perspective* (Lullymore?, n.d.).

Kee, Robert, *The Green Flag* (London, 1972).

Kelly, Matthew, 'Radical Nationalisms, 1882–1916', in Thomas Bartlett (ed), *The Cambridge History of Ireland*, iv (4 vols, Cambridge, 2018), pp.33–61.

Laffan, Michael, *The Resurrection of Ireland: The Sinn Féin party 1916–1923* (Cambridge, 1999).

Lawlor, Chris, *A Revolutionary Village: Dunlavin, County Wicklow 1900–25* (Naas, 2021).

Idem, *The Little Book of Kildare* (Dublin, 2015).

Idem, *The Little Book of Wicklow* (Dublin, 2014).

Idem, 'Constance Markievicz: Papal Countess and Irish Rebel', in *Dunlavin Diversions* (Naas, 2020), pp.109–15.

Idem, 'Robert Barton: Wicklow revolutionary and statesman', in Deane, Ciaran (ed), *Wicklow and the War of Independence* (Wicklow, 2021), pp.203–211.

Lee, J. J., *Ireland 1912–1985* (Cambridge, reprint, 1990).

Lee, Kevin, 'The assassination of Coollatin land agent, Frank Brooke, 30 July 1920', in Deane, Ciaran (ed), *Wicklow and the War of Independence* (Wicklow, 2021), pp.83–8.

Levenson, Samuel, *James Connolly: A Biography* (London, 1977).

Llywelyn, Morgan, *Pocket History of Irish Rebels* (Dublin, 2001).

Local Government Archivists and Records Managers, *Democracy and Change: The 1920 Local Elections in Ireland* (Dublin, 2020).

Longford, Lord (Pakenham, Frank), *Peace by Ordeal: An account, from first-hand sources, of the negotiation and signature of the Anglo-Irish Treaty 1921* (London, 1935; reprint 1972).

Lyons, F. S. L., *Charles Stewart Parnell* (Bungay, Suffolk, 1978).

Idem, *Ireland Since the Famine* (London, 4th ed., 1976).

Macardle, Dorothy, *The Irish Republic* (London, 1937; reprint, 1968).

Maguire, Martin, 'Protestant Republicans in the revolution and after', in Ian d'Alton and Ida Milne, *Protestant and Irish* (Cork, 2019), pp.191–212.

Mais, S. P. B., *I Return to Ireland* (London, 1948).

McCabe, Brian, 'A little bit of Bulgaria in Ireland: Pierce O'Mahony (1850–1930), politician and philanthropist', in *Journal of the West Wicklow Historical Society*, xii (Naas, 2023), pp.54–6.

McCullagh, David, 'Truce and Treaty: Why did de Valera not lead the delegation sent to London?', *The Irish Times*, 25 May 2021.

McGee, Owen, *Arthur Griffith* (Sallins, 2015).

McKenna, Kathleen, *A Dáil Girl's Revolutionary Recollections* (Dublin, 2014).

McMahon, Sean, *Rebel Ireland: from Easter Rising to Civil War* (Cork, 2001).

Meehan, Ciara, 'The propaganda war over the Anglo-Irish treaty', in Gannon, Darragh and McGarry, Fearghal (eds), *Ireland 1922: Independence, Partition, Civil War* (Dublin, 2022), pp.71–5.

Milne, Ida, *Stacking the Coffins: Influenza, War and Revolution in Ireland 1918–19* (Manchester, 2018).

Eadem, '"The jersey is all that matters, not your Church": Protestants and the G.A.A. in the rural Republic', in d'Alton and Milne (eds), *Protestant and Irish*, pp.171–190.

Nevin, Donal (ed), *James Connolly: political writings 1893–1916* (Dublin, 2011).

Ó Corráin, Daithí, 'Catholicism in Ireland, 1880–2015: rise, ascendancy and retreat', in Thomas Bartlett (ed), *The Cambridge History of Ireland*, iv (4 vols, Cambridge, 2018), pp.726–64.

O'Donnell, Ruán, *The Rebellion in Wicklow 1798* (Dublin, 1998).

Idem, *Aftermath: Post-Rebellion Insurgency in Wicklow 1799–1803* (Dublin, 2000)

O'Donnell, Peadar, *There Will be Another Day* (Dublin, 1963).

O'Donoghue, Florence, *No Other Law* (Dublin, 1986).

O'Meara, Liam, *From Richmond Barracks to Keogh Square* (Dublin, 2014).

O'Riordan, Manus, 'Larkin in America: the road to Sing Sing', in Donal Nevin (ed), *James Larkin: Lion of the Fold* (Dublin, 1998).

O'Sullivan Greene, Patrick, 'A century on: the Dáil loan that set the State on the road to financial sovereignty', *The Irish Times*, 4 April 2019.

Pakenham, Valerie, *The Big House in Ireland* (London, 2000).

Pyne, Peter, 'The third Sinn Féin party 1923–1926: (1) Narrative account', in *Economic and Social Review*, vol. 1 (Dublin, 1969), pp.29–50.

Riddell, George, *Lord Riddell's Intimate Diary of the Peace Conference and After, 1918–1923* (London, 1933).

Roddie, Robert P., 'Padraig and Eily O'Horan: A story of rebellion and redemption', in *Dublin Historical Record*, vol. 55, no. 1 (2002), pp.75–87.

Ryle Dwyer, T., *De Valera: The Man and the Myths* (Dublin, 1991).

Sloan, Geoffrey, 'Hide seek and negotiate: Alfred Cope and counter intelligence in Ireland 1919–1921', in *Intelligence and National Security*, vol. 33, no. 2 (Oxford, 2018), pp.176–95.

Steglich, Wolfgang, 'The fatal decision', in *History of the Twentieth Century*, no. 24 (2nd ed, London, 1973), pp.646–51.

Timmons, Martin, *Wicklow and the 1916 Rising* (Greystones, 2016).

Townshend, Charles, *The Republic: The Fight for Irish Independence* (London, 2013).

Tynan O'Mahony, Peter (ed), *Eamon De Valera* (Dublin, 1976).

Whelan, Kevin, *Fellowship of Freedom: The United Irishmen and 1798* (Cork, 1998).

Whittle, James (ed), *Sons of St Nicholas: A History of Dunlavin GAA Club* (Dunlavin, 1984).

Wright, Catherine, 'The Barton papers in Wicklow County Archives', in *History Ireland*, no. 4, vol. 29 (July–August, 2021).

Younger, Calton, *Arthur Griffith* (Dublin, 1981).

Idem, *A State of Disunion* (London, 1972).

Unpublished Theses and Essays

Cullen, Kevin, 'The humanitarian wing of Irish Republicanism: the Irish National Aid and Volunteer Dependents' Fund' (M.A. thesis, St Patrick's College, Drumcondra, a college of D.C.U., 2012).

Farrell, Mel, '"Few supporters and no organisation"? Cumann na nGaedheal organisation and policy, 1923–33' (Ph.D. thesis, Maynooth, 2011).

Electronic Sources

Callanan, Frank, 'Healy, Timothy Michael', www.dib.ie/biography/
healy-timothy-michael-a3903

Census of Ireland 1911, form A, 31 Upper Fitzwilliam Street, Dublin, www.census.
nationalarchives.ie/reels/nai000207160

Civil List, www.britannica.com/topic/Civil-List

Clarke, Frances, 'Ceannt, Áine', www.dib.ie/biography/ceannt-aine-a1580

Clearinghouse (finance), www.britannica.com/topic/clearinghouse

Coleman, Marie, 'O'Connor, Bartholomew ('Batt', Phartalán)', www.dib.ie/
biography/oconnor-bartholomew-batt-phartalan-a6582

Coleman, Marie, 'Ó Buachalla (Ua Buachalla), Domhnall (Donal/Daniel Richard
Buckley)', www.dib.ie/biography/o-buachalla-ua-buachalla-domhnall-
donaldaniel-richard-buckley-a6284

D.O.R.A. at Westminster, www.rarebooks.ie/shop/books/d.o.r.a.-at-westminster

Debate on the treaty, 19 December 1921, www.oireachtas.ie/en/debates/debate/
dail/1921-12-19/2

Debate on the treaty, 20 December 1921, www.oireachtas.ie/en/debates/debate/
dail/1921-12-20/2

Debate on the treaty, 21 December 1921, www.oireachtas.ie/en/debates/debate/
dail/1921-12-21/2

Debate on the treaty, 22 December 1921, www.oireachtas.ie/en/debates/debate/
dail/1921-12-22/2

Debate on the treaty, 3 January 1921, www.oireachtas.ie/en/debates/debate/
dail/1922-01-03/2

Debate on the treaty, 4 January 1921, www.oireachtas.ie/en/debates/debate/
dail/1922-01-04/2

Dempsey, Pauric and Boylan, Shaun, 'Barton, Robert Childers', www.dib.ie/
biography/barton-robert-childers-a0485

Dempsey, Pauric, and Boylan, Shaun, 'Broy, Eamon ("Ned")', www.dib.ie/
biography/broy-eamon-ned-a1067

Dempsey, Pauric, 'Byrne, Christopher Michael ("Christy", "C. M.")', www.dib.ie/
biography/byrne-christopher-michael-christy-c-m-a1321

Dolan, Anne, 'Lemass, Noel Denis Joseph', www.dib.ie/biography/lemass-noel-
denis-joseph-a4785

Donegan, Conor, 'Charlie McGuinness and the Freida gun run to Waterford,
November 1921', tidesandtales.ie/charlie-mcguinness-and-the-freida-gun-run-
to-waterford-november-1921

Draft Treaty A, https://celt.ucc.ie/published/E900019/index.html

Dredge, John, online lecture about Robert Barton at www.richmondbarracks.ie/
festival-of-history-2019/robert-barton-the-wicklow-landlord-who-became-a-
key-player-in-the-struggle-for-independence-1918-1922

Fanning, Ronan, 'Mulcahy, Richard', www.dib.ie/biography/mulcahy-richard-a6029

Ferriter, Diarmaid, 'Peace by ordeal: how the treaty was signed', www.rte.ie/
history/treaty/2021/1108/1258552-how-the-treaty-was-signed

Field Marshal Sir John French, www.iwm.org.uk/collections/item/
  object/205016677

Gallagher, Niav, 'Hoey, Patricia', www.dib.ie/biography/hoey-patricia-a10154

Gallagher, Michael, 'The 1922 pact election', www.rte.ie/history/
  pact-election/2022/0404/1290254-the-1922-pact-election

Gaughan, Anthony J., 'Stack, Austin', www.dib.ie/biography/stack-austin-a8231

General election in the United Kingdom, www.dail100.ie/en/timeline

History Ireland hedge school, 'Robert Barton: forgotten man of the Irish
  Revolution?' heritage.wicklowheritage.org/new-contributions/latest-wicklow-
  podcast-robert-barton-forgotten-man-of-the-irish-revolution

History of 1877: the old Portsmouth Gaol, www.cityandcountry.co.uk/history-of-
  1877-the-old-portsmouth-gaol

Irish general election 1922, irishpoliticalmaps.blogspot.com/2012/08/irish-general-
  election-1922.html

Kildare Wicklow 1922, https://electionsireland.org/result.
  cfm?election=1922&cons=144

Lawlor, Chris, 'The Dunlavin tragedy: murder, suicide and the execution of
  William Mitchell in 1921', https://heritage.wicklowheritage.org/places/
  dunlavin-2/the-dunlavin-tragedy-murder-suicide-and-the-execution-of-
  william-mitchell-in-1921

Lawlor, Chris, 'Robert Barton, Sinn Féin M.P.', https://heritage.wicklowheritage.
  org/topics/together-apart-wicklow-2020-stories/dunlavin-diversions/dunlavin-
  diversions-21-30/25-robert-barton-sinn-fein-mp#_ednref12

Letters of 1916, Robert Barton to Kathleen Lynn, https://letters1916.ie/item/842

Letters of 1916, Robert Barton to Mabel Fitzgerald, https://letters1916.ie/item/1471

Maolmhuire, www.libraryireland.com/names/men/maolmhuire-meyler.php

Maume, Patrick, 'Walsh, James Joseph', www.dib.ie/biography/walsh-
  james-joseph-a8874

Maume, Patrick, 'Beaslaí, Piaras', www.dib.ie/biography/beaslai-piaras-a0515

Maume, Patrick, 'Sears, David', www.dib.ie/biography/sears-david-a7965

Maume, Patrick, 'Sears, William', www.dib.ie/biography/sears-william-a7966

Maume, Patrick, 'McKenna, Kathleen Napoli', www.dib.ie/biography/mckenna-
  kathleen-napoli-a9612

Message to the free nations of the world, www.difp.ie/docs/1919/Message-to-the-
  Free-Nations-of-the-World/2.htm

Minutes of Cabinet meeting on 8 December 1921, www.difp.ie/volume-1/1921/
  minutes-of-a-cabinet-meeting-held-on-8-december-1921/215/#section-
  documentpage

Mr James O'Connor, www.theyworkforyou.com/mp/15651/james_o%27connor/
  wicklow_west

Murphy, Meadhbh, 'Mother, father and ideal friend' https://ucdculturalheritagecol-
  lections.com/2018/10/04/mother-father-and-ideal-friend

Murphy, William, 'Figgis, Darrell', www.dib.ie/biography/figgis-darrell-a3078

Murphy, William, 'O'Connor, Arthur James Kickham ("Art")', www.dib.ie/
biography/oconnor-arthur-james-kickham-art-a6581

Noel Lemass (1897 – 1923) in the I.M.S.C., https://militarypensions.wordpress.
com/2023/07/03/noel-lemass-1897-1923-in-the-mspc

Notes by Erskine Childers on a Cabinet meeting, 8 December 1921, www.difp.ie/
volume-1/1921/cabinet-meeting-of-december-8-1921-copy-of-notes-taken-by-
erskine-childers/216/#section-documentpage

Nowlan, Emer, 'Arthur Griffith's contribution to Irish independence', https://
theanglo-irishtreatydelegations1921.org/arthur-griffith

Number 23 Campden Hill Square, Kensington, www.flickr.com/photos/24671749@
N07/5597713567

O'Connor Lysaght, D. R., 'Plunkett, Count George Noble', www.dib.ie/
biography/plunkett-count-george-noble-a7384

O'Halpin, Eunan, 'Cosgrave, William Thomas', www.dib.ie/biography/cosgrave-
william-thomas-a2077

Paseta, Senia, 'Markievicz, Constance Georgine', www.dib.ie/biography/
markievicz-constance-georgine-a5452

Peace negotiations, www.oireachtas.ie/en/debates/debate/dail/1921-09-14/2

Phoenix Park, www.facebook.com/BarroughterAndClonmoylanBogsActionGroup

Quinn, James, 'Brugha, Cathal', www.dib.ie/biography/brugha-cathal-a1077

Raising the Banner: The East Clare By-Election, July 1917, https://erinascendant-
wordpress.wordpress.com/2020/07/10/raising-the-banner-the-east-clare-by-
election-july-1917

Ratification of plenipotentiaries, 14 September 1921 (Dáil debates, 2nd Dáil, vol. S,
no. 10), www.oireachtas.ie/en/debates/debate/dail/1921-09-14/3

Report on agriculture, 17 August 1921 (Dáil debates, 2nd Dáil, vol. S, no. 2), www.
oireachtas.ie/en/debates/debate/dail/1921-08-17/16

Richmond Barracks, www.dublincity.ie/residential/environment/waste-and-
recycling/find-recycling-centre/dun-richmond

RTE archives, *Standing for Election 1919*, 'Interview with Robert Barton', www.rte.
ie/archives/exhibitions/920-first-dail-eireann-1919/139408-an-chead-dail-1919

Sinn Féin Weekly, www.irishnewsarchive.com/sinn-fein-weekly-

The 10th battalion, Royal Dublin Fusiliers, www.wartimememoriesproject.com/
greatwar/allied/battalion.php?pid=6090

The 1918 Representation of the People Act, www.parliament.uk/about/living-
heritage/transformingsociety/electionsvoting/womenvote/case-study-the-
right-to-vote/the-right-to-vote/birmingham-and-the-equal-franchise/1918-
representation-of-the-people-act

The burning of the Customs House, www.gov.ie/en/press-release/eb1c0-100-years-
ago-today-the-burning-of-the-custom-house

The Republican Loan film 1919, www.youtube.com/watch?v=5CfrkvE7_hs

The treaty debates, www.oireachtas.ie/en/visit-and-learn/centenaries/
treaty-debates/explore-the-treaty-debates

Tierney, Mark, 'Sweetman, John Francis', www.dib.ie/biography/sweetman-john-francis-a8407

Traynor, Jack, 'Jan Smuts and the Anglo-Irish truce of July 1921', www.theirishstory.com/2023/02/14/jan-smuts-and-the-anglo-irish-truce-of-july-1921/#_edn33

Truce Liaison and Evacuation Papers (1921–1922), www.militaryarchives.ie/collections/reading-room-collections/truce-liaison-and-evacuation-papers-1921-1922

Walter Leonard Cole, 3 Mountjoy Square, www.oliversearsgallery.com/walter-leonard-cole-3-mountjoy-square

West, Trevor, 'Plunkett, Sir Horace Curzon', www.dib.ie/biography/plunkett-sir-horace-curzon-a7385

White, Lawrence William, 'O'Connor, Roderick (Rory)', www.dib.ie/biography/oconnor-roderick-rory-a6614

White, Lawrence William, 'MacDonagh, Joseph', www.dib.ie/biography/macdonagh-joseph-a5162

Wicklow 1923, https://electionsireland.org/result.cfm?election=1923&cons=235

Wicklow election poster (1918), catalogue.nli.ie/Record/vtls000266109

Wicklow West (1918), https://electionsireland.org/result.cfm?election=1918&cons=237

Woods, C. J., 'Gill, Thomas Patrick', www.dib.ie/biography/gill-thomas-patrick-a3476

Works of Reference

Webster's Third New International Dictionary, vol. ii (Chicago, 1986).

Endnotes

INTRODUCTION

Rationale and Background

1   This 'Hedge School' is available online at heritage.wicklowheritage.org/
    new-contributions/latest-wicklow-podcast-robert-barton-forgotten-man-of-
    the-irish-revolution (visited on 25 January 2024).

A Note on Sources

2   Chris Lawlor, *The Little Book of Wicklow* (Dublin, 2014).
3   Michael Fewer, 'R. C. Barton and Glendalough House', in *Roundwood and
    District Historical and Folklore Journal*, no. 19 (Greystones, 2008).
4   Catherine Wright, 'The Barton papers in Wicklow County Archives', in *History
    Ireland*, no. 4, vol. 29 (Jul–Aug, 2021).
5   Turtle Bunbury, 'Barton and Childers of Glendalough House', in *The Landed
    Gentry and Aristocracy of County Wicklow*, vol. 1 (Dublin, 2005).
6   Pauric Dempsey and Shaun Boylan, 'Barton, Robert Childers', in *Dictionary of
    Irish Biography*, available at www.dib.ie/biography/barton-robert-childers-a0485
    (visited on 9 January 2023).
7   Lord Longford (Frank Pakenham), *Peace by Ordeal: an account, from first-hand sources, of
    the negotiation and signature of the Anglo-Irish Treaty 1921* (London, 1935; reprint 1972).
8   Dorothy Macardle, *The Irish Republic* (London, 1937; reprint, 1968).
9   Chris Lawlor, *A Revolutionary Village: Dunlavin, County Wicklow 1900–25* (Naas, 2021).
10 Patrick J. Corish, 'The Cromwellian regime, 1650–1660', in T. W. Moody,
    F. X. Martin and F. J. Byrne (eds), *A New History of Ireland: Early Modern Ireland
    1534–1691*, vol. iii (Oxford, 1976), pp.385–6.

CHAPTER 1

1   Kevin Whelan, *Fellowship of Freedom: the United Irishmen and 1798* (Cork, 1998), p.25 and Morgan Llywelyn, *Pocket history of Irish Rebels* (Dublin, 2001), p.29. Tone's father was a successful businessman.

2   F. S. L. Lyons, *Charles Stewart Parnell* (Bungay, Suffolk, 1978), p.21. Lyons says that Parnell's father, John Henry, 'took naturally to the life of a country gentleman, acting right by his tenants and playing his part as a squire of the manor in the duties, as well as the pleasures, of the countryside'.

3   Chris Lawlor, 'Constance Markievicz: Papal Countess and Irish Rebel', in *Dunlavin Diversions* (Naas, 2020), p.109. See also Senia Paseta, 'Markievicz, Constance Georgine', in *Dictionary of Irish Biography* (hereafter D.I.B.), available at www.dib.ie/biography/markievicz-constance-georgine-a5452 (visited on 1 January 2021).

4   Pauric Dempsey and Shaun Boylan, 'Barton, Robert Childers', in *D.I.B.*, available at www.dib.ie/biography/barton-robert-childers-a0485 (visited on 9 January 2023).

5   Wicklow County Archive [hereafter WW.C.A.], Barton Papers, Abstinence card of Robert Barton, 14 September 1894, WWCA/PP1/16.

6   Irish Military Archives [hereafter I.M.A.], Bureau of Military History [hereafter B.M.H.], witness statement of Robert C. Barton, Glendalough House, Annamoe, Co. Wicklow, WS979, p.9.

7   R. F. Foster, 'Parnell and his neighbours', in Ken Hannigan and William Nolan (eds), *Wicklow History and Society* (Dublin, 1994), p.908. Foster refers to Barton senior as 'John', rather than 'Charles'.

8   Fewer, 'R. C. Barton and Glendalough House', p.6.

9   Ibid., p.1.

10 Valerie Pakenham, *The Big House in Ireland* (London, 2000), p.13.

11 Terence Dooley, *Burning the Big House: The Story of the Irish Country House in a Time of War and Revolution* (Yale, 2022), p.5. For example, the smaller, more modest Tynte Park House, Dunlavin (like Glendalough House also dating from the 1830s), is a case in point.

12 Mark Bence Jones, *Burke's Guide to Country Houses: Ireland* (London, 1978), pp.137–8.

13 S.P.B. Mais, *I Return to Ireland* (London, 1948), pp.129–33 passim.

14 On Thomas Hugo's anti-insurgency activity during this turbulent period, see Ruán O'Donnell, *The Rebellion in Wicklow 1798* (Dublin, 1998), pp.55, 75–6, 92, 125, 128 183, 227, 308 and 369; and Ruán O'Donnell, *Aftermath: Post-Rebellion Insurgency in Wicklow 1799–1803* (Dublin, 2000), pp.41, 52–3, 59, 98, 187 and 190.

15 RTE archives, *Standing for election 1919*, 'Interview with Robert Barton', available at www.rte.ie/archives/exhibitions/920-first-dail-eireann-1919/139408-an-chead-dail-1919 (visited on 12 August 2021).

16 One could draw a comparison here with the boyhood of Douglas Hyde (another Protestant), who also absorbed quite a lot of national sympathies as a boy. On Hyde's absorption of the unwritten Irish tradition, see Dominic Daly, *The Young Douglas Hyde* (Dublin, 1974), passim, especially pp.1–29. However, in Hyde's

case, his interest manifested itself mainly in language and culture, while Barton's was much more political in nature.

17 National Archives of Ireland [hereafter N.A.I.], Private accession 1093, Robert Barton papers, 'Glendalough House and Annamoe: history, reminiscences and folklore', PRIV1093/13.

18 RTE archives, *Standing for Election 1919*, 'Interview with Robert Barton', available at www.rte.ie/archives/exhibitions/920-first-dail-eireann-1919/139408-an-chead-dail-1919 (visited on 12 August 2021).

19 Mais, *I Return to Ireland*, p.133.

20 For a brief account of the fortunes of the agricultural labourers in County Wicklow during the existence of the Irish Free State, see Ross M. Connolly, 'A rightful place in the sun – the struggle of the farm and rural labourers in County Wicklow', in Hannigan and Nolan (eds), *Wicklow History and Society* (Dublin, 1994), pp.917–24.

21 Conversations with two local people in the County Wicklow village of Dunlavin in 1998. Both of them have since died, but both retained a sense of being wronged by the Land Commission, which came forcefully to the fore during our conversations.

CHAPTER 2

1 Dempsey and Boylan, 'Barton, Robert Childers', in *D.I.B.* available at www.dib.ie/biography/barton-robert-childers-a0485 (visited on 9/1/2023). See also WW.C.A., Barton Papers, Diploma examination docket from the Royal Agricultural College, Cirencester, WWCA/PP1/17. Unfortunately, this document is merely dated 'December 18'; there is no year mentioned. I am indebted to Peter Brooks, Archivist, Royal Agricultural University, Cirencester, who confirmed that Barton was awarded Membership of the College by Diploma (MRAC) in 1901.

2 WW.C.A., Barton Papers, Diploma in Economics from the University of Oxford, 13 June 1908, WWCA/PP1/19.

3 Brian McCabe, 'A little bit of Bulgaria in Ireland: Pierce O'Mahony (1850–1930), politician and philanthropist', in *Journal of the West Wicklow Historical Society*, xii (Naas, 2023), p.55.

4 Ibid.

5 *The Times*, 24 April 1975.

6 Mais, *I Return to Ireland*, p.10.

7 Ibid., p.12. The acronym O.T.C. stands for Officers' Training Corps.

8 Longford (Pakenham), *Peace by Ordeal*, p.113.

9 I.M.A., B.M.H., witness statement of Dulcibella Barton, Hazelbrook, Terenure Road West, Dublin, WS936, p.1. She goes on to describe how 'our mother, who was English, would be reading the *London Times*, and we two would be devouring *Sinn Féin*'.

10 www.irishnewsarchive.com/sinn-fein-weekly- (visited on 27 April 1923).

11   Dempsey and Boylan, 'Barton, Robert Childers', in *D.I.B.*, available at www. dib.ie/biography/barton-robert-childers-a0485 (visited on 9 January 2023).

12   Economically, Griffith believed that Ireland should be as self-sufficient as possible, and he advocated a policy of protectionism for indigenous Irish industries, akin to the Frederick List-influenced economic policies in Germany after the unification of the empire in 1871. See Arthur Griffith, *The Resurrection of Hungary: A Parallel for Ireland* (Dublin, 1904), passim. For an overview of and commentary on Griffith's political and economic policies, see Owen McGee, *Arthur Griffith* (Sallins, 2015) pp.73–95.

13   R. F. Foster, *Modern Ireland 1600–1972* (London, 1988), p.504.

14   Trevor West, 'Plunkett, Sir Horace Curzon', in *D.I.B.* available at www.dib.ie/ biography/plunkett-sir-horace-curzon-a7385 (visited on 26 January 2024).

15   John Dredge, online lecture about Robert Barton at www.richmondbarracks. ie/festival-of-history-2019/robert-barton-the-wicklow-landlord-who-became-a-key-player-in-the-struggle-for-independence-1918-1922 (visited on 3 August 2021). See also Bunbury, *The Landed Gentry … of County Wicklow*, p.117.

16   Martin Maguire, 'Protestant Republicans in the revolution and after', in Ian d'Alton and Ida Milne, *Protestant and Irish* (Cork, 2019), p.196.

17   Lawlor, *The Little Book of Wicklow*, p.105.

18   On Griffith, see McGee, *Arthur Griffith*, and Calton Younger, *Arthur Griffith* (Dublin, 1981).

19   Eoin MacNeill, 'The North Began', *An Claidheamh Soluis,* 1 November 1913.

20   On the various small Irish revolutionary organisations during this period, see Matthew Kelly, 'Radical Nationalisms, 1882–1916', in Thomas Bartlett (ed), *The Cambridge History of Ireland*, iv (4 vols, Cambridge, 2018), pp.33–61.

21   I.M.A., B.M.H., Robert C. Barton, WS979, p.8. Barton uses the term 'Sinn Féin leaders' to denote those who went on to stage the Easter Rising, as Sinn Féin were erroneously but serendipitously blamed for staging the rebellion during its immediate aftermath.

22   Childers, the author of *The Riddle of the Sands* (London, 1903), was an expert on nautical matters. His naval intelligence officer's notebook contains a wealth of information and sketches of vessels that would be of interest to any student of naval warfare during the early twentieth century. Manuscripts and Archives Library, Trinity College Dublin, Papers of Robert Erskine and Mary Childers, TCD, MS 11299, ff 1–23v.

23   I.M.A., B.M.H., Robert C. Barton, WS979, p.9.

24   W.W.C.A., Barton Papers, Recommendation from Captain Booth for Robert Childers Barton, 17 December 1915, WWCA/PP1/21. Captain Erskine Booth was later appointed as Assistant Director of Vegetable Supplies, Ministry of Food. [*Supplement to the London Gazette*, 7 June 1918, p.6696.] This letter is reproduced in full in Appendix 1.

25   Dempsey and Boylan, 'Barton, Robert Childers', in *D.I.B.*, available at www. dib.ie/biography/barton-robert-childers-a0485 (visited on 9 January 2023).

CHAPTER 3

1   I.M.A., B.M.H., Robert C. Barton, WS979, p.1. The effect of the Rising on the city centre may also be seen by viewing a number of postcards in WW.C.A., Barton Papers, Postcards of historic interest, WWCA/PP1/33.

2   I.M.A., B.M.H., Robert C. Barton, WS979, p.1.

3   I.M.A., B.M.H., Dulcibella Barton, WS936, p.3.

4   I.M.A., B.M.H., Robert C. Barton, WS979, p.1.

5   I.M.A., B.M.H., Dulcibella Barton, WS936, p.3.

6   Liam O'Meara, *From Richmond Barracks to Keogh Square* (Dublin, 2014), p.269.

7   Richmond Barracks www.dublincity.ie/residential/environment/waste-and-recycling/find-recycling-centre/dun-richmond (visited on 8 May 2023).

8   I.M.A., B.M.H., Robert C. Barton, WS979, pp.1–2. This information is confirmed in I.M.A., B.M.H., Dulcibella Barton, WS936, p.3. She cites the case of the recovery of a watch from a 'high-ranking British officer'. The watch had been 'stolen from a publican in Camden Street'.

9   O'Meara, *From Richmond Barracks to Keogh Square*, p.299.

10 Longford (Pakenham), *Peace by Ordeal*, p.113.

11 I.M.A., B.M.H., Robert C. Barton, WS979, p.2.

12 Letters of 1916, Robert Barton to Mabel Fitzgerald, letters1916.ie/item/1471 (visited on 9 May 2023). Mabel Fitzgerald was the wife of Irish Volunteer Desmond Fitzgerald. She had been a governess in London, and she actively lobbied her former Liberal friends in London to support Francis Sheehy Skeffington during his hunger strike in 1915. Skeffington opposed the First World War and had become increasingly involved with pacifism. He was incarcerated in 1915 for 'making statements likely to prejudice recruitment of His Majesty's forces'. He went on hunger strike and was released under the 'Cat and Mouse Act' shortly afterwards. Both Mabel and Desmond Fitzgerald would serve in the G.P.O. garrison during Easter Week, but Padraig Pearse didn't want both parents of young children involved, so he sent her home.

13 I.M.A., B.M.H., Robert C. Barton, WS979, p.3.

14 Letters of 1916, Robert Barton to Kathleen Lynn, letters1916.ie/item/842 (visited on 9 May 2023). Kathleen Lynn was a medical doctor, an Irish nationalist, a female suffragist and a revolutionary. She was also involved in the Labour movement and supported the workers during the 1913 lockout. She supported and befriended James Connolly, becoming involved with the Irish Citizens' Army [I.C.A.]. She was the I.C.A.'s Chief Medical Officer during the Easter Rising, and was stationed at City Hall. She took command of the garrison there after the death of Seán Connolly, who was killed on the first day of hostilities. She was arrested and imprisoned after the Rising.

15 Joseph E. A. Connell Jr., 'The executions after the Easter Rising', in *History Ireland*, vol. 24, no. 3 (May/June 2016), editorial. Connell notes that 'while Major Heathcote was identified as the commander, the regiment followed the custom of not identifying the men who were in the firing squad, and the regimental records have no listing of the squad members'.

16   I.M.A., B.M.H., Robert C. Barton, WS979, p.4.

17   On Connolly, see Samuel Levenson, *James Connolly: A Biography* (London, 1977) and Donal Nevin (ed), James Connolly: *Political Writings 1893–1916* (Dublin, 2011).

18   I.M.A., B.M.H., Robert C. Barton, WS979, pp.4–5.

19   O'Meara, *From Richmond Barracks to Keogh Square*, pp.280–1. For accounts of some of the courts martial held at the barracks, see pp.280–98.

20   On MacEntee, see Tom Feeney, *Seán McEntee: A Political Life* (Dublin, 2009).

21   I.M.A., B.M.H., Robert C. Barton, WS979, p.6.

22   The Wartime Memories Project www.wartimememoriesproject.com/greatwar/allied/battalion.php?pid=6090 (visited on 15 May 2023).

23   *Irish Independent*, 26, 27, 28, 29 April and 1, 2, 3, 4 May 1916.

24   *Weekly Irish Times*, 29 April and 6 and 13 May 1916.

25   *The Irish World and American Industrial Liberator*, 13 May 1916.

26   *Leinster Leader and Nationalist and Leinster Times*, both 13 May 1916.

27   I.M.A., B.M.H., Robert C. Barton, WS979, p.8.

28   Darrell Figgis was a writer and propagandist for the Irish nationalist cause. He was involved in the Howth gun running of 1914. He was not directly involved in the 1916 Rising, but was imprisoned during its aftermath. [William Murphy, 'Figgis, Darrell', in *D.I.B.*, available at www.dib.ie/biography/figgis-darrell-a3078 (visited on 18 May 2023)].

29   I.M.A., B.M.H., William O'Brien, WS1766, pp.20–1.

30   I.M.A., B.M.H., Robert C. Barton, WS979, p.10.

31   Following the party's árd fheis (convention) in October 1917, this energised, resurgent, 'second' Sinn Féin party had a younger demographic. It was led by de Valera as president (with Griffith as vice-president) and, crucially, it now aimed at a republic rather than a dual monarchy.

32   I.M.A., B.M.H., Robert Kinsella, WS1346, p.11. Kinsella was a member of the Irish volunteers and was involved the Rising in County Wexford. He was arrested in Ferns and imprisoned for a while after the Rising. Following his release, he became a member of the North Wexford flying column and took the pro-treaty side in the Civil War, joining the National Army in 1922. (Information taken from his witness statement.)

33   I.M.A., B.M.H., Mrs Batt O'Connor, WS330, pp.3–4. Batt O'Connor was a member of the Gaelic League and the Irish Volunteers, but was not directly involved in the Easter Rising. Nonetheless, he was arrested and held for a time in Richmond Barracks, before being shipped off to Wandsworth Prison and eventually to Frongoch, North Wales. He was involved in the War of Independence, took the pro-treaty side in the Civil War and later became a Cumann na nGaedheal T.D. His wife, Bridget (nee Dennehey), was also an activist, and she hosted many republican meetings at her house, which she also provided for use as a safe house during the War of Independence. The national loan (raised by Michael Collins and in which Batt O'Connor was also involved) was also hidden on the premises. [Marie Coleman, 'O'Connor, Bartholomew ('Batt', Phartalán), in *D.I.B.*, available at www.dib.ie/biography/oconnor-bartholomew-batt-phartalan-a6582 (visited on 19 May 2023).]

34 A member of the Dublin volunteers, Hehir was holidaying for Easter 1916 in his native Clare. On hearing of the Rising, he hurried back to the city, but was arrested on arrival and eventually interned in Frongoch. He was released in August 1916. Having been fired from his job in the civil service, Hehir returned to Clare, where he claimed credit for the setting up of one of the first Sinn Féin clubs in the county. He was later involved in the republican courts in County Clare. [erinascendantwordpress.wordpress.com/2020/07/10/raising-the-banner-the-east-clare-by-election-july-1917 (visited on 19 May 2023).]
35 I.M.A., B.M.H., Hugh Hehir, WS683, p.6.
36 Chris Lawlor, 'Robert Barton: Wicklow revolutionary and statesman', in Ciaran Deane (ed), *Wicklow and the War of Independence* (Wicklow, 2021), p.203.
37 Macardle, *The Irish Republic*, p.176.
38 Longford (Pakenham), *Peace by Ordeal*, p.113.

CHAPTER 4

1 Thomas Patrick Gill served as Secretary of the Department of Agriculture and Technical Instruction for Ireland from its inception in 1900 until he retired from the post in 1923. [C. J. Woods, 'Gill, Thomas Patrick' in *D.I.B.*, available at www.dib.ie/biography/gill-thomas-patrick-a3476 (visited on 22 May 2023).]
2 On the decision to renew unrestricted U-boat warfare and its consequences, see Wolfgang Steglich, 'The fatal decision', in *History of the twentieth century*, no. 24 (2nd ed, London, 1973), pp.646–51. Though effective in the short term, the principal long-term consequence of the decision was that it prompted the U.S.A. to enter the war.
3 I.M.A., B.M.H., Robert C. Barton, WS979, p.7.
4 In his witness statement, Barton makes this point in relation to another officer. Ibid., pp.6–7.
5 Mais, *I Return to Ireland*, p.131. Writing in 1948, Mais was referring to Barton's incarceration during the War of Independence (1919–21). However, Barton's conversion to republicanism was completed by late 1918.
6 Foster, 'Parnell and his neighbours', p.908.
7 I.M.A., B.M.H., Robert C. Barton, WS979, p.8.
8 Census of Ireland, 1901, Form A, Residents of a house 23 in Drummin (Glendalough, Wicklow), available online at census.nationalarchives.ie/pages/1901/Wicklow/Glendalough/Drummin/1812581 (visited on 22 February 2024). Agnes was 53 in 1901.
9 W.W.C.A., Barton Papers, Inland Revenue form regarding property chargeable with estate duty on the death of Agnes Barton (18 November 1918), undated, but 1919, WWCA/PP1/22.
10 RTE archives, *Standing for election 1919*, 'Interview with Robert Barton', available at www.rte.ie/archives/exhibitions/920-first-dail-eireann-1919/139408-an-chead-dail-1919 (visited on 12 August 2021).

11 Wicklow County Archive, Wicklow County Council Minute Book 1916, ff 650 and 660.
12 Ibid., f. 663.
13 Brian Donnelly, *For the Betterment of the People: A History of Wicklow County Council* (Wicklow, 1999), p.35.
14 Wicklow County Archive, Wicklow County Council Minute Book 1916, f. 685.
15 Martin Timmons, *Wicklow and the 1916 Rising* (Greystones, 2016), p.42.
16 *Leinster Leader*, 17 June 1916.
17 Timmons, *Wicklow and the 1916 Rising*, p.42.
18 *Wicklow People*, 30 December 1916.
19 *Wicklow People*, 14 April 1917.
20 Younger, *Arthur Griffith*, pp.60–7. See also McGee, *Arthur Griffith*, pp.163–172.
21 National Library of Ireland [hereafter N.L.I.], 1918 Election Handbill, Department of Ephemera, EPH B231.
22 www.rarebooks.ie/shop/books/d.o.r.a.-at-westminster (visited on 17 January 2019). Other speakers at the meeting included Alderman Walter Cole, personal friend of Arthur Griffith and honorary secretary of Sinn Féin in 1917. [ucdculturalheritagecollections.com/2018/10/04/mother-father-and-ideal-friend (visited on 17 January 2019)].
23 *Nationalist and Leinster Times*, 27 October 1917.
24 *Leinster Leader*, 8 August 1917.
25 Younger, *Arthur Griffith*, p.67. See also *Nationality*, 3 November 1917.
26 *The Irish Nation*, 3 November 1917.
27 I.M.A., I.R.A. brigade activity reports, MSPC/A67, f. 73.
28 Ida Milne, *Stacking the Coffins: Influenza, War and Revolution in Ireland 1918–19* (Manchester, 2018), p.5.
29 Ibid., pp.21–9 and 63–6.
30 *Evening Herald*, 31 October 1918.
31 I am indebted to the Hon. Bernard Barton for this information.
32 Lloyd George had adopted a conciliatory approach to the Irish problem at this stage, mindful of the need to mollify American public opinion regarding events in Ireland, in order to persuade the U.S.A. to join the war on the Allied side.
33 Plunkett was widely respected on both sides of the politico-religious divide because of his work with the Irish co-operative movement. Trevor West, 'Plunkett, Sir Horace Curzon', in *D.I.B.*, available at www.dib.ie/biography/plunkett-sir-horace-curzon-a7385 (visited on 22 May 2023).
34 I.M.A., B.M.H., Dulcibella Barton, WS936, p.8.
35 I am indebted to the Hon. Bernard Barton for this information.
36 I.M.A., B.M.H., Dulcibella Barton, WS936, p.9.
37 Piaras Beaslaí, *Michael Collins and the Making of a New Ireland* (2 vols, London, 1926), vol. ii, p.110.
38 I.M.A., B.M.H., Dulcibella Barton, WS936, p.4.

CHAPTER 5

1   WW.C.A., Barton Papers, Recommendation from Captain Booth for Robert Childers Barton, 17 December 1915, WWCA/PP1/21.

2   I.M.A., B.M.H., Robert C. Barton, WS979, p.10. See also I.M.A., B.M.H., Dulcibella Barton, WS936, p.4.

3   Sinn Féin was in a very strong position, enjoying the support of the Volunteers, Cumann na mBan, the Gaelic League and many other nationalist organisations. They had over 100,000 members in about 1,200 active Cumainn across the island. The inactive and declining Irish Parliamentary Party, on the other hand, failed to run candidates in opposition to Sinn Féin in twenty-five constituencies, Even John Dillon was despondent about the lack of organisation within his party. [Diarmaid Ferriter, *A Nation and Not a Rabble: The Irish Revolution 1913–1923* (London, 2015), pp.170–84 passim.]

4   McCabe, 'A little bit of Bulgaria in Ireland', p.55.

5   I.M.A., B.M.H., Robert C. Barton, WS979, p.10.

6   The reference to the 'dead votes' concedes that some votes in this election were cast by deceased people. Some voters cast more than one vote, in the spirit of the slogan 'vote early and often'. However, given the large majority of the Sinn Féin victory, it is inconceivable that these tactics materially affected the overall result.

7   I.M.A., B.M.H., Robert C. Barton, WS979, pp.10–11.

8   Parliamentary Archives, London, Representation of the People Act, 1918, c. 64.

9   www.parliament.uk/about/living-heritage/transformingsociety/electionsvoting/womenvote/case-study-the-right-to-vote/the-right-to-vote/birmingham-and-the-equal-franchise/1918-representation-of-the-people-act/ (visited on 12 November 2019). The franchise was also extended to all males of 21 years of age and over.

10   catalogue.nli.ie/Record/vtls000266109 (visited on 12 November 2019).

11   I.M.A, M.P.S.C., pension claim 42858 of William Esmonde, p.5 and pension claim 44810 of Thomas Kirwan, p.5. It is probably safe to assume that the rest of the county's volunteer force was also engaged in these and similar activities.

12   *Irish Weekly Independent*, 25 May 1918.

13   *Irish Independent*, 30 December 1918. Robert Barton's poll in West Wicklow is given as 6,289 both in this newspaper and on electionsireland.org/result.cfm?election=1918&cons=237 (visited on 22 January 2019).

14   *Wicklow People*, 4 January 1919. The figure for Robert Barton is erroneously given as 6,839 in this newspaper.

15   Fleming's percentage was slightly inaccurate. Over 75 per cent of voters had chosen Robert Barton. In the general election of 1918, the West Wicklow electorate of 11,683 (7,898 men and 3,775 women) had a total poll of 7,609 (65.18 per cent) who voted thus: 6,239 (82 per cent) for Robert Barton (Sinn Féin) and 1,370 (18 per cent) for The O'Mahony (Irish Party); a Sinn Féin majority of 64 per cent. [electionsireland.org/result.cfm?election=1918&cons=237 (visited on 22 January 2019)].

16   *Nationalist and Leinster Times*, 4 January 1919.

17 Paul Gorry, *Baltinglass Chronicles 1851–2001* (Dublin, 2006), p.172.
18 I.M.A., B.M.H., Robert C. Barton, WS979, pp.11–12.
19 www.flickr.com/photos/24671749@N07/5597713567 (visited on 23 May 2023).
    The address is erroneously given as 'Camden Hill' in Barton's witness statement.
20 James O'Connor was elected as M.P. for West Wicklow on 4 July 1892. He
    served until 1 October 1900, when he was re-elected, sitting for a further ten
    years until 12 March 1910. He succeeded Garret Byrne and was succeeded by
    Edward O'Kelly. [www.theyworkforyou.com/mp/15651/james_o%27connor/
    wicklow_west (visited on 12 April 2015).] O'Connor's Christian name is
    erroneously given as 'Charles' in Barton's witness statement.
21 I.M.A., B.M.H., Robert C. Barton, WS979, p.12.
22 www.dail100.ie/en/timeline (visited on 23 May 2023).
23 *Evening Telegraph*, 22 January 1919.
24 J. J. Lee, *Ireland 1912–1985* (Cambridge, reprint, 1990), pp.40–1.
25 Lawlor, *The Little Book of Wicklow*, p.105. The text of the 'Message to the Free
    Nations of the World' is available at www.difp.ie/docs/1919/Message-to-the-
    Free-Nations-of-the-World/2.htm (visited on 31 July 2020).
26 *Cork Examiner*, 22 January 1919.
27 *Evening Telegraph* and *Cork Examiner*, 22 January 1919.

CHAPTER 6

1 I.M.A., B.M.H., Robert C. Barton, WS979, p.14.
2 This was evidently an overt reference to the executions that followed the Easter
   Rising of 1916.
3 I.M.A., B.M.H., Robert C. Barton, WS979, p.14.
4 Ibid.
5 Dom John Francis Sweetman of Ferns, Co. Wexford, entered Downside Abbey,
   Somerset in 1891. In 1905, Abbot Ford of Downside accepted an offer from
   the Sweetman family of a house in Ballinapierce, Enniscorthy, with a view to
   opening a Benedictine school there. Sweetman was appointed superior, and he
   rechristened the building 'Mount St Benedict'. Following the Easter Rising,
   he supported Sinn Féin. In 1917 he attended the funeral of hunger striker
   Thomas Ashe. He supported the anti-conscription campaign and attended the
   first meeting of the Dáil. Bishop Codd disapproved of Sweetman's political
   involvement and he suffered an ecclesiastical ban, which was only lifted in 1939.
   He died in 1953. [Mark Tierney, 'Sweetman, John Francis', in *D.I.B.*, available at
   www.dib.ie/biography/sweetman-john-francis-a8407 (visited on 24 May 2023).]
6 French served as Chief of the Imperial General Staff, gaining the rank of field
   marshal in 1913. French was given command of the British Expeditionary Force
   on the outbreak of the First World War but was replaced by Haig in 1915. He
   was given command of the British Home Front and was kept busy in Ireland
   from 1916 onwards. He was in charge of operations against the I.R.A. during
   the Anglo-Irish War. French died in 1925. [www.iwm.org.uk/collections/item/
   object/205016677 (visited on 24 May 2023).]

7   Brooke was Deputy Lieutenant of County Wicklow and a Justice of the Peace. He was regarded as a fair-minded land agent, but he was also a member of the seven-man privy council established by French, who also took the ultra-loyalist Brooke on as a private advisor. These activities put Brooke on the I.R.A.'s wanted list, and Michael Collins ordered his squad (known as the 'twelve apostles') to assassinate him. Following an unsuccessful attempt on his life in December 1919, Brooke was eventually killed by the squad in his office at Westland Row station in Dublin on 30 July 1920. [Kevin Lee, 'The assassination of Coollatin land agent, Frank Brooke, 30 July 1920', in Deane (ed), *Wicklow and the War of Independence*, pp.85–7.]

8   I.M.A., B.M.H., Robert C. Barton, WS979, pp.11 and 14.

9   Lee, 'The assassination of Coollatin land agent, Frank Brooke', p.86.

10 I.M.A., B.M.H., Robert C. Barton, WS979, p.13.

11 I.M.A., B.M.H., Dulcibella Barton, WS936, p.4.

12 I.M.A., B.M.H., Robert C. Barton, WS979, p.11.

13 I.M.A., B.M.H., Dulcibella Barton, WS936, p.4.

14 Henry Cairns and Owen Gallagher, *Aspects of the War of Independence and Civil War in Wicklow 1913–1923* (Bray, 2009), p.17.

15 *Wicklow News-Letter*, 22 March 1919.

16 The general 'list of operations carried out by the 6th Battalion, Carlow Brigade' includes no operations from 1919. All events on the list happened in either 1920 or 21. I.M.A., I.R.A. brigade activity reports, MSPC/A67, ff 27-35. Geographically, this battalion covered much of Barton's West Wicklow constituency.

17 Kevin Cullen, 'The R.I.C. and the I.R.A. in Wicklow's War of Independence' in *Journal of the West Wicklow Historical Society*, vii (Naas, 2013), p.64.

18 I.M.A., B.M.H., Robert C. Barton, WS979, p.13. However, Barton seems mistaken here. Specifically, he seems to be confused about Sears' Christian name. In the 1918 general election, Walsh was elected in Cork. [Patrick Maume, 'Walsh, James Joseph', in *D.I.B.*, available at www.dib.ie/biography/walsh-james-joseph-a8874] and Beaslaí was elected in Kerry [Patrick Maume, 'Beaslaí, Piaras', in *D.I.B.*, available at www.dib.ie/biography/beaslai-piaras-a0515], but David Sears was not elected [Patrick Maume, 'Sears, David', in *D.I.B.*, available at www.dib.ie/biography/sears-david-a7965.] However, Barton's apparent confusion may be explained by the fact that David's father, William Sears, was elected in Mayo. [Patrick Maume, 'Sears, William', in *D.I.B.*, available at www.dib.ie/biography/sears-william-a7966 (all visited on 25 May 2023).]

19 Lawlor, 'Robert Barton: Wicklow revolutionary and statesman', in Deane (ed), *Wicklow and the War of Independence*, p.204.

20 Richard ('Dick') Mulcahy was a politician, general and military commander-in-chief, He was involved in the 1916 Easter Rising, and served as Chief of Staff of the I.R.A. during the War of Independence. In 1922, he succeeded Michael Collins as commander-in-chief of the national army during the Civil War. Later, he served in W. T. Cosgrave's Cumann na nGaedheal government,

and was leader of Fine Gael from 1944 to 1948. He died in 1971. [Ronan
Fanning, 'Mulcahy, Richard', in *D.I.B.*, available at www.dib.ie/biography/
mulcahy-richard-a6029 (visited on 25 May 2023).]

21 I.M.A., B.M.H., Robert C. Barton, WS979, p.13.

22 Beaslaí, *Michael Collins*, i, p.185.

23 Lawlor, 'Robert Barton: Wicklow revolutionary and statesman', in Deane
(ed), *Wicklow and the War of Independence*, p.204. See also Beaslaí, *Michael
Collins*, i, p.186.

24 Rory O'Connor was the I.R.A.'s Director of Engineering during the
Anglo-Irish War. He vehemently opposed the treaty and was chairman of
the republican military council that eventually morphed into the Anti-Treaty
I.R.A. He was one of the main polemicists for the anti-treaty side in the
lead-up to the Civil War. He led the occupation of the Four Courts, but was
captured when the Free State Army attacked the building. Following a period
of imprisonment, he was executed on 8 December 1922 with Liam Mellows,
Richard Barrett and Joe McKelvey, in retaliation for the killing of the Free State
T.D. Sean Hales. [Lawrence William White, 'O'Connor, Roderick (Rory)', in
D.I.B., available at www.dib.ie/biography/oconnor-roderick-rory-a6614 (visited
on 25 May 2023).]

25 I.M.A., B.M.H., Robert C. Barton, WS979, p.16.

26 I.M.A., B.M.H., Dulcibella Barton, WS936, p.4.

27 Born Frances Mary O'Brennan in 1880, Áine Ceannt was the widow of
executed 1916 leader, Éamonn Ceannt. She was a vice-president of Cumann na
mBan from 1917 to 1924. During the Anglo-Irish War, she was a District Justice
in the republican courts, and she was also involved in the Irish White Cross
organisation, established to aid civilians during that war. She presided over the
Cumann na mBan convention that voted overwhelmingly against the Treaty in
February 1922. She took the anti-treaty side in the Civil War, but was a member
of a Sinn Féin peace committee that tried to end hostilities. In later years, she
was active in the Irish Red Cross, She died in 1954 and is buried in Deansgrange
Cemetery. [Frances Clarke, 'Ceannt, Áine', in *D.I.B.*, available at www.dib.ie/
biography/ceannt-aine-a1580 (visited on 25 May 2023).] On Éamonn Ceannt,
see William Henry, *Éamonn Ceannt: Supreme Sacrifice* (Cork, 2nd ed, 2012).

28 *Wicklow News-Letter*, 22 March 1919.

29 Kevin Cullen, 'The humanitarian wing of Irish Republicanism: the Irish
National Aid and Volunteer Dependents' Fund' (M.A. thesis, St. Patrick's
College Drumcondra, a college of D.C.U., 2012), p.42.

30 Patrick O'Sullivan Greene, 'A century on: the Dáil loan that set the State on the
road to financial sovereignty', *The Irish Times*, 4 April 2019.

31 www.youtube.com/watch?v=5CfrkvE7_hs (visited on 24 October 2023).

32 Material regarding the Dáil loans is found in leaflets, programmes and other
ephemera in N.L.I., Dulcibella Barton Papers 1916-1927, MS 8786/1.

33 I.M.A., B.M.H., Dulcibella Barton, WS936, p.4.

34 N.A.I., Department of the Taoiseach papers (April 1919–January 1922),
Ministerial appointments: Robert Childers Barton, TSCH/3/S10013.

35 Art O'Connor T.D., Report on agriculture, 17 August 1921 (Dáil debates, 2nd Dáil, vol. S, no. 2), available online at www.oireachtas.ie/en/debates/debate/dail/1921-08-17 (visited on 25 May 2023). While given charge of their specific portfolios, Dáil directors were not full ministers as they did not sit in Cabinet.

36 On the pursuit of land reform, see Terence Dooley, 'Irish land questions, 1879–1923', in Thomas Bartlett (ed), *The Cambridge History of Ireland*, iv (4 vols, Cambridge, 2018), pp.117–44.

37 I.M.A., B.M.H., Robert C. Barton, WS979, pp.16–17.

38 The probability of Barton being recognised and informed upon was increased by the fact that peers within his own social circle were generally sympathetic to the British authorities. Dublin was the administrative centre of Ireland and many of Barton's social set spent a lot of time there, adding to his necessity to remain incognito.

39 I.M.A., B.M.H., Robert C. Barton, WS979, p.17.

40 The Black and Tans were recruited in response to the escalating violence in Ireland, which seemed to be on a downward spiral to destruction as the year 1920 progressed. The advertised remuneration of 10s per day was very attractive at a time of unemployment and poverty in the aftermath of military demobilisations following the First World War. The first English police recruits arrived in Ireland on 25 March 1920. A shortage of dark green R.I.C. uniforms led to the new constables being attired in a mixture of dark green and khaki, giving rise to the colourful but derogatory nickname 'Black and Tans'. [Richard Bennett, *The Black and Tans* (London, revised ed., 1970), pp.28–30.] A clearing house is an institution established by firms engaged in similar activities to enable them to offset transactions with one another. Clearing houses play an important role in settling transactions related to banks. www.britannica.com/topic/clearinghouse (visited on 25 May 2023).

41 Calton Younger, *A State of Disunion* (London, 1972), p.53.

42 www.oireachtas.ie/en/debates/debate/dail/1921-08-17/16/ (O'Connor, Report on agriculture, 17 August 1921).

43 I.M.A., B.M.H., Robert C. Barton, WS979, p.20.

44 www.oliversearsgallery.com/walter-leonard-cole-3-mountjoy-square (visited on 25 May 2023).

45 www.oireachtas.ie/en/debates/debate/dail/1921-08-17/16 (O'Connor, Report on agriculture, 17 August 1921). Cole's brief report was as follows: 'My work began towards the end of last August. Some ten weeks only were available to circularise the whole country, get all the Cumainn to work, stir up the County and Urban Councils, write to all educational institutions in rural districts, to each School Manager and all Clergymen in ditto, to Societies interested in Forestry, and to call forth and reply to endless queries and problems that arose in individual instances. The main result is that in practically every case the work was got in hand, and, as nearly as we can reckon, some 250,000 to 300,000 trees were planted.'

46 Art O'Connor was born in 1888 and in his youth became a member of the Gaelic League and Sinn Féin. He was arrested at the time of the 'German plot'

and imprisoned in Durham. He was elected for Kildare South in the 1918 general election. He was appointed substitute Director for Agriculture in the first Dáil, after the arrest of Robert Barton. In September 1920, O'Connor convinced the Dáil to create the Land Commission. He took the anti-treaty side in the Civil War and was interned in Mountjoy and Kilmainham. He succeeded de Valera as 'President of the Republic' in 1926, when the latter resigned. O'Connor also resigned the position in 1927, read law and was called to the bar. He became counsel to the revenue commissioners (1944–7) and a circuit court judge in Cork (1947–50), resigning when he was appointed chairman of the Military Services Pensions Tribunal, but he died later in 1950. [William Murphy, 'O'Connor, Arthur James Kickham ('Art')', in *D.I.B.*, available at www.dib.ie/biography/oconnor-arthur-james-kickham-art-a6581 (visited on 26 May 2023).]

47 www.oireachtas.ie/en/debates/debate/dail/1921-08-17/16 (O'Connor, Report on agriculture, 17 August 1921).

48 *Nationalist and Leinster Times*, 3 January 1920.

49 I am indebted to the late Mr Dudley Kirwan of Uppertown, Dunlavin, for this information.

50 Domhnall Ó Buachalla was born in Maynooth in 1866. An ardent member of the Gaelic League, in 1905 he was prosecuted for using the Irish form of his name on his cart. He also joined the I.R.B. and was active in the Irish Volunteers. He travelled from Maynooth to join the G.P.O. garrison in 1916. He was imprisoned until December 1916. He was elected for Kildare North in the 1918 general election. He fought with the anti-treaty I.R.A. during the Civil War and was imprisoned in Dundalk in 1922–3. He was elected as Fianna Fáil T.D. for Kildare in both 1927 general elections. He always addressed the Dáil in Irish. In November 1932 he was appointed governor general of the Irish Free State by de Valera. He cycled to work, did not occupy the Governor General's official residence and never performed any public duties. Hence, when the office was abolished in 1936, it had virtually ceased to exist. From 1936, Ó Buachalla lived in retirement in Dublin. He died on 30 October 1963. [Marie Coleman, 'Ó Buachalla (Ua Buachalla), Domhnall (Donal/Daniel Richard Buckley)', in *D.I.B.*, available at www.dib.ie/biography/o-buachalla-ua-buachalla-domhnall-donaldaniel-richard-buckley-a6284 (visited on 26 May 2023).]

51 www.oireachtas.ie/en/debates/debate/dail/1921-08-17/16/ (O'Connor, Report on agriculture, 17 August 1921).

52 www.oireachtas.ie/en/debates/debate/dail/1921-08-17/16/ (O'Connor, Report on agriculture, 17 August 1921). According to O'Connor: 'A circular was issued pointing out the manifold advantages of the scheme, and calling attention to the remarkable fact that every year we export from this country 800,000 fat and store cattle and 650,000 sheep and lambs at a value of £21,000,000. The circular stated: "By purchasing in Ireland, £21,000,000 worth of raw material, the English promote an almost unending chain of industries subsidiary to that of dressing the meat and preparing it for consumption."'

53 I.M.A., B.M.H., Robert C. Barton, WS979, p.24.

54 Barton remained on the run for ten months before he was re-arrested. [Lawlor, *The Little Book of Wicklow*, p.105.]

55 Patricia Hoey was a suffragist and nationalist who was active in Sinn Féin after the 1916 Rising. She was temporarily employed by the British government and was offered a permanent civil service position in exchange for renouncing Sinn Féin and taking the oath of allegiance. She refused and was dismissed. During the War of Independence Hoey worked as a propagandist for Sinn Féin and as Griffith's confidential secretary. She supported the pro-treaty side in the Civil War. She was enlisted in the National Army as assistant military censor. After the Civil War, despite financial hardship, she organised a dispensary for the treatment of sick animals of the poor in Portobello, Dublin, in 1926. She died on 9 November 1930. [Niav Gallagher, 'Hoey, Patricia', in *D.I.B.*, available at www.dib.ie/biography/hoey-patricia-a10154 (visited on 1 June 2023).]

56 Although I have not discovered her Christian name, Mrs McGarry was the mother of Milo McGarry. He mentions her repeatedly in his witness statement; she was evidently a staunch republican. He also mentions that the Cabinet 'met periodically at the[ir] house'. [I.M.A., B.M.H., Milo McGarry, WS356, p.9.] Sixteen-year-old 'Maolmuire' appears in the 1911 census, living with his father, Seumás (51) and brother, Sosamh (22). Milo's mother does not appear on the form. [Census of Ireland 1911, form A, 31 Upper Fitzwilliam Street, Dublin, available at www.census.nationalarchives.ie/reels/nai000207160 (visited on 1 June 2023).] The name 'Maolmhuire' translates as 'Myles' or 'Miles'. [www.libraryireland.com/names/men/maolmhuire-meyler.php (visited on 1 June 2023).]

57 I.M.A., B.M.H., Robert C. Barton, WS979, p.21.

58 www.oireachtas.ie/en/debates/debate/dail/1921-08-17/16/ (O'Connor, Report on agriculture, 17 August 1921).

59 I.M.A., B.M.H., Robert C. Barton, WS979, p.17.

60 www.oireachtas.ie/en/debates/debate/dail/1921-08-17/16/ (O'Connor, Report on agriculture, 17 August 1921).

61 I.M.A., B.M.H., Robert C. Barton, WS979, p.17. Barton added: 'Conor Maguire, now President of the High Court, was one of these.'

62 www.oireachtas.ie/en/debates/debate/dail/1921-08-17/16/ (O'Connor, Report on agriculture, 17 August 1921).

CHAPTER 7

1 Eamon ('Ned') Broy was born on 22 December 1887 in Ballinure, Co. Kildare, the son of Patrick Broy, farmer, and his wife, Mary (née Barry). He joined the R.I.C. in 1910 and the D.M.P. a year later. In 1915 he moved to the detective branch, and was later assigned to the headquarters of G division (British secret service) as a confidential clerk. The Easter Rising and its aftermath led to a political conversion, and in March 1917 Broy made the decision to assist Sinn Féin and the volunteers. He became one of the principal sources of information

for Michael Collins. Initially, Broy established his credibility by warning
about the imminent arrest of two middle-ranking members of Sinn Féin, and
shortly afterwards began to pass on confidential documents and police codes. In
April 1919, Broy smuggled Collins into G division headquarters at Brunswick
Street (later Pearse Street), enabling him to trawl through secret files for five
hours. Many junior detectives were threatened and warned off. The policy of
shooting detectives began in July 1919. Broy was arrested in December 1920
following the discovery of documents typed by him in the house of Eileen
McGrane, an ardent Sinn Féin sympathiser. Broy was incarcerated in Arbour
Hill prison until the truce. Following his release, he travelled to London with
the treaty delegation as Collins' private secretary and bodyguard. Following
independence, he served in the Free State army air corps and in 1925 he was
appointed a chief superintendent in An Garda Síochána. In 1933, de Valera
appointed him as Garda Commissioner. He retired in 1938 and eventually died
in Dublin in 1972. [Pauric Dempsey and Shaun Boylan, 'Broy, Eamon ("Ned")',
in *D.I.B.*, available at www.dib.ie/biography/broy-eamon-ned-a1067 (visited on
3 July 2023).]

2   I.M.A., B.M.H., Robert C. Barton, WS979, pp.21–2.
3   Lawlor, 'Robert Barton: Wicklow revolutionary and statesman', in Deane (ed),
    Wicklow and the War of Independence, p.204.
4   I.M.A., B.M.H., Robert C. Barton, WS979, pp.14–5.
5   Fewer, 'R. C. Barton and Glendalough House', p.6.
6   Mais, *I Return to Ireland*, pp.131–2.
7   I.M.A., B.M.H., Robert C. Barton, WS979, p.15.
8   I.M.A., B.M.H., Dulcibella Barton, WS936, pp.4–6.
9   Local Government Archivists and Records Managers, *Democracy and Change: The
    1920 Local Elections in Ireland* (Dublin, 2020), p.24.
10 In County Wicklow, the results for the twenty available seats broke down as
    follows: Sinn Féin 14, Sinn Féin Labour 3, Farmers' Association 2, Nationalist
    1. [Ibid., p.61.]
11 Christopher Michael ('C. M.') Byrne was born in the 1880s in Glenealy, Co.
    Wicklow. He became involved in politics at a young age and began to organise the
    Irish Volunteers in County Wicklow in 1913. During the War of Independence,
    he was an I.R.A. quartermaster and his home was repeatedly raided by the
    military. He was elected to Wicklow County Council in 1920, and he succeeded
    Robert Barton as chairman, serving for seventeen of the years between June
    1922 and 1945. Beyond Wicklow, he played a significant role in national politics,
    beginning with his election as a Sinn Féin T.D. for Kildare-Wicklow in 1921. He
    took the pro-treaty side in the Civil War and was re-elected to the Dáil in 1922,
    and again in 1923 as a Cumann na nGaedheal T.D. for Wicklow. A member
    of the commission on agriculture (1922), in 1924 he served a period as acting
    party whip. Disillusioned by the outcome of the 1925 boundary commission,
    he was involved in forming a short-lived new party, Clann Éireann, and later
    joined Fianna Fáil. He was a member of the Fianna Fáil national executive in the

1940s. He died in St John of God Nursing Home, Stillorgan, Co. Dublin, on 12 April 1958. [Pauric Dempsey, 'Byrne, Christopher Michael ('Christy', 'C. M.'), in *D.I.B.*, available at www.dib.ie/biography/byrne-christopher-michael-christy-c-m-a1321 (visited on 3 July 2023).]

12 Donnelly, *For the Betterment of the People*, pp.40–3, 53, 163, 167. See also *Wicklow News-Letter*, 19 June 1920.

13 *Nationalist and Leinster Times*, 17 July 1920.

14 Much was made of this fact in the locality, as the courthouse had been used to house United Irish prisoners prior to their execution in the village during the 1798 rebellion. I am indebted to the late Mr Joe Deering of Milltown, Dunlavin, for this information.

15 *Nationalist and Leinster Times*, 17 July 1920.

16 *The Freeman's Journal*, 13 September 1919.

17 Manus O'Riordan, 'Larkin in America: the road to Sing Sing' in Donal Nevin (ed), *James Larkin: Lion of the Fold* (Dublin, 1998), p.71.

18 *Nationalist and Leinster Times*, 17 July 1920.

19 Henry Cairns (ed), *Wicklow in Revolt: a History of County Wicklow from 1913–1923* (Bray, 2016) p.104.

20 I.M.A., B.M.H., Dulcibella Barton, WS936, pp.8–9.

21 On this incident, see Chris Lawlor, 'The Dunlavin tragedy: murder, suicide and the execution of William Mitchell in 1921', available online at heritage. wicklowheritage.org/places/dunlavin-2/the-dunlavin-tragedy-murder-suicide-and-the-execution-of-william-mitchell-in-1921 (visited on 20 August 2023).

22 Mais, *I Return to Ireland*, p.131. See also I.M.A., B.M.H., Robert C. Barton, WS979, p.15.

23 Piaras Beaslaí, *Michael Collins*, vol. ii, p.99.

24 James Quinn, 'Brugha, Cathal', in *D.I.B.*, available at www.dib.ie/biography/ brugha-cathal-a1077 (visited on 3 July 2023).

25 I.M.A., B.M.H., Robert C. Barton, WS979, p.26.

26 Portsmouth Gaol opened in 1877 as a local prison. It was the last of nineteen 'Pentonville' radial prisons to be constructed, with an octagonal central hall and five wings leading into it. ['History of 1877: the old Portsmouth Gaol, available at www.cityandcountry.co.uk/history-of-1877-the-old-portsmouth-gaol (visited on 21 August 2023).]

27 I.M.A., B.M.H., Robert C. Barton, WS979, p.27.

28 'The burning of the Customs House', available at www.gov.ie/en/press-release/ eb1c0-100-years-ago-today-the-burning-of-the-custom-house (visited on 21 August 2023).

29 Joseph E. A. Connell Jr., 'The burning of the Custom House, 25 May 1921', in *History Ireland*, vol. 29, no. 3 (May–June, 2021), p.29.

30 Ostensibly, this was done to avoid splitting the nationalist/republican vote, but there may also have been a certain level of intimidation used in some cases.

31 See, for example, N.L.I., Dulcibella Barton papers 1916–1927, MS 8786/2/6, MS 8786/2 and MS 8786/1/48.

32 N.L.I., Erskine Childers Papers, Augustus Cullen to Erskine Childers, 14 May 1921, MS 48,052/14.

33 George Riddell, *Lord Riddell's Intimate Diary of the Peace Conference and After, 1918–1923* (London, 1933), p.302.

34 Macardle, *The Irish Republic*, p.431.

35 Mais, *I Return to Ireland*, pp.131–2.

36 Dempsey and Boylan, 'Barton, Robert Childers', in *D.I.B.*, available at www. dib.ie/biography/barton-robert-childers-a0485 (visited on 9 January 2023).

37 De Valera is quoted in T. Ryle Dwyer, *De Valera: The Man and the Myths* (Dublin, 1991), p.70.

38 Dempsey and Boylan, 'Barton, Robert Childers', in *D.I.B.*, available at www. dib.ie/biography/barton-robert-childers-a0485 (visited on 9 January 2023).

39 Jack Traynor, 'Jan Smuts and the Anglo-Irish truce of July 1921', available at www.theirishstory.com/2023/02/14/jan-smuts-and-the-anglo-irish-truce-of-july-1921/#_edn33 (visited on 21 August 2023).

40 Dempsey and Boylan, 'Barton, Robert Childers', in *D.I.B.*, available at www. dib.ie/biography/barton-robert-childers-a0485 (visited on 9/1/2023). Eamon Duggan was a solicitor and Sinn Féin T.D. for Meath South constituency. He played a leading role in negotiating the truce and, later, the Anglo-Irish treaty of 1921. On Duggan, see Peter Connell (in association with Mary Hayes), *Eamon Duggan: Counsel to the Revolution* (Meath County Council, 2021).

41 Smuts is quoted in Charles Townshend, *The Republic: The Fight for Irish Independence* (London, 2013), p.307.

42 Nevil Macready, *Annals of an Active Life* (2 vols, London, 1924), ii, pp.572–3.

43 'Truce Liaison and Evacuation Papers (1921–1922)', available at www.militaryarchives.ie/collections/reading-room-collections/truce-liaison-and-evacuation-papers-1921-1922 (visited on 12 February 2023).

44 Dempsey and Boylan, 'Barton, Robert Childers', in *D.I.B.*, available at www. dib.ie/biography/barton-robert-childers-a0485 (visited on 9 January 2023).

45 I.M.A, M.P.S.C., pension claim 2431 of Eamon Duggan, p.24.

46 Longford (Pakenham), *Peace by Ordeal*, p.70.

47 Macready, *Annals*, ii, p.579.

48 McGee, *Arthur Griffith*, p.257.

49 Longford (Pakenham), *Peace by Ordeal*, p.70.

CHAPTER 8

1 I.M.A., B.M.H., Robert C. Barton, WS979, pp.24–5. Barton continued in his witness statement: 'There was never an open rupture, so far as I remember. I think Cathal Brugha felt that Michael Collins was getting too much control of the Army. Brugha was Minister of Defence, and Dick Mulcahy was Chief of Staff. Cathal Brugha, I think, felt that Michael Collins's duties as Director of Intelligence were being stretched so as to undermine Brugha's control of the Army. I think that possibly was one cause. There was not the close harmony

between Michael Collins and Cathal Brugha that there had been before I was arrested. I do not remember any open friction between Austin Stack and Mick Collins at these meetings.'

2   Austin Stack (1879–1929), from Tralee, County Kerry, was involved in the G.A.A. and the Gaelic League as a young man. Stack joined the I.R.B., the Volunteers, the Young Ireland Society and the Irish National Foresters, and was very interested in Irish history. In 1916, he made arrangements to receive arms from the ill-fated Aud gun-running, but he was arrested and sentenced to penal servitude for life. However, he was released with the other Irish prisoners in 1917 and he helped to reorganise the Kerry Volunteers and the local branch of Sinn Féin. He was rearrested in August and went on hunger strike in prison, in which his companion Thomas Ashe died from force-feeding. Stack was elected for Kerry West in the 1918 general election. In October 1919 he escaped from Strangeways, and he was Minister for Home Affairs from November 1919 to January 1922, establishing the republican courts. He sided with Cathal Brugha against Michael Collins, and supported the anti-treaty side during the Civil War. He was captured in April 1923 and remained imprisoned until July 1924. He remained active in Sinn Féin until his death on 27 April 1929. Anthony J. Gaughan, 'Stack, Austin', in *D.I.B.*, available at www.dib.ie/biography/stack-austin-a8231 (visited on 24 August 2023).

3   Count George Plunkett (1851–1948) was a Papal count and the father of executed 1916 leader Joseph Mary Plunkett. He supported Home Rule and, surprisingly, supported Parnell in the face of opposition from the Catholic hierarchy. Joseph Plunkett swore his father into the I.R.B. in April 1916, sending him to seek German aid and a Papal blessing for the planned Easter Rising. Following the rebels' defeat and the execution of his son, Plunkett was elected in the Roscommon North by-election, paving the way for the Sinn Féin victory in the 1918 general election. Plunkett and Griffith became vice-presidents of the party, which was by then under de Valera's leadership. Plunkett became Minister for Foreign Affairs in the first Dáil, but he was inactive in the post. He opposed the treaty and was imprisoned during the Civil War. However, he topped the poll in Roscommon in August 1923 and was released in December. He continued to support Sinn Féin until his death on 12 March 1948. D. R. O'Connor Lysaght, 'Plunkett, Count George Noble', in *D.I.B.*, available at www.dib.ie/biography/plunkett-count-george-noble-a7384 (visited on 24 August 2023).

4   Macardle, *The Irish Republic*, p.439. Laurence O'Neill and Kathleen O'Connell also travelled in the group.

5   Stack (quoted in Longford (Pakenham), *Peace by Ordeal*, p.71) recalled: 'All the Irish in London seemed to be awaiting the train at Euston and it was with difficulty that we reached our hotel.'

6   Macardle, *The Irish Republic*, p.439.

7   I.M.A., B.M.H., Robert C. Barton, WS979, p.29.

8   Longford (Pakenham), *Peace by Ordeal*, p.72.

9   I.M.A., B.M.H., Robert C. Barton, WS979, p.29.

10 Barton is quoted in Longford (Pakenham), *Peace by Ordeal*, p.72.

11 Lawlor, *Dunlavin Diversions*, p.91.

12 Michael Laffan, *The Resurrection of Ireland: The Sinn Féin Party 1916–1923* (Cambridge, 1999), p.346.

13 I.M.A., B.M.H., Robert C. Barton, WS979, pp.30–1.

14 Ferriter, *A Nation and Not a Rabble*, p.247.

15 Longford (Pakenham), *Peace by Ordeal*, p.77.

16 *Freeman's Journal*, 1 October 1921.

17 Longford (Pakenham), *Peace by Ordeal*, p.76.

18 McGee, *Arthur Griffith*, p.259.

19 *Webster's Dictionary* defines a 'plenipotentiary' as 'a person invested with full power to transact any business'. *Webster's Third New International Dictionary*, vol. ii (Chicago, 1986), p.1739.

20 Gavan Duffy and de Valera, Ratification of plenipotentiaries, 14 September 1921 (Dáil debates, 2nd Dáil, vol. S, no. 10), available online at www.oireachtas. ie/en/debates/debate/dail/1921-09-14/3 (visited on 12 October 2023). See also Beaslaí, *Michael Collins*, vol. ii, p.99.

21 Macardle, *The Irish Republic*, p.483.

22 William Thomas Cosgrave was born in Dublin on 5 June 1880. He was involved with Sinn Féin from its inception in 1905 and later joined the Volunteers. He fought in the 1916 Rising and was sentenced to death, but reprieved and was released in 1917. He was elected as the Sinn Féin representative for Kilkenny in a by-election in 1917 and became Minister for Local Government in the first Dáil. He was one of the T.D.s who chose the delegates for the treaty negotiations and crucially, at Cabinet level, he later supported the document's referral to the Dáil. He took the pro-treaty side in the Civil War and served as a minister under Griffith. He succeeded Michael Collins as president of the Dáil after the latter was killed at Béal na mBláth. He presided over hard-line policies, including the executions of republican prisoners during the Civil War, but he organised free elections in late 1923 and freed most republican prisoners by the following year. He rebranded pro-treaty Sinn Féin as Cumann na nGaedheal in 1923. With Cosgrave as its leader, this new party remained in government until 1932, when it was defeated by Fianna Fáil in a general election. Cosgrave handed over power peacefully. He led Cumann na nGaedheal's successor, Fine Gael, in opposition from 1934 to 1943, retiring from politics in 1944. W. T. Cosgrave died on 16 November 1965. [Eunan O'Halpin, 'Cosgrave, William Thomas' in *D.I.B.*, available at www.dib.ie/biography/cosgrave-william-thomas-a2077 (visited on 12 October 2023).]

23 The letter referred to was de Valera's reply of 12 September 1921 to Lloyd George's letter of 7 September 1921. Both letters are reproduced in Appendix 2. [www.oireachtas.ie/en/debates/debate/dail/1921-09-14/2/ (visited on 12 October 2023).]

24 Cosgrave and de Valera, Ratification of plenipotentiaries, 14 September 1921 (Dáil debates, 2nd Dáil, vol. S, no. 10), available online at www.oireachtas.ie/en/debates/debate/dail/1921-09-14/3/ (visited on 12 October 2023).
25 I.M.A., B.M.H., Robert C. Barton, WS979, p.36.
26 Longford (Pakenham), *Peace by Ordeal*, p.84.
27 I.M.A., B.M.H., Dulcibella Barton, WS936, p.9.
28 I.M.A., B.M.H., Robert C. Barton, WS979, p.37.
29 Beaslaí, *Michael Collins*, vol. ii, p.193. Collins did not travel until the following day.
30 Kathleen McKenna, *A Dáil Girl's Revolutionary Recollections* (Dublin, 2014), p.149.

CHAPTER 9

1   Kathleen McKenna, *A Dáil Girl's Revolutionary Recollections* (Dublin, p.153).
2   Macardle, *The Irish Republic*, p.485.
3   Beaslaí, *Michael Collins*, vol. ii, p.193.
4   Macardle, *The Irish Republic*, p.486.
5   Ratification of plenipotentiaries, 14 September 1921 (Dáil debates, 2nd Dáil, vol. S, no. 10), available online at www.oireachtas.ie/en/debates/debate/dail/1921-09-14/3 (visited on 12 October 2023).
6   Peadar O'Donnell, *There Will be Another Day* (Dublin, 1963), p.14. O'Donnell continued: 'This difference was to explode, and startle both of them by its shattering power, in the conflict of the Treaty versus Document No. 2.'
7   Ratification of plenipotentiaries, 14 September 1921 (Dáil debates, 2nd Dáil, vol. S, no. 10), available online at www.oireachtas.ie/en/debates/debate/dail/1921-09-14/3 (visited on 12 October 2023).
8   Éamon de Valera to Joseph McGarrity, 27 December 1921 (N.L.I., McGarrity Papers, MS 17440/4). McGarrity was a prominent member of the Irish-American organisation, Clan na Gael.
9   Longford (Pakenham), *Peace by Ordeal*, p.214.
10 De Valera to McGarrity, 27 December 1921 (N.L.I., McGarrity Papers, MS 17440/4).
11 Ibid. However, Ryle Dwyer has pointed out: 'If he [de Valera] really suspected that Griffith and Collins would be so weak, why did he not include Childers in the delegation proper? It would have been idiotic to think a secretary could control the delegation through his influence with a younger cousin.' Ryle Dwyer, *De Valera*, p.70.
12 Foster, *Modern Ireland 1600–1972*, p.505.
13 I.M.A., B.M.H., Robert C. Barton, WS979, p.32.
14 Ibid., p.43.
15 F. S. L. Lyons, *Ireland since the Famine* (London, 4th ed., 1976), p.430.

16 Both men are quoted in Tim Pat Coogan, *Michael Collins: A Biography* (London, 2nd ed., 1991), p.241.

17 Lyons, for example, referred to the British negotiating team as 'formidable'. [Ibid., p.430.] Beckett informed us that, 'Lloyd George played skilfully on their doubts and fears.' [J. C. Beckett, *The Making of Modern Ireland 1603–1923* (London, reprint, 1973), p.453.]

18 N.A.I., Private accession 1093, Robert Barton papers, 'Correspondence with Marjorie Forester (1964) and Andrew Boyle (1974)', PRIV1093/12 and 'Miscellaneous – Notes for a lecture', PRIV1093/14.

19 This suspicion was well founded. Collins discovered that Childers was sending secret reports to de Valera. Coogan, *Michael Collins*, p.244. See also Ferriter, *A Nation and Not a Rabble*, p.250.

20 I.M.A., B.M.H., Robert C. Barton, WS979, p.42.

21 Longford (Pakenham), *Peace by Ordeal*, p.85.

22 I.M.A., B.M.H., Robert C. Barton, WS979, p.28.

23 Ibid., p.33.

24 Ryle Dwyer, *De Valera*, p.59.

25 David McCullagh, 'Truce and Treaty: Why did de Valera not lead the delegation sent to London?', *The Irish Times*, 25 May 2021.

26 Longford (Pakenham), *Peace by Ordeal*, p.79; and Coogan, *Michael Collins*, p.226.

27 N.A.I., Private accession 1093, Robert Barton papers, 'Miscellaneous – Notes for a lecture', PRIV1093/14.

28 Tim Pat Coogan, *De Valera: Long Fellow, Long Shadow* (London, 1993), p.249.

29 Griffith's account of this incident was as follows: 'The first I heard of External Association was when Dev was pressing me to go over as a plenipotentiary. I went in to him one day and found him with Cathal and Austin at his desk, all three sitting. I was standing. He told me he wanted me to go to London. I said to him; "You are my Chief, and if you tell me to go, I'll go. But I know, and you know, that I can't bring back a Republic." Then he produced this External Association idea – the first I ever heard of it – and after half-an-hour's persuasion, Cathal gave a reluctant consent to it. Stack said nothing, but sat there, sullen. I said nothing. Then the other two left, and left me alone with him. I said, "Look here Dev, what is the meaning of this External Association idea? What are you getting at with it?" He replied by getting a pencil and paper and drew the line thus: [At this point Griffith too produced paper and pencil and drew a line AB at a sixty-degree angle.] (sic. the line AB was vertical) "That," said he, "is me, in the straightjacket of the Republic. I must get out of it." Then he drew another line, a curved line [from A] AC. "That," said he, "is External Association. The purpose of it is to bring Cathal along." Then he drew another straight line. [Here Griffith drew the

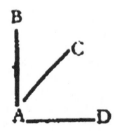

line AD] "That," said he, is where we'll eventually get to." Then I was satisfied, and said no more about it.' This account was published in P.S. O'Hegarty, *The Victory of Sinn Féin* (Dublin, 1924), pp.86–7.

30 Foster, *Modern Ireland 1600–1972*, p.505.
31 Longford (Pakenham), *Peace by Ordeal*, p.95.
32 McCullagh, 'Truce and Treaty', *The Irish Times*, 25 May 2021.
33 This memorandum is quoted in Coogan, *Michael Collins*, p.230.
34 Longford (Pakenham), *Peace by Ordeal*, p.100.
35 Dempsey and Boylan, 'Barton, Robert Childers', in *D.I.B.* available at www. dib.ie/biography/barton-robert-childers-a0485 (visited on 9 January 2023).
36 Burke Wilkinson, *The Zeal of the Convert: the Life of Erskine Childers* (London, 1976; reprint, New York, 1985), p.185.
37 Lawlor, 'Robert Barton: Wicklow revolutionary and statesman', in Deane (ed), *Wicklow and the War of Independence*, p.205.
38 *Irish Weekly Independent*, 15 October 1921.

CHAPTER 10

1 N.A.I., Private accession 1093, Robert Barton papers, 'Treaty negotiations: memoranda and correspondence', PRIV 1093/4/52.
2 Both documents are reproduced in Macardle, *The Irish Republic*, pp.482–3.
3 Younger, *Arthur Griffith*, p.102.
4 Dempsey and Boylan, 'Barton, Robert Childers', in *D.I.B.* available at www. dib.ie/biography/barton-robert-childers-a0485 (visited on 9 January 2023).
5 Frederick Winston Furneaux Smith, *Frederick Edwin, Earl of Birkenhead: The Last Phase* (London, 1933), p.150.
6 Diarmaid Ferriter, 'Peace by Ordeal: how the treaty was signed', online article (part of the War of Independence project coordinated by U.C.C.), available at www.rte.ie/history/treaty/2021/1108/1258552-how-the-treaty-was-signed (visited on 2 November 2023).
7 Chris Lawlor, 'Robert Barton, Sinn Féin M.P.', online article (part of Wicklow Co. Council's Together Apart project), available at heritage.wicklowheritage. org/topics/together-apart-wicklow-2020-stories/dunlavin-diversions/dunlavin-diversions-21-30/25-robert-barton-sinn-fein-mp#_ednref12 (visited on 2 November 2023).
8 Connell (in association with Hayes), *Eamon Duggan*, p.106.
9 Longford (Pakenham), *Peace by Ordeal*, p.145.
10 I.M.A., B.M.H., Robert C. Barton, WS979, p.37.
11 Mais, *I Return to Ireland*, p.134.
12 I.M.A., B.M.H., Robert C. Barton, WS979, pp.37–8.
13 Longford (Pakenham), *Peace by Ordeal*, p.104.
14 Ferriter, *A Nation and Not a Rabble*, p.249.
15 Longford (Pakenham), *Peace by Ordeal*, pp.122–3.
16 Macardle, *The Irish Republic*, p.493.

17 I.M.A., B.M.H., Robert C. Barton, WS979, p.32.
18 Conor Donegan, 'Charlie McGuinness and the Freida gun run to Waterford, November 1921', available at tidesandtales.ie/charlie-mcguinness-and-the-freida-gun-run-to-waterford-november-1921 (visited on 6 November 2023).
19 Macardle, *The Irish Republic*, p.493.
20 Lyons, *Ireland Since the Famine*, p.69.
21 Both prices and wages must be taken into account when comparing costs of living.
22 Longford (Pakenham), *Peace by Ordeal*, p.127.
23 Draft Treaty A is available online at celt.ucc.ie/published/E900019/index.html (visited on 6 November 2023).
24 Ryle Dwyer, *De Valera*, p.71.
25 Longford (Pakenham), *Peace by Ordeal*, p.144.
26 Lawlor, *The Little Book of Wicklow*, p.107.
27 Emer Nowlan, 'Arthur Griffith's contribution to Irish independence', online article available at theanglo-irishtreatydelegations1921.org/arthur-griffith (visited on 7 November 2023).
28 Coogan, *Michael Collins*, p.241.
29 I.M.A., B.M.H., Robert C. Barton, WS979, pp.42–3.
30 Ferriter, *A Nation and Not a Rabble*, p.250.
31 I.M.A., B.M.H., Robert C. Barton, WS979, p.38.
32 Coogan, *Michael Collins*, p.243; and Ryle Dwyer, *De Valera*, p.76.
33 N.A.I., Private accession 1093, Robert Barton papers, 'Miscellaneous – Notes for a lecture', PRIV1093/14.
34 Longford (Pakenham), *Peace by Ordeal*, pp.159–61.
35 Excerpt taken from an untitled collection of documents compiled by Robert Barton, later loaned to Coogan by Dr T. P. O'Neill and quoted in Coogan, *Michael Collins*, p.253 [hereafter cited as Barton compilation, quoted in Coogan, *Michael Collins*.]
36 N.A.I., Private accession 1093, Robert Barton papers, 'Anglo-Irish treaty 1921: minutes of conference', PRIV1093/1/3.
37 Macardle, *The Irish Republic*, pp.506–7.
38 Longford (Pakenham), *Peace by Ordeal*, pp.166–9.
39 Barton compilation, quoted in Coogan, *Michael Collins*, p.254.

Chapter 11

1 I.M.A., B.M.H., Robert C. Barton, WS979, p.38.
2 Longford (Pakenham), *Peace by Ordeal*, p.190.
3 Macardle, *The Irish Republic*, p.508.
4 Coogan, *Michael Collins*, p.244.
5 Macardle, *The Irish Republic*, p.508.

6 I.M.A., B.M.H., Robert C. Barton, WS979, p.38.
7 Longford (Pakenham), *Peace by Ordeal*, p.190.
8 Beaslaí, *Michael Collins*, vol. ii, p.192.
9 Longford (Pakenham), *Peace by Ordeal*, p.191.
10 Ibid., p.173.
11 However, the British may not have shared the Irish perspective on this point; the Unionists most certainly did not! There seemed to be an acceptance that some 'islands' (such as nationalist West Belfast) would have to accept the preferred government of their surrounding populations. Macardle, *The Irish Republic*, p.517.
12 *The Irish Press*, 18 January 1933.
13 Younger, *Arthur Griffith*, p.110.
14 Macardle, *The Irish Republic*, p.518.
15 Barton compilation, quoted in Coogan, *Michael Collins*, p.254.
16 Longford (Pakenham), *Peace by Ordeal*, p.193.
17 Younger, *Arthur Griffith*, p.110–1.
18 Macardle, *The Irish Republic*, p.522.
19 Longford (Pakenham), *Peace by Ordeal*, p.194.
20 Macardle, *The Irish Republic*, p.522.
21 McKenna, *A Dáil Girl's Revolutionary Recollections*, p.166.
22 This is the list of sums appropriated annually by parliament to pay the expenses of the sovereign and his or her household. [www.britannica.com/topic/ Civil-List (visited on 14 November 2023).]
23 I.M.A., B.M.H., witness statement of Mrs Austin Stack, Seabank, Strand Road, Merrion, Dublin, WS418, pp.50–1. Much of this statement is in Austin Stack's own words, taken directly from his notes.
24 Younger, *Arthur Griffith*, p.111.
25 I.M.A., B.M.H., Mrs Austin Stack, WS418, p.51
26 Longford (Pakenham), *Peace by Ordeal*, p.202.
27 Macardle, *The Irish Republic*, p.523.
28 I.M.A., B.M.H., Mrs Austin Stack, WS418, p.51.
29 Macardle, *The Irish Republic*, p.525.
30 Coogan, *Michael Collins*, pp.265–6.
31 Longford (Pakenham), *Peace by Ordeal*, pp.206–7.
32 Ibid., p.208.
33 I.M.A., B.M.H., Mrs Austin Stack, WS418, p.53.
34 Coogan, *Michael Collins*, p.266.
35 Ibid.
36 Macardle, *The Irish Republic*, pp.527–8.
37 Longford (Pakenham), *Peace by Ordeal*, p.209.
38 Macardle, *The Irish Republic*, p.528.
39 I.M.A., B.M.H., Mrs Austin Stack, WS418, p.53.
40 I.M.A., B.M.H., Robert C. Barton, WS979, p.36.
41 Macardle, *The Irish Republic*, p.528.
42 Ibid.

43 Longford (Pakenham), *Peace by Ordeal*, p.211.
44 McKenna, *A Dáil Girl's Revolutionary Recollections*, p.169. See also Coogan, *Michael Collins*, p.268.
45 Connell (in association with Hayes), *Eamon Duggan*, p.108.
46 N.A.I., Private accession 1093, Robert Barton papers, 'Miscellaneous – Notes for a lecture', PRIV1093/14.
47 T. M. (Tim) Healy was born on 17 May 1855 in Bantry, County Cork. As a young man he emigrated to England and worked as a railway clerk. In 1878 he became the parliamentary correspondent for the *Nation* at a time when the Land War was beginning. He became close to nationalist leader Charles Stewart Parnell and was arrested for Land League activities, but was elected as M.P. for Wexford in 1880. He was deeply involved in the Land Question and the 'Healy Clause' of the 1881 Land Act, which protected tenant improvements from rent increases by landlords increased his popularity. He was called to the Irish Bar in 1884, but he fell out with Parnell in 1886 and remained at odds with later leaders of the Irish Parliamentary Party, though he remained a supporter of Home Rule. Disappointed by the Irish Party after the Easter Rising, he switched his allegiance to Sinn Féin. By now regarded as an elder statesman, he was an acceptable choice in both British and Irish eyes for the post of Governor General of the fledgling Irish Free State. He held the post until his resignation in 1928. Healy died in Dublin on 26 March 1931. [Frank Callanan, 'Healy, Timothy Michael', in *D.I.B.*, available at www.dib.ie/biography/healy-timothy-michael-a3903 (visited on 16 November 2023).]
48 Coogan, *Michael Collins*, p.269.

Chapter 12

1   Macardle, *The Irish Republic*, p.530.
2   Coogan, *Michael Collins*, p.269.
3   I.M.A., B.M.H., Robert C. Barton, WS979, p.35.
4   I.M.A., B.M.H., Mrs Austin Stack, WS418, pp.54–5.
5   Longford (Pakenham), *Peace by Ordeal*, p.216.
6   Macardle, *The Irish Republic*, p.531.
7   I.M.A., B.M.H., Robert C. Barton, WS979, p.35.
8   Barton compilation, quoted in Coogan, *Michael Collins*, p.269.
9   I.M.A., B.M.H., Robert C. Barton, WS979, p.39.
10 *Daily Express*, 5 December 1921.
11 *Daily Chronicle*, 5 December 1921.
12 *The Irish Press*, 18 January 1933.
13 Longford (Pakenham), *Peace by Ordeal*, p.229.
14 Barton compilation, quoted in Coogan, *Michael Collins*, p.272.
15 Macardle, *The Irish Republic*, p.533.
16 Longford (Pakenham), *Peace by Ordeal*, pp.236–7.
17 Macardle, *The Irish Republic*, p.534.

18 Ronan Fanning, *Fatal Path: The British Government and the Irish Revolution* (London, 2013), p.309.
19 Longford (Pakenham), *Peace by Ordeal*, p.237.
20 Macardle, *The Irish Republic*, p.535.
21 Coogan, *Michael Collins*, p.274. Coogan actually suggests that Lloyd George was bluffing for Barton's benefit. However, Ferriter has suggested that (had the Irish not signed) 'there seems much truth in Pakenham's observation that ... the British army [would be] still more or less in control in Ireland'. Diarmaid Ferriter, *The Transformation of Ireland 1900–2000* (London, 2005), p.242.
22 Debate on the treaty, 19 December 1921 (Dáil debates, 2nd Dáil, vol. T, no. 6) available online at www.oireachtas.ie/en/debates/debate/dail/1921-12-19/2 (visited on 18 November 2023).
23 Anne Dolan and William Murphy, *Michael Collins: The Man and the Revolution* (Cork, 2018), p.152. Their second exemplar is Collins' shock when de Valera rejected the treaty.
24 Longford (Pakenham), *Peace by Ordeal*, p.236.
25 N.A.I., Private accession 1093, Robert Barton papers, 'Miscellaneous – Notes for a lecture', PRIV1093/14.
26 Macardle, *The Irish Republic*, p.537.
27 Lawlor, *The Little Book of Wicklow*, p.107.
28 Longford (Pakenham), *Peace by Ordeal*, p.243.
29 Lawlor, *The Little Book of Wicklow*, p.107.
30 Coogan, *Michael Collins*, p.274.
31 I.M.A., B.M.H., Robert C. Barton, WS979, p.42.
32 Longford (Pakenham), *Peace by Ordeal*, p.243.
33 Lawlor, *The Little Book of Wicklow*, p.108.
34 Debate on the treaty, 19 December 1921 (Dáil debates, 2nd Dáil, vol. T, no. 6) available online at www.oireachtas.ie/en/debates/debate/dail/1921-12-19/2/ (visited on 18 November 2023).
35 Lawlor, *The Little Book of Wicklow*, p.108.
36 Longford (Pakenham), *Peace by Ordeal*, p.244.
37 Connell (in association with Hayes), *Eamon Duggan*, p.111.
38 Longford (Pakenham), *Peace by Ordeal*, p.244.
39 Childers is quoted in Coogan, *Michael Collins*, p.275.
40 I.M.A., B.M.H., Dulcibella Barton, WS936, p.8.
41 Coogan, *Michael Collins*, p.275.
42 Lawlor, *The Little Book of Wicklow*, p.108.
43 I.M.A., B.M.H., Robert C. Barton, WS979, p.42.
44 Macardle, *The Irish Republic*, p.537.
45 Wilkinson, *The Zeal of the Convert*, pp.190–1.
46 Longford (Pakenham), *Peace by Ordeal*, p.244.
47 Macardle, *The Irish Republic*, p.537.
48 N.A.I., Dáil Éireann papers, notes by Robert Barton of two sub-conferences held on December 5/6, 1921 at 10 Downing St, London, 5–6 December 1921,

DE 2 (number 304/1), available online at www.difp.ie/volume-1/1921/anglo-irish-treaty/213/#section-documentpage (visited on 20 November 2023). The first sub-conference was at 3 p.m. on 5 December, and the second began at 11.15 p.m. that night and continued until 2.20 a.m. on the morning of 6 December. Barton's notes provide an account of proceedings, which brought about only minor changes in wording.

49 I.M.A., B.M.H., Robert C. Barton, WS979, p.34.

50 Lawlor, 'Robert Barton: Wicklow revolutionary and statesman', in Deane (ed), *Wicklow and the War of Independence*, p.207.

51 Kathleen Napoli McKenna (Kenna) was born on 9 September 1897 into a nationalist family in Oldcastle, County Meath. Her father, William Kenna, was active in the Land League. In her teenage years, Kathleen changed her surname to 'McKenna', but her parents remained 'Kenna'. In October 1919, she began work for the Propaganda Department of the newly formed Dáil. She was involved the production of the *Irish Bulletin*, a clandestine newspaper set up to counteract British propaganda during the Anglo-Irish War. She travelled to London with the Irish delegation in the autumn of 1921. She acted as Arthur Griffith's private secretary during the treaty negotiations. She supported the treaty and, after the Civil War, became a secretary in the Department of Foreign Affairs. She married Vittorio Napoli in 1931 and moved abroad, spending time in Libya and Albania before eventually moving to Rome. In her retirement, McKenna often visited Ireland, and contributed articles to Irish publications. McKenna died in Rome on 22 March 1988. She never published a full, definitive version of her experiences, but her papers were edited by her daughter and niece and published as *A Dáil Girl's Revolutionary Recollections* in 2014. [Patrick Maume, 'McKenna, Kathleen Napoli', in *D.I.B.*, available at www.dib.ie/biography/mckenna-kathleen-napoli-a9612 (visited on 21 November 2023).]

52 McKenna, *A Dáil Girl's Revolutionary Recollections*, p.175.

53 I.M.A., B.M.H., Robert C. Barton, WS979, p.34.

54 *Drogheda Independent*, 12 February 1927.

55 *The Irish Times*, 11 October 1944.

56 I.M.A., B.M.H., Robert C. Barton, WS979, pp.34–5.

57 I.M.A., B.M.H., witness statement of Dan MacCarthy, 1 Malahide, Clontarf, Dublin, WS722, pp.22–3.

58 Longford (Pakenham), *Peace by Ordeal*, p.263.

CHAPTER 13

1 *The Irish Times*, 7 December 1921.

2 *The Weekly Freeman*, 10 December 1921.

3 I.M.A., B.M.H., Mrs Austin Stack, WS418, pp.56–7.

4 Macardle, *The Irish Republic*, p.543.

5 I.M.A., B.M.H., Robert C. Barton, WS979, pp.39–40.

6 I.M.A., B.M.H., Mrs Austin Stack, WS418, pp.59–60.

7 Ryle Dwyer, *De Valera*, p.85.
8 I.M.A., B.M.H., Robert C. Barton, WS979, p.40.
9 Peter Tynan O'Mahony (ed), *Eamon De Valera* (Dublin, 1976), p.44.
10 According to Childers' rough notes of this meeting, when Griffith said, 'I stand over the document,' Barton assented with words to the effect of, 'I do too. I was intimidated. I had to declare war on my own behalf.' U.C.D. Archive [hereafter U.C.D.A.], Papers of Eamon de Valera, number 216, P150/1930, Cabinet meeting of 8 December 1921, copy of notes taken by Erskine Childers, available online at www.difp.ie/volume-1/1921/cabinet-meeting-of-december-8-1921-copy-of-notes-taken-by-erskine-childers/216/#section-documentpage (visited on 23 November 2023).
11 I.M.A., B.M.H., Robert C. Barton, WS979, p.40.
12 N.A.I., Dáil Éireann papers, Minutes of a Cabinet meeting held on 8 December 1921, DE 1/3 (number 215), available online at www.difp. ie/volume-1/1921/minutes-of-a-cabinet-meeting-held-on-8-december-1921/215/#section-documentpage (visited on 23 November 2023).
13 N.L.I., Dulcibella Barton Papers 1916–1927, Thomas Fleming, Shillelagh (West Wicklow Comhairle Ceanntair) to Robert Barton, 11 December 1921, MS 8796/2/46.
14 www.oireachtas.ie/en/visit-and-learn/centenaries/treaty-debates/explore-the-treaty-debates (visited on 22 November 2023).
15 Macardle, *The Irish Republic*, pp.555–6.
16 Barton is quoted in Wilkinson, *The Zeal of the Convert*, p.201.
17 Richard Aldous, *Great Irish Speeches* (London, 2007), p.71.
18 Longford (Pakenham), *Peace by Ordeal*, p.256. Pakenham continued: 'It was surely not asking too much of collective statesmanship to take precautions so that, whatever else ensued, there should be no Civil War.' This, however, was easier said than done!
19 Aldous, *Great Irish Speeches*, p.74.
20 Younger, *A State of Disunion*, p.81.
21 Debate on the treaty, 19 December 1921 (Dáil debates, 2nd Dáil, vol. T, no. 6) available online at www.oireachtas.ie/en/debates/debate/dail/1921-12-19/2 (visited on 18 November 2023). The full text of Barton's speech is reproduced in Appendix 3.
22 Ibid.
23 Ferriter, *A Nation and Not a Rabble*, p.253.
24 Debate on the treaty, 21 December 1921 (Dáil debates, 2nd Dáil, vol. T, no. 8) available online at www.oireachtas.ie/en/debates/debate/dail/1921-12-21/2 (visited on 22 November 2023).
25 Alfred William Cope to Winston Churchill, 23 December 1921 (University of Cambridge, Churchill Archives Centre, Winston Churchill Papers, CHAR22/8/14-20). On Alfred Cope, see Geoffrey Sloan, 'Hide seek and negotiate: Alfred Cope and counter intelligence in Ireland 1919–1921', in *Intelligence and National Security*, vol. 33, no. 2 (Oxford, 2018), pp.176–195.

26 Debate on the treaty, 20 December 1921 (Dáil debates, 2nd Dáil, vol. T, no. 7) available online at www.oireachtas.ie/en/debates/debate/dail/1921-12-20/2 (visited on 22 November 2023).

27 Debate on the treaty, 21 December 1921 (Dáil debates, 2nd Dáil, vol. T, no. 8) available online at www.oireachtas.ie/en/debates/debate/dail/1921-12-21/2 (visited on 22 November 2023).

28 Debate on the treaty, 22 December 1921 (Dáil debates, 2nd Dáil, vol. T, no. 9) available online at www.oireachtas.ie/en/debates/debate/dail/1921-12-22/2 (visited on 22 November 2023).

29 *Nationalist and Leinster Times*, 10, 24 and 31 December 1921; and *Leinster Leader*, 18 and 31 December 1921.

30 *Nationalist and Leinster Times* and *Leinster Leader*, 7 January 1922.

31 Debate on the treaty, 3 January 1921 (Dáil debates, 2nd Dáil, vol. T, no. 10) available online atwww.oireachtas.ie/en/debates/debate/dail/1922-01-03/2 (visited on 22 November 2023).

32 Longford (Pakenham), *Peace by Ordeal*, p.114.

33 Debate on the treaty, 4 January 1921 (Dáil debates, 2nd Dáil, vol. T, no. 11) available online at www.oireachtas.ie/en/debates/debate/dail/1922-01-04/2 (visited on 22 November 2023).

34 Aldous, *Great Irish Speeches*, p.77.

CHAPTER 14

1 I.M.A., B.M.H., Robert C. Barton, WS979, p.43.

2 Eoin MacNeill to Desmond Fitzgerald, 13 January 1922, (U.C.D.A., Papers of Desmond and Mabel Fitzgerald, P80/258).

3 Younger, *Arthur Griffith*, p.287.

4 Kenneth Griffith and Timothy O'Grady, *Curious Journey: An Oral History of Ireland's Unfinished Revolution* (Cork, 1988), p.285.

5 Ciara Meehan, 'The propaganda war over the Anglo-Irish treaty', in Darragh Gannon and Fearghal McGarry (eds), *Ireland 1922: Independence, Partition, Civil War* (Dublin, 2022), p.71.

6 Younger, *Arthur Griffith*, p.287.

7 Robert Barton, *The Truth about the Treaty and Document No. 2* (Dublin, 1922), p.3.

8 Ibid., p.7.

9 Ibid., p.8.

10 I.M.A., B.M.H., Robert C. Barton, WS979, p.46.

11 Barton, *The Truth About the Treaty*, p.9.

12 Ibid., pp.14–5.

13 I.M.A., B.M.H., Robert C. Barton, WS979, p.46.

14 Marie Coleman, 'Women activists during the Civil War', in Gannon and McGarry (eds), *Ireland 1922*, p.54. The organisation rejected the treaty by a margin of 87 per cent to 13 per cent.

15 Diarmaid Ferriter, *Between Two Hells: the Irish Civil War* (London, 2022), p.21. Ferriter suggests that up to three quarters of I.R.A. members disapproved of the treaty, but not all of them would fight to oppose it.

16 Peter Hart, *The I.R.A. and its Enemies: Violence and Community in Cork, 1916–1923* (London, 1998), p.269.

17 Robert Kee, *The Green Flag* (London, 1972), p.733.

18 *The Freeman's Journal*, 27 March 1922 and *Poblacht na h-Eireann/The Republic of Ireland*, 29 March 1922.

19 I.M.A., B.M.H., Robert C. Barton, WS979, p.43.

20 Typescript copy article ridiculing Robert Barton's position (U.C.D.A., Papers of Desmond and Mabel Fitzgerald, P80/274).

21 Edgar Holt, *Protest in Arms: The Irish Troubles 1916–1923* (New York, 1960), p.293.

22 Kildare County Archives, Local Studies collection, June 1922 election poster (collection currently being re-catalogued).

23 I.M.A., B.M.H., Robert C. Barton, WS979, p.43.

24 *Leinster Leader*, 10 June 1922.

25 Michael Gallagher, 'The 1922 pact election', available online at www.rte.ie/history/pact-election/2022/0404/1290254-the-1922-pact-election (visited on 4 December 2023).

26 Holt, *Protest in Arms*, p.293.

27 The pro-treaty side won fifty-eight seats with 45.3 per cent of the votes; the anti-treaty side won thirty-six seats with 28.1 per cent of the votes; Labour, the Farmers' Party and independents [almost all pro-treaty] won thirty-four seats with 26.6 per cent of the votes. [(irishpoliticalmaps.blogspot.com/2012/08/irish-general-election-1922.html (visited on 30 March 2020).]

28 Kildare-Wicklow, 16 June 1922 [electionsireland.org/result.cfm?election=1922&cons=144 (visited on 25 November 2023).]

29 James Durney, *The Civil War in Kildare* (Cork, 2011), pp.70–1.

30 De Valera is quoted in Holt, *Protest in Arms*, p.287.

31 I.M.A., B.M.H., Robert C. Barton, WS979, p.45.

32 Coogan, *Michael Collins*, p.331.

33 I.M.A., B.M.H., Robert C. Barton, WS979, p.45.

34 Dolan and Murphy, *Michael Collins: The Man and the Revolution*, p.123.

35 I.M.A., B.M.H., Robert C. Barton, WS979, pp.45–6.

36 Ibid., p.46.

37 Ferriter, *Between Two Hells*, p.46.

38 I.M.A., B.M.H., Robert C. Barton, WS979, p.46.

39 C. S. (Todd) Andrews, *Dublin Made Me* (Cork, 1979), p.234.

40 Holt, *Protest in Arms*, p.298.

41 I.M.A., B.M.H., Robert C. Barton, WS979, p.46.

42 *Leinster Leader*, 8 July 1922.

43 B.M.H., Robert C. Barton, WS979, p.47.

44 Joseph MacDonagh was born on 18 May 1883 in Cloughjordan, Co. Tipperary. Prior to the execution of his eldest brother, the 1916 proclamation signatory

Thomas MacDonagh, he had no involvement in politics. However, he was arrested in the aftermath of the Rising and was also forced to resign from his civil service job in the Customs and Excise department. He moved to Dublin and served as headmaster in Thomas' former school, St Enda's, for a while. By 1918 he had become a tax consultant and in 1919 he became a partner in an insurance firm, which traded as MacDonagh and Boland from 1920. From 1917 onwards, MacDonagh was also active in the resurgent Sinn Féin Party. He was sentenced to six months in prison for supporting Éamon de Valera in the Clare by-election, and was a participant in the hunger strike in which Thomas Ashe died. In October 1917 he was elected to the Sinn Fein executive and, following more stints in prison, he was elected for Tipperary North in the 1918 general election. He was often 'on the run' during the War of Independence and served as acting Minister for Labour from January 1921. He administered the 'Belfast Boycott' efficiently, and opposed the Anglo-Irish treaty. He was arrested soon after the outbreak of the Civil War, but escaped during a mass breakout in July. However, he was re-arrested on 30 September and imprisoned in Mountjoy, where he fell ill with acute appendicitis. He would not sign the form for medical release because it recognised the Free State. Despite this, he was eventually transferred to the Mater hospital – but too late. He died on 25 December 1922 and is buried in Glasnevin cemetery. [Lawrence William White, 'MacDonagh, Joseph' in *D.I.B.*, available at www.dib.ie/biography/ macdonagh-joseph-a5162 (visited on 5 January 2024).]

45 Noel Lemass was born in Dublin on 15 December 1897. He joined the Volunteers in 1915 and fought with his brother Seán in the 1916 Rising. Wounded in combat, Noel spent three months in prison, after which he worked for the Great Southern Railway and, later, Dublin Corporation. He remained active in the Volunteers and was promoted to captain in 1919, but was arrested for possession of arms in November of that year and he spent a year in prison, which he served in Mountjoy, Derry and Kilkenny. He was released, but re-arrested in 1921, spending time in Dublin Castle, Collinstown Camp and Kilmainham Gaol before moving to Rath Camp, where he became Officer Commanding. He took the anti-treaty side in the Civil War, during which he was involved in intelligence work for the anti-treatyites. He was arrested on 14 August 1922, but escaped from Gormanstown Camp. He was re-arrested at Glencullen, but escaped again and went to England, where he stayed until the Civil War ended in May. However, he was kidnapped, tortured and murdered, and his body was discovered in the remote, mountainous area of Featherbed on 12 October 1923. His corpse was unrecognisable and he had to be identified by his clothing. His death has been attributed to the C.I.D., but nobody was ever charged in connection with the incident. Speculation also surrounds the motive for the killing – possibly it happened because of his involvement in the death of Seán Hales or because he intercepted the incoming and outgoing mail of Michael Collins. His death, after hostilities had ended, caused outrage within old anti-treaty circles. He is buried in Glasnevin cemetery. [Anne Dolan,

'Lemass, Noel Denis Joseph', in *D.I.B.*, available at www.dib.ie/biography/
lemass-noel-denis-joseph-a4785 (visited on 5 January 2024).]

46 Noel Lemass (1897-1923) in the I.M.S.C., I.M.A., militarypensions.wordpress.
com/2023/07/03/noel-lemass-1897-1923-in-the-mspc (visited on 5 January 2024).

47 Born in 1902, Pádraig Ó Horan (P.K. Horan) was a 19-year-old Gaelic League
teacher who modelled himself on Pádraig Pearse when he rushed to the aid of
the anti-treatyites in Dublin following the bombardment of the Four Courts at
the beginning of the Civil War. He was captured and held as a political prisoner
at Gormanstown Camp. He spent a year and a half in captivity, during which
he became disillusioned with the leaders of both the republican movement
and the Roman Catholic Church. Once released, he converted to Methodism,
joining the Dublin Methodist Mission. He then studied to become a Methodist
minister at Cliff Methodist College, Derbyshire, before moving to Belfast in
1926, where he continued his studies at Edgehill Theological College. He was
highly critical of the republican leadership and the futility of the anti-treaty
position during the Civil War. He married Elizabeth Dolan at Knock, Belfast,
on 2 July 1928. The couple converted to Anglicanism in 1930, and later carried
out ministries in Somerset, Nottingham, Achill Island, Bath, Priddy and
Sampford before Pádraig's death in 1951. [Robert P. Roddie, 'Padraig and Eily
O'Horan: A story of rebellion and redemption', in *Dublin Historical Record*, vol.
55, no. 1, (2002), pp.75–87.]

48 P.K. Horan, 'Thro' red days', in *Irish Christian Advocate*, 9 March 1928.

49 P.K. Horan, 'Prisoners in Portobello', in *Methodist Magazine* (1928), pp.434–8.

50 Michael Farry, *The Aftermath of Revolution: Sligo 1921–23* (Dublin, 2000),
pp.116–20 passim.

51 I.M.A., B.M.H., Robert C. Barton, WS979, p.47.

52 Sean McMahon, *Rebel Ireland: From Easter Rising to Civil War* (Cork, 2001), p.145.
See also Ryle Dwyer, *De Valera*, p.59.

53 Ryle Dwyer, *De Valera*, p.59.

54 Lawlor, *The Little Book of Wicklow*, p.108.

55 I.M.A., B.M.H., Robert C. Barton, WS979, p.47.

56 I.M.A., B.M.H., Dulcibella Barton, WS936, pp.5–6.

57 Wilkinson, *The Zeal of the Convert*, pp.221.

58 Fewer, 'R. C. Barton and Glendalough House', p.4.

59 I.M.A., B.M.H., Dulcibella Barton, WS936, p.6.

60 Ferriter, *Between Two Hells*, p.90.

61 John M. Feehan, *The Shooting of Michael Collins* (Cork, reprint, 1987), pp.52 *et seq.*

62 Erskine Childers to Ivor Lloyd Jones, 24 November 1922 (University of
Cambridge, Trinity College Library [Special Collections], Additional
manuscripts, Add. MS a. 599). Ivor Gordon Lloyd Jones (1869–1946) was born
on 12 April 1869 at Blackheath, Kent. Like Childers, he attended Haileybury
school and went to Cambridge, entering Trinity College in 1888. He obtained
his B.A. in 1891, and taught at Orley Farm School, Harrow and Forest School,
Walthamstow, from 1894–9. He moved to Cheltenham College in 1899, and

obtained his M.A. in 1901. He moved to Uppingham School in 1909, and served in the First World War in 1914–18. He returned to teaching after the war and retired from Uppingham in 1931. He died at Uppingham on 6 February 1946. [archives.trin.cam.ac.uk/index.php/jones-ivor-gordon-lloyd-c-1869-1946-schoolmaster-friend-of-robert-erskine-childers (visited on 4 February 2023).]
63 Lawlor, *The Little Book of Wicklow*, p.114.
64 N.A.I., Records of the courts services in Ireland, Childers, Robert Erskine: will and associated papers, CS/HC/PO/4/76/1082.
65 Fewer, 'R. C. Barton and Glendalough House', p.2.
66 Florence O'Donoghue, *No Other Law* (Dublin, 1986), pp.304 *et seq.*
67 Chris Lawlor, *The Little Book of Kildare* (Dublin, 2015), p.113.
68 I.M.A., B.M.H., Robert C. Barton, WS979, p.47.
69 electionsireland.org/result.cfm?election=1923&cons=235 (visited on 6 January 2024).
70 Fewer, 'R. C. Barton and Glendalough House', p.2.

CHAPTER 15

1 O'Higgins is quoted in R. F. Foster, *Vivid Faces: The Revolutionary Generation in Ireland* (London, 2014), p.25.
2 Matthew Kelly, 'Radical Nationalisms, 1882–1916', in Thomas Bartlett (ed), *The Cambridge History of Ireland*, vol. iv, p.33.
3 Lyons, *Ireland since the Famine*, pp.471–510 passim.
4 WW.C.A., Barton Papers, Members of West Wicklow Comhairle Ceanntair of Sinn Féin to Robert Barton, 8 June 1924, WWCA/PP1/24. The full text of this letter is reproduced in Appendix 4.
5 See, for example, James Whittle (ed), *Sons of St Nicholas: A History of Dunlavin GAA club* (Dunlavin, 1984), pp.16–19 passim.
6 Ida Milne, '"The jersey is all that matters, not your Church": Protestants and the G.A.A. in the rural Republic', in d'Alton and Milne (eds), *Protestant and Irish*, pp.180–7 passim.
7 Barry Coldrey, *Faith and Fatherland: the Christian Brothers and the development of Irish nationalism 1838–1921* (Dublin, 1988), passim, especially pp.251–70.
8 Mel Farrell, '"Few supporters and no organisation?" Cumann na nGaedheal organisation and policy, 1923–33' (Ph.D. thesis, Maynooth, 2011), pp.225–257 passim.
9 *Irish Independent* and *Irish Times*, both 26 October 1922.
10 Constitution published in *Freeman's Journal*, 26 October 1922. The relevant articles are three, eight and nine.
11 Patrick J. Corish, *The Irish Catholic Experience: A Historical Survey* (Dublin, reprint, 1986), p.244.
12 Daithí Ó Corráin, 'Catholicism in Ireland, 1880–2015: rise, ascendancy and retreat', in Bartlett (ed), *The Cambridge History of Ireland*, iv, p.733.
13 d'Alton and Milne (eds), *Protestant and Irish*, p.xx.

14 Peter Pyne, 'The third Sinn Féin party 1923–1926: (1) Narrative account', in *Economic and Social Review*, vol. 1 (Dublin, 1969), p.45.
15 Ibid., p.46.
16 Brian Farrell, *Seán Lemass* (Dublin, 1983), p.18.
17 Coogan, *De Valera*, p.404.
18 Lee, *Ireland 1912–85*, p.155.
19 Ferriter, *The Transformation of Ireland*, p.268.
20 I.M.A., B.M.H., Robert C. Barton, WS979, p.44. The process of 'getting more as time went by' happened, with progress being made at imperial conferences under Cumann na nGaedheal, various steps being taken by Fianna Fáil to 'dismantle the treaty', and the introduction of the Republic of Ireland Act by the first inter-party government during the three decades following the acceptance of the Anglo-Irish treaty.
21 Dempsey and Boylan, 'Barton, Robert Childers', in *D.I.B.*, available at www.dib.ie/biography/barton-robert-childers-a0485 (visited on 9 January 2023).
22 I am indebted to Ciarán McGann of the Houses of the Oireachtas Service for this information.
23 Dempsey and Boylan, 'Barton, Robert Childers', in *D.I.B.*, available at www.dib.ie/biography/barton-robert-childers-a0485 (visited on 9 January 2023).
24 I.M.A., B.M.H., Robert C. Barton, WS979, pp.44–5.
25 Tynan O'Mahony (ed), *Eamon de Valera*, p.103.
26 WW.C.A., Barton Papers, Lease of sporting rights on lands at Drummin, 26 May 1936, WWCA/PP1/25.
27 Ferriter, *The Transformation of Ireland*, p.312.
28 Lyons, *Ireland Since the Famine*, p.503.
29 Dempsey and Boylan, 'Barton, Robert Childers', in *D.I.B.*, available at www.dib.ie/biography/barton-robert-childers-a0485 (visited on 9 January 2023).
30 Ferriter, *The Transformation of Ireland*, pp.312 and 741.
31 Dempsey and Boylan, 'Barton, Robert Childers', in *D.I.B.*, available at www.dib.ie/biography/barton-robert-childers-a0485 (visited on 9 January 2023).
32 Lyons, *Ireland Since the Famine*, p.608.
33 Dempsey and Boylan, 'Barton, Robert Childers', in *D.I.B.*, available at www.dib.ie/biography/barton-robert-childers-a0485 (visited on 9 January 2023).
34 C. S. Andrews, *Man of No Property* (Dublin, 1982; reprint, 2001), p.127.
35 Irish Peatland Conservation Council, *Bogs: A New Perspective* (Lullymore?, n.d.), pp.1–3).
36 Significantly, these three sites were all associated with turf development – peat briquette factories at Lullymore and Littleton and a peat-burning power station at Lanesboro.
37 Andrews, *Man of No Property*, p.132.
38 www.facebook.com/BarrougherAndClonmoylanBogsActionGroup (visited on 12 November 2023).
39 Lyons, *Ireland Since the Famine*, p.618.
40 Dempsey and Boylan, 'Barton, Robert Childers', in *D.I.B.*, available at www.

dib.ie/biography/barton-robert-childers-a0485 (visited on 9 January 2023).
41 Mais, *I Return to Ireland*, pp.134 and 129.
42 Dempsey and Boylan, 'Barton, Robert Childers', in *D.I.B.*, available at www.
    dib.ie/biography/barton-robert-childers-a0485 (visited on 9 January 2023).
43 Fewer, 'R. C. Barton and Glendalough House', p.5.
44 Dempsey and Boylan, 'Barton, Robert Childers', in *D.I.B.*, available at www.
    dib.ie/biography/barton-robert-childers-a0485 (visited on 9 January 2023).
45 Fewer, 'R. C. Barton and Glendalough House', p.7.
46 Dempsey and Boylan, 'Barton, Robert Childers', in *D.I.B.*, available at www.
    dib.ie/biography/barton-robert-childers-a0485 (visited on 9 January 2023).
47 Tynan O'Mahony (ed), *Eamon de Valera*, p.135.
48 Fewer, 'R. C. Barton and Glendalough House', p.7.

CONCLUSION

1   I am indebted to Brian Crowley of Kilmainham Gaol Museum for
    this information.
2   On Irish Catholicism during this period, see Patrick J. Corish, *The Irish Catholic
    Experience: A Historical Survey* (Dublin, reprint, 1986), pp.226–46.
3   On Irish-Irelandism and other dimensions of cultural nationalism, see Brian Ó
    Conchubhair, 'The culture war: the Gaelic League and Irish Ireland', in Bartlett
    (ed), *The Cambridge History of Ireland*, iv, pp.168–95.
4   I am grateful to Dr Ida Milne for sharing her thoughts on this 'Wicklow
    Nationalist Protestant' proposition with me at a lecture in Baltinglass.
5   By this I mean 'republican' in the post-Enlightenment sense, often taken
    as originating in Ireland during the 1790s with the doctrine of the United
    Irish organisation.
6   Peter O'Shaughnessy (ed), *Rebellion in Wicklow: General Joseph Holt's personal
    account of 1798* (Dublin, 1998), pp.20–1.
7   W.W.C.A., Barton Papers, Recommendation from Captain Booth for Robert
    Childers Barton, 17 December 1915, WWCA/PP1/21.
8   Debate on the treaty, 19 December 1921 (Dáil debates, 2nd Dáil, vol. T,
    no. 6) available online at www.oireachtas.ie/en/debates/debate/dail/1921-
    12-19/2 (visited on 18 November 2023).
9   Roy Foster, 'The Protestant accent', in d'Alton and Milne (eds), *Protestant and
    Irish*, pp.xxi–xxiv.
10 I.M.A., B.M.H., Robert C. Barton, WS979, pp.33–4, 47 and 44.
11 Mais, *I Return to Ireland*, p.134.

Index